On Muslim Democracy

RELIGION AND GLOBAL POLITICS

Series Editor

John L. Esposito
University Professor and Director
Prince Alwaleed Bin Talal Center for Muslim-Christian Understanding
Georgetown University

ISLAMIC LEVIATHAN
Islam and the Making of State Power
Seyyed Vali Reza Nasr

RACHID GHANNOUCHI
A Democrat Within Islamism
Azzam S. Tamimi

BALKAN IDOLS
Religion and Nationalism in Yugoslav States
Vjekoslav Perica

ISLAMIC POLITICAL IDENTITY IN TURKEY
M. Hakan Yavuz

RELIGION AND POLITICS IN
POST-COMMUNIST ROMANIA
Lavinia Stan and Lucian Turcescu

PIETY AND POLITICS
Islamism in Contemporary Malaysia
Joseph Chinyong Liow

TERROR IN THE LAND OF THE HOLY SPIRIT
Guatemala under General Efrain Rios Montt,
1982–1983
Virginia Garrard-Burnett

IN THE HOUSE OF WAR
Dutch Islam Observed
Sam Cherribi

BEING YOUNG AND MUSLIM
New Cultural Politics in the Global South and North
Asef Bayat and Linda Herrera

CHURCH, STATE, AND DEMOCRACY IN
EXPANDING EUROPE
Lavinia Stan and Lucian Turcescu

THE HEADSCARF CONTROVERSY
Secularism and Freedom of Religion
Hilal Elver

THE HOUSE OF SERVICE
The Gülen Movement and Islam's Third Way
David Tittensor

ANSWERING THE CALL
Popular Islamic Activism in Sadat's Egypt
Abdullah Al-Arian

MAPPING THE LEGAL BOUNDARIES OF
BELONGING
Religion and Multiculturalism from Israel to Canada
Edited by René Provost

RELIGIOUS SECULARITY
A Theological Challenge to the Islamic State
Naser Ghobadzadeh

THE MIDDLE PATH OF MODERATION IN ISLAM
The Qur'ānic Principle of Wasaṭiyyah
Mohammad Hashim Kamali

ONE ISLAM, MANY MUSLIM WORLDS
Spirituality, Identity, and Resistance Across Islamic Lands
Raymond William Baker

CONTAINING BALKAN NATIONALISM
Imperial Russia and Ottoman Christians (1856–1914)
Denis Vovchenko

INSIDE THE MUSLIM BROTHERHOOD
Religion, Identity, and Politics
Khalil al-Anani

POLITICIZING ISLAM
The Islamic Revival in France and India
Z. Fareen Parvez

SOVIET AND MUSLIM
The Institutionalization of Islam in Central Asia
Eren Tasar

ISLAM IN MALAYISA
An Entwined History
Khairudin Aljunied

SALAFISM GOES GLOBAL
From the Gulf to the French Banlieues
Mohamed-Ali Adraoui

UNDER THE BANNER OF ISLAM
Turks, Kurds, and the Limits of Religious Unity
Gülay Türkmen

JIHADISM IN EUROPE
European Youth and the New Caliphate
Farhad Khosrokhavar

ISLAM AND NATIONHOOD IN MODERN
GREECE, 1821–1940
Stefanos Katsikas

WAHHABISM AND THE WORLD
Understanding Saudi Arabia's Global Influence on Islam
Peter Mandaville

THEOCRATIC SECULARISM
A Religious Rational for Political Separation in Iran
Naser Ghobadzadeh

UMMAH YET PROLETARIAT
Islam, Marxism, and the Making of the Indonesian
Republic
Lin Hongxuan

ON MUSLIM DEMOCRACY
Essays and Dialogues
Rached Ghannouchi with Andrew F. March

On Muslim Democracy

Essays and Dialogues

By
RACHED GHANNOUCHI
with
ANDREW F. MARCH

Translated by
JONATHAN WRIGHT AND ANDREW F. MARCH

OXFORD
UNIVERSITY PRESS

Oxford University Press is a department of the University of Oxford. It furthers
the University's objective of excellence in research, scholarship, and education
by publishing worldwide. Oxford is a registered trade mark of Oxford University
Press in the UK and certain other countries.

Published in the United States of America by Oxford University Press
198 Madison Avenue, New York, NY 10016, United States of America.

© Oxford University Press 2023

All rights reserved. No part of this publication may be reproduced, stored in
a retrieval system, or transmitted, in any form or by any means, without the
prior permission in writing of Oxford University Press, or as expressly permitted
by law, by license, or under terms agreed with the appropriate reproduction
rights organization. Inquiries concerning reproduction outside the scope of the
above should be sent to the Rights Department, Oxford University Press, at the
address above.

You must not circulate this work in any other form
and you must impose this same condition on any acquirer.

Library of Congress Control Number: 2023938501

ISBN 978–0–19–766687–6

DOI: 10.1093/oso/9780197666876.001.0001

Printed by Integrated Books International, United States of America

Contents

From Islamic Democracy to Muslim Democracy: Rached
Ghannouchi in Thought and Action (Andrew F. March)   1

ESSAYS ON FREEDOM, DEMOCRACY, AND CONSTITUTIONALISM (RACHED GHANNOUCHI)

1. Basic Freedoms in Islam   35

2. The Dialectic of Unity, Difference, and Political Pluralism in Islam   57

3. When Is Islam the Solution?   78

4. Freedom First   83

5. Between Sayyid Qutb and Malek Bennabi: Ten Points   91

6. Islam and Citizenship   100

7. The Problems of Contemporary Islamist Discourse   108

8. Secularism and the Relation Between Religion and the State from the Perspective of the Ennahda Party   120

9. The Implications and Requirements of a Post-Revolutionary Constitution   130

10. Human Rights in Islam   137

Philosophical-Theological Dialogues on Democracy, Pluralism, and Islam (Rached Ghannouchi and Andrew F. March)   145
    Biography and Formation   145
    Democracy, Sovereignty, and Morality   181
    The Universal Caliphate, Democracy, and the Meaning of the *Shari'a*   194
    Freedom, Pluralism, and Toleration   214

Index   237

From Islamic Democracy
to Muslim Democracy

Rached Ghannouchi in Thought and Action

Andrew F. March

It is December 2021 and Rached Ghannouchi is sitting in his book-lined office in the home he has occupied in Tunis since returning from exile a little more than ten years before. It is barely five months since Tunisian president Kais Saied froze parliament and suspended the government in a temporary move that quickly turned into an indefinite coup against the often messy and deeply unpopular, but nonetheless impeccably democratic, constitutional order painstakingly created by Tunisian political parties after the 2011 Jasmine Revolution.[1] Much of the popular acclamation for the July 25, 2021, constitutional coup was directed against Ghannouchi's Ennahda Party, but a remarkable feature of the support for Saied at that time was how much of it consisted in a generalized anti-political attitude. Politics itself, especially in its chaotic and ineffectual parliamentary form, seemed to be on trial in the wake of the coup, a deeply depressing coda to the ten years in which Tunisia had avoided both civil war and authoritarian counterrevolution to remain the last democracy standing from the 2011 Arab Spring.

Ghannouchi maintained his usual phlegmatic demeanor as we discussed the fallout from the coup and the growing broad anti-coup coalition, which now included a wide range of secular parties and civil society organizations in addition to Ennahda.[2] Ghannouchi's political thought had naturally evolved

---

[1] See Sharan Grewal, "Kais Saied's Power Grab in Tunisia," *Order from Chaos* (blog), Brookings Institution, July 26, 2021, https://www.brookings.edu/blog/order-from-chaos/2021/07/26/kais-saieds-power-grab-in-tunisia/.
[2] See Monica Marks, "Can a Fragmented Opposition Save Tunisia's Democracy from Saied?," Democracy for the Arab World Now, February 1, 2022, https://dawnmena.org/can-a-fragmented-opposition-save-tunisias-democracy-from-saied/.

On Muslim Democracy. Rached Ghannouchi and Andrew F. March, Oxford University Press.
© Oxford University Press 2023. DOI: 10.1093/oso/9780197666876.003.0001

over the past years, in which he had been at the center of brokering coalition deals between ideologically antagonistic parties and most recently served as Speaker of parliament. Over the previous decades Ghannouchi's political theory was noteworthy for the role he imagined for an active, engaged, and deliberative democratic populus. Unlike Montesquieuian and Madisonian theories of the separation of powers and institutional pluralism as the ultimate check against tyranny, Ghannouchi had long stressed popular virtue and public opinion. Unlike traditional Islamic theories that placed custodianship of the law in the hands of jurists exclusively, Ghannouchi imagined the realization of Islamic law as largely a public deliberative process involving not only experts but also ordinary citizen-believers. But on this day he repeatedly turned to the theme of elite consensus as the check against authoritarianism and the path back to democracy.

It is not hard to see why this might be the case given Tunisian history over the preceding ten years. Tunisia's transition from authoritarianism was uncommonly democratic. Unlike in Egypt, the democratic transition was not overseen by a de facto sovereign like the armed forces or the security apparatus, and still less by a coalition of foreign occupying powers. The political parties that emerged in the wake of the democratic revolution had free rein to found and run a political system grounded on nothing other than their own will and agreement. While the lengthy and conflictual constituent process resulted eventually in a constitutional consensus, Tunisia's deep ideological divides and mistrust remained evident in all subsequent elections. Years of state propaganda had poisoned the well for wide swaths of the Tunisian electorate against Ennahda. While celebrated in the West as "moderate Islamists" committed to the democratic process, many Tunisians continued to regard Ennahda as no different from more conservative Muslim Brotherhood parties in other countries, or even on a continuum with militant Islamist organizations. Simultaneously Tunisia's most popular and most detested party, Ennahda was frequently the object of scaremongering in electoral campaigns by old-regime forces that reconstituted themselves after 2011, especially after the horrors of the civil war in Syria.

While much of the tension that plagued Tunisian democracy between 2011 and 2021 was a result of elite competition, and particularly efforts to avoid accountability for financial corruption and political repression under the Ben Ali regime, there was no escaping the fact that ideological disagreement and mistrust ran deep within Tunisian society itself, a society not otherwise riven by ethnic or sectarian divides. There was no underlying supermajority of Tunisian citizens united around a single vision of what the post-revolutionary order ought to look like that could be mobilized against a minority of corrupt elites, at least not one that manifested itself in electoral results in parliamentary, presidential, and local elections after 2014. If elite competition and rivalry, enhanced by a constitutional order that distributed power between the president and the prime minister, was the bane of Tunisian politics after 2011, it would also seem that the capacity and willingness of those same elites to grind out agreements and coalitions was what held Tunisian democracy together. Perhaps the greatest, and most notorious, example of this was the working relationship that developed between Ghannouchi and President Beji Caid Essebsi (in office 2014–2019), the founder of the big-tent secularist party Nidaa Tunis and a former official under both Habib Bourguiba and Zine El Abidine Ben Ali, whose 2014 election campaign largely consisted in playing on fears of an Islamist or jihadist threat to Tunisia. Time and again crises were resolved and governments narrowly assembled on the basis of elite consensus. Whatever underlying contempt or mistrust parties had for each other, there seemed to be no will to use a crisis to justify a counterrevolutionary coup like what brought an end to the Egyptian revolution in 2013.

That is, until the actions of an unlikely autocrat, an unaffiliated and little-known law professor who swept to power in 2019 on the back of broad opposition to media plutocrat and Essebsi loyalist Nabil Karoui. Saied's moves to suspend the constitutional system were cheered by many in Tunisian society because of the many discontents of democratic politics: economic stagnation, real and perceived corruption, a circus-like atmosphere at times in parliament, and an ineffectual response to the COVID-19 crisis. But five months on, Saied's seizure of power had not resulted in a more effective state approach to the economy or the pandemic, and some of the bloom was off the presidential rose by December. I attended dueling rallies on December 17, 2021 (the anniversary of the outbreak of the revolution in 2010), that suggested far more popular energy and confidence for the anti-coup coalition than for the supporters of the president, at least measured in terms of willingness to turn to the streets. (One year on, this seems confirmed by the paltry 11 percent turnout for Saied's sham legislative elections of December 17, 2022.)[3]

[3] "Tunisia Election Board Edges Vote Turnout up to 11 Percent," France 24, December 19, 2022, https://www.france24.com/en/live-news/20221219-tunisia-election-board-edges-vote-turnout-up-to-11-percent.

4 ON MUSLIM DEMOCRACY

Ghannouchi expressed to me cautious optimism and hope for a return to constitutional government through a combination of elite consensus and popular protest. (Although in the year subsequent to this conversation, Saied has done much to entrench his authoritarian rule, including a July 25, 2022, referendum to ratify a hyper-presidentialist constitution, which was passed with a meager 30.5 percent voter turnout.)

Nonetheless, at age eighty and approaching the end of his political career, Ghannouchi must have felt acutely that the coup and the ongoing threat to recriminalize Ennahda or somehow exclude it from the political order represented an ambivalent, if not quite tragic, end to his life's work, which above all can be characterized as the mission to secure a place in Tunisian political life for Islam as a public religion—by making Islam safe for democracy, so to speak, and also by making the post-colonial secular state safe for Islam and practicing Muslims. Despite ten years of consensus-based politics in which Ennahda neither could nor seemed to want to monopolize power for itself, the image of "Islamists" as a threat to the gains of state-driven secularism and feminism could not be completely dislodged in the minds of many Tunisians. Ghannouchi's willingness to strike political bargains with secularist political rivals (and former enemies) did not so much seem to enhance trust for the party as associate it with the perception that post-revolutionary parties were corrupt as well as ineffectual, and responsible for the failure of the revolution to deliver a better life.[4]

Yet even these conversations from 2021 and 2022 now seem optimistic. As this book goes to press (April 2023), Ghannouchi has been arrested and is presently being held in prison while awaiting trial on the politically-motivated charges of "committing a conspiracy to attack the internal security of the state and a deliberate assault that intends to change the state's structure and force residents to attack each other."[5] His attempts between 2011 and 2023 to form a multiparty democratic alternative to authoritarianism may represent his final legacy.

*

[4] On this theme, see Sharan Grewal and Shadi Hamid, "The Dark Side of Consensus in Tunisia: Lessons from 2015–2019," Brookings Institution, January 2020, https://www.brookings.edu/research/the-dark-side-of-consensus-in-tunisia-lessons-from-2015-2019/.

[5] "Tunisia: Ghannouchi Faces Death Sentence as Judge Charges Him with Conspiracy against the State," *Middle East Monitor*, April 20, 2023. https://www.middleeastmonitor.com/20230420-tunisia-ghannouchi-faces-death-sentence-as-judge-charges-him-with-conspiracy-against-the-state/.

Ghannouchi's personal and political biography is by this point well known.[6] Born in 1941 in the small village of Hamah, near Gabes, in southeastern Tunisia, he studied in the capital, Tunis, briefly in Egypt, and then more consequentially in Syria and Paris before returning to Tunisia to help organize the Islamist political movement there. On the cusp of legal recognition for the Islamic Tendency Movement (MTI) that he cofounded, he was imprisoned between 1981 and 1984 along with many of his fellow activists. A second prison stint followed in 1987, and he was nearly sentenced to death by long-ruling Tunisian president Habib Bourguiba, only to be spared by the coup that brought Zine El Abidine Ben Ali to power. After his Ennahda Party (the new name of the Islamic Tendency Movement) posted an impressive showing in local elections in 1989, he fled into exile, fearing another state crackdown on his party and its senior leadership.

Ghannouchi's more than two decades in exile were productive both intellectually and politically. He published his most important work of political theory, *Public Freedoms in the Islamic State*, which he had been working on since his lengthy prison terms, in 1993.[7] He continued to lead the Ennahda movement from London and became an increasingly prominent member of the global Islamist public sphere, emerging as an influential figure in international debates on democracy, pluralism, and the reinterpretation of Islamic law for contemporary circumstances. He might have remained primarily an intellectual and civil society figure indefinitely had it not been for the shock of the 2010–2011 Jasmine Revolution, which unleashed the wave of popular revolts across the Arab world and allowed Ghannouchi to return home to Tunisia, in which Ennahda could now contest fully free and democratic elections.

Islamism and the Tunisian Democratic Transition (Interlude?)

In October 2011, Tunisians elected a National Constituent Assembly (NCA) that, despite a series of political, security, and economic crises, was able to

---

[6] For the following, see Azzam S. Tamimi, *Rachid Ghannouchi: A Democrat Within Islamism* (New York: Oxford University Press, 2001); Anne Wolf, *Political Islam in Tunisia: The History of Ennahda* (New York: Oxford University Press, 2017); and the conversation between Ghannouchi and myself in this volume.

[7] Rāshid al-Ghannūshī, *Al-ḥurriyyāt al-ʿamma fi'l-dawla al-Islāmiyya* (Beirut: Markaz Dirāsāt al-Wiḥdah al-ʿArabiyya, 1993). See the recent English translation: Rached Ghannouchi, *Public Freedoms in the Islamic State*, trans. David Johnston (New Haven, CT: Yale University Press, 2022), based on the updated edition published in 2015 by *Dār al-Mujtahid li'l-Nashr Wa'l-Tawzī'*.

6   ON MUSLIM DEMOCRACY

adopt a new constitution on January 26, 2014. The length of time it took the NCA to arrive at a consensus around that document and other foundational issues of a new political order (such as a law on transitional justice and the status of former regime officials) is a testament to the deep political and ideological divisions in Tunisia, but also to the capacity of elites both in and out of the NCA[8] to create a new political order through political bargaining alone.[9] Even before the July 2021 coup, this process had not been successfully completed. The Constitutional Court had not yet been established, since the governing parties had still been unable to agree on nominees to it,[10] which contributed to Kais Saied's ability to unilaterally suspend the constitution on the basis of his own understanding of presidential powers. While the new system remained in place, it was less an ideological agreement to share in the formation of a new democratic society and more a kind of bargained competition over political resources through tenuous power-sharing agreements.[11] But if Nathan Brown is correct that new constitutions can attain "stability and justice" not from technocratic bargaining over interests and reasons alone but from "the ways that bargaining, short-term interest, and passions are engaged directly by the constitutional process,"[12] then the Tunisian process had the advantage at least of being forged through the passionate, even narrowly self-interested, political bargaining of democratically representative actors. This is part of the tragedy of July 2021 and the joy with which many Tunisians greeted it.

Ghannouchi's Ennahda Party, which held 41 percent of the seats in the NCA, was central to this transitional bargaining process and thus claimed a

---

[8] The so-called Tunisian National Dialogue Quartet won the Nobel Peace Prize in 2015 for its role in mediating the crisis of the summer of 2013, which allowed the NCA to ultimately adopt the new constitution in January 2014.

[9] On the politics of the NCA, see Sami Zemni, "The Extraordinary Politics of the Tunisian Revolution: The Process of Constitution Making," *Mediterranean Politics* 20, no. 1 (2015): 1–17; Hamadi Redissi and Rihab Boukhayatia, "The National Constituent Assembly of Tunisia and Civil Society Dynamics," EU Spring Working Paper No. 2, July 8, 2015; and Abrak Saati, "Negotiating the Post-Revolution Constitution for Tunisia: Members of the National Constituent Assembly Share Their Experiences," *International Law Research* 7, no. 1 (2018): 235–246. For the reflections of a member of the National Constituent Assembly, see Mabrouka M'Barek, "Makers of Our Own History: Upholding the Revolution and Unsettling Coloniality in the Drafting of Tunisia's 2014 Constitution," in *Constitution Makers on Constitution Making: New Cases*, edited by Tom Ginsburg and Sumit Bisarya, 151–193 (Cambridge, UK: Cambridge University Press, 2022).

[10] The 2014 constitution stipulates that "the President of the Republic, the Assembly of the Representatives of the People, and the Supreme Judicial Council shall each appoint four members, three quarters of whom must be legal specialists" (Art. 118).

[11] Amel Boubekeur, "Islamists, Secularists and Old Regime Elites in Tunisia: Bargained Competition," *Mediterranean Politics* 21, no. 1 (2016): 107–127.

[12] Nathan J. Brown, "Reason, Interest, Rationality, and Passion in Constitution Drafting," *Perspectives on Politics* 6, no. 4 (2008): 676.

significant measure of the authorship of the new constitution.[13] It is, to say the least, not the constitution of an Islamic republic, but one that reflects a political community with significant divides based on identity and competing ways of life.[14] The sole mention of Islam outside of the preamble (which makes reference to "our people's commitment to the teachings of Islam") is that the state's religion is defined as Islam (Art. 1). But, apart from the fact that the president must be Muslim (Art. 74), this is given no substance in a document that immediately also declares that the state is a "civil state based on citizenship, the will of the people, and the supremacy of law" (Art. 2) and that "the people are sovereign and the source of authority, which is exercised through the people's representatives and by referendum" (Art. 3). Indeed, the concessions made by Ennahda on matters of religion and Islamist ideology have been widely observed.[15] Most notable are giving up the demand for some reference to *shari'a* as a source or inspiration of law, the question of the language used to describe the status of women, the description of human rights as "universal," backing down on a provision against blasphemy, and, perhaps most important, agreeing to a mixed presidential-parliamentary system as opposed to the pure parliamentary system preferred by Ennahda.[16] Even an NCA member from the rival Nida Tounès party asks, "Why did Ennahda concede as much to the opposition, when it had a parliamentary majority and the possibility, with the help of some independents in the assembly, to muster the required two-thirds majority?"[17]

However, the mystery is not why a party like Ennahda would make the calculation to endorse this new constitutional order, and still less how an ideologically defined party could possibly participate in creating a constitution that does not reflect its ideal political vision. Rather, the question is what the subsequent ideological and moral endorsement of this new order means for

[13] An English translation of the 2014 Tunisian constitution is available at https://www.constitute project.org/constitution/Tunisia_2014.pdf (accessed April 9, 2022).

[14] Malika Zeghal, "Competing Ways of Life: Islamism, Secularism, and Public Order in the Tunisian Transition," *Constellations* 20, no. 2 (2013): 254–274.

[15] See M'Barek, "Makers of Our Own History," for one version of an inside story.

[16] See Malika Zeghal, "Constitutionalizing a Democratic Muslim State Without Shari'a: The Religious Establishment in the Tunisian 2014 Constitution," in *Shari'a Law and Modern Muslim Ethics*, edited by Robert W. Hefner (Bloomington: Indiana University Press, 2016), 107–134; Monica Marks, "Convince, Coerce, or Compromise? Ennahda's Approach to Tunisia's Constitution," Brookings Doha Center Analysis Paper No. 10, February 2014; and Kasper Ly Netterstrøm, "The Islamists' Compromise in Tunisia," *Journal of Democracy* 26, no. 4 (2015): 110–124.

[17] Sélim Ben Abdesselem, "The Making of a Constitution: A Look Back at Tunisia's Thorny Consensus-Building Process," ConstitutionNet, March 26, 2014, http://constitutionnet.org/news/making-constitution-look-back-tunisias-thorny-consensus-building-process.

8 ON MUSLIM DEMOCRACY

the idea of an Islamist ideology built on the sovereignty of a particular kind of people committed in some way to a public, deliberative creation of Islamic legal meaning and legitimacy through its own political action. Temporary political compromises need not raise this kind of intellectual or ideological crisis. But they might, particularly if the adherents of an alternative moral-ideological vision reveal their own belief that the ideal doctrine is in some way unrealizable and give increasingly strong reasons for endorsing the non-ideal compromise. That this is the case in the Tunisian context is most supported by Ennahda's historical declaration at their 2016 party congress to have gone beyond the label of "political Islam" and identified themselves as "Muslim democrats."[18]

It is tempting to reduce this to a question of pragmatism, compromise, or "moderation." The pragmatism (if we wish to avoid the more overused term "moderation") of political Islam is almost an essential feature of a movement that is based on Islam's presumed flexibility and applicability to all mundane historical conditions. But there is, nonetheless, something distinctive about the post-2011 condition. It is one thing to choose to accommodate or collaborate with a political order not of one's making. This can always be portrayed as a tactical decision or compromise that defers to the future some moment in which the ideological vision can be realized, whether through revolution, societal transformation, or a democratic refounding moment. And so the non-utopian, non-ideal outcomes of post-2011 constituent politics are, I submit, a special moment for the trajectory of Islamism as ideology. In Egypt, that process was obviously destroyed by the military coup of July 2013, and thus an ideological reckoning can be deferred by pointing to the overwhelming anti-democratic power of the military and the permanent "deep state." But in Tunisia, the new constitutional and political order was one produced solely by the ideological and demographic divisions internal to the political community, and the Islamist party was as much a democratic author of this order as any other political formation. If something like the pluralist constitution of 2014 was not an authoritarian or colonial imposition but rather a reflection of what the broadest segment of a particular political community could consent to, and this political order reflected very little of what was previously theorized as an "Islamic democracy," then what is the remaining force of that prior ideal

---

[18] Rached Ghannouchi, "From Political Islam to Muslim Democracy: The Ennahda Party and the Future of Tunisia," *Foreign Affairs* 95, no. 5 (September–October 2016): 58–67.

theory and what is the most sophisticated theoretical defense of the new order from a doctrinal perspective?

Partly this raises questions about the authoritativeness of various registers or levels of discourse. Certain systematic treatises, written and published for the broad Muslim public sphere, can be presumed to represent some of the most considered reflections on sovereignty, law, and legitimacy. These works (paradigmatically Ghannouchi's *Public Freedoms in the Islamic State*) are not merely scholarly elaborations, because they are contributions by activist intellectuals to an ongoing public discourse seeking to define the commitments of political movements. But they are also not immediate reactions to current events or political crises, where the logic of shorter-term partisan interest predominates over theoretical consistency. They represent attempts to give the most persuasive ideal theory for Islamic government in this historical context. By contrast, much of the political discourse during and after negotiated constituent moments is ad hoc, unsystematic, and provisional. To put it bluntly: if an ideal theory of a democratic Islamic state was elaborated through complex and sophisticated treatises, does the post-utopian, non-ideal order that Islamists have participated in creating need an equally complex, sophisticated, and systematic theory? What would a complete political theory, or political theology, of "public freedoms in the pluralist state" look like?

This introduction (and the entire volume) seeks to address these questions. First, what are the ideological contours of the idea of "Muslim democracy," in contrast with the ideal Islamist theory developed in the decades prior to the 2011 revolution? How different is the non-ideal, post-utopian ideology from the previous ideal theory? Second, given this knowledge of a gap between the two iterations, what kind of moral commitment or consensus undergirds the commitment to something like the 2014 constitutional order in Tunisia—again, given the fact that this order was the result of free democratic negotiation rather than authoritarian imposition? Of course, this can only be speculative, and doctrinal factors are hardly the only test of democratic commitment. But, insofar as there has traditionally been a very powerful alternative theory of legitimacy and sovereignty, it is worth asking how deep and persuasive the theoretical commitment to a new order might be.

In order to answer these questions, it is necessary to say something about the vision of an Islamic political order before the turn to "Muslim democracy." What is that turn being compared to and measured against? This volume is

10 · ON MUSLIM DEMOCRACY

largely about Ghannouchi's legacy and transformation as a political thinker, and it is thus appropriate here to take stock of Ghannouchi's ideal theory of democracy and rule of law in an "Islamic state" as it was expressed in its most elaborate form in the first edition of *Public Freedoms in the Islamic State*.

Islamic Democracy as Ideal Theory

From the founding of the Islamic Tendency Movement, Ghannouchi and his associates pronounced support for multiparty democracy, and collaboration with a wide range of anti-authoritarian parties and forces has been part of the practice of the MTI and then Ennahda throughout their history. But Ghannouchi's own political philosophy should not be confused with a mere endorsement of political pluralism within a parliamentary system. In fact, at its most comprehensive and elaborate (particularly in *Public Freedoms in the Islamic State*), Ghannouchi's contribution to modern Islamic political theory took the form of an ideal Islamic democracy that sought to harmonize the principle of divine sovereignty with the ideal of the people as the source of all political authority and the ultimate check on authoritarianism and tyranny. While this vision endorses extensive public freedoms and the rights of non-Muslims, and non-Islamic parties, to participate in political life, it is quite distinct from an endorsement of a pluralist democratic order held together by a constitution that separates and balances political powers. It is a vision of a democratic order built on substantial moral and religious unity within the demos in which Islam is hegemonic without fully suppressing or excluding other visions or ways of life. Ghannouchi's and Ennahda's formal turn to a quite distinct ideology of "Muslim democracy" can only be fully appreciated by examining the contours of the idea of an "Islamic democracy."[19]

On my reading of this text, Ghannouchi provides a theory of democratic regime for a more or less morally unified people. It is in many ways a regime of tolerance of non-Islamic doctrines and ways of life, and accommodates significant political pluralism, but its core animating commitment is morally perfectionist rather than secular or liberal. It is significant for its democratic commitments given the ambivalence about democracy on the part of many

---

[19] The following draws from the analysis and arguments in Andrew F. March, *The Caliphate of Man: Popular Sovereignty in Modern Islamic Thought* (Cambridge, MA: Belknap Press of Harvard University Press, 2019), 150–200.

modern Islamic thinkers. But it is nonetheless an ideal theory of how a religiously committed Muslim people can be fully self-governing.

Ghannouchi writes that the Islamic conception of politics is based on a metaphysical account of the totality of existence, premised on the beliefs "that God is the creator and master of all existence, more knowledgeable than His creatures and the highest legislator and commander, and that man has been distinguished from the rest of God's creatures by his designation as God's deputy [or 'caliph'], through which he has been entrusted with reason, will, freedom, responsibility, and the divinely ordered path for his life."[20] The universal caliphate is the foundation for a kind of democratic theory since it holds that "the people" is entrusted by God with His authority, with no intermediaries prior to their appointment and delegation by the people itself.

This doctrine represents a significant democratic turn within Islamism. The people is described as "the source of all political authority," and even the traditional religious scholars enjoy legislative and judicial powers only at the pleasure of the people. But it is a democracy of a *believing* people, and a social contract to collectively carry out a covenant with God while pursuing the community's own welfare and prosperity. In this section I want to briefly highlight those features of this ideal theory that bring it into tension not only with the realities of Tunisian society but also with Ghannouchi's later turn to "Muslim democracy." Of particular note are Ghannouchi's moral perfectionism and his vision of a constitutional democracy characterized by moral unity and collective virtue.

Perfectionism

The basic metaphysical foundation of divine sovereignty and the universal caliphate is used by Ghannouchi to distinguish Islamic approaches to freedom, human rights, public justification, and the state from "Western" conceptions, which he tends to see in a reductive way as all based on a kind of arbitrary, foundationless human will and purposeless philosophical anthropology. Ghannouchi frames his project around a very specific, perfectionist vision of politics and statecraft. As late as his 2012 book, *Al-Dīmuqrāṭiyya wa ḥuqūq al-insān fi'l-Islām* (Democracy and human rights in Islam),

---

[20] Ghannūshī, *Al-ḥurriyyāt al-ʿāmma*, 37 (2015 ed., 35).

12 ON MUSLIM DEMOCRACY

Ghannouchi distinguished the Islamic vision of politics as being about "the unity of matter and spirit, politics and morality, this world and religion" and for "which the Islamic state is an irreplaceable means as long as people remain social by nature and as long as Islam is a comprehensive system of life that calls for constructing a social environment that allows for the greatest possible number of people to live spiritually and materially in an innate accord with the law that Islam brought." Stronger yet, in words that were written on the cusp of the democratic revolution in Tunisia: "Imagining life in accordance with the example of Islam in terms of justice, charity, piety, and cooperation toward the good without establishing Islamic public authority to protect its lands, guard its frontiers, and defend freedom of religion far from any form of coercion 'until there is no sedition' [Qur'an 8:39] is a mere deceptive fantasy, severe deviation, and fall into sin and error. In other regards, it is surrender to the enemies of Islam and giving them power over its fate."[21] This is an almost verbatim restatement of his formulation from 1993.[22]

Democracy and Moral Unity

Because Ghannouchi is a democrat, he wants to assign to the people not only full powers of appointment and removal over rulers and the apparatus of government but also significant powers to design and authorize the political system itself. But because he is an *Islamic* democrat (in *Public Freedoms in the Islamic State*), he has to hold that the delegation of authority to a government is a form of contract to enforce the Islamic *shari'a* and safeguard public welfare. All other points are negotiable, but this is a significant constraint on democratic pluralism.[23]

Ghannouchi outlines some more specific parameters for the concept of popular constituent power in a discussion of the relevance of Western republican principles of the separation of powers (Montesquieu and Madison

---

[21] Rāshid al-Ghannūshī, *Al-dīmuqrāṭiyya wa ḥuqūq al-insān fi'l-Islām* (Doha: Markaz al-Jazīra li'l-dirāsat, 2012), 14.

[22] "Everything else is just a means, insofar as man is social by nature and Islam is a comprehensive system for life, for creating a social environment for enabling the largest possible number of people to live spiritually and materially in accord with the law of human nature [*al-qānūn al-fiṭrī*] that came from God, i.e., Islam. The Islamic state is nothing other than the political apparatus [*jihāz*] for realizing Islam's exalted ideal of a community founded on good and justice, realizing truth and invalidating falsehood on the entire earth" (Ghannūshī, *Al-ḥurriyyāt al-'āmma*, 93 [2015 ed., 103]).

[23] Ghannūshī, *Al-ḥurriyyāt al-'āmma*, 170 (2015 ed., 192).

FROM ISLAMIC DEMOCRACY TO MUSLIM DEMOCRACY   13

are referred to) for Islam. Under the basic principle that "supreme legitimacy both in ideology and values belongs to the Qur'an and Sunna, which are independent from all state institutions and which provide the framework within which Islamic scholars and their institutions can carry out the task of interpreting the texts and apply them to challenges arising," he outlines a set of principles for the legitimacy of any constitutional order that involves multiple distinct branches and powers of government.

Again, Ghannouchi's views at this stage are quite radically democratic within the tradition of Islamic political thought. But more noteworthy for our present purposes are the non-liberal features of this kind of democratic theory.[24] For example, Ghannouchi insists that Islam favors cooperation and integration over a (Madisonian) conflict model: "The notion of struggle between the state powers must be completely set aside in favor of a cooperative, mutually supportive model, which then becomes a model for all human relationships." In rejecting Madison's arguments from Federalist 10, he writes that "mutual consultation entails a variety of interpretations of the *shari'a*, while it strongly refuses and resists the principle of conflict between Muslims as individuals and communities. It calls them to unity on the basis of creed and as social groupings." Not only is the separation of powers in a Muslim society not justified by the fear of the tyranny of the majority, but he holds that the separation of powers alone is insufficient to prevent oligarchy. Rather, "even if the Islamic system of governance decides to adopt a pluralistic form, it remains immune to creedal conflicts and special interests, because of its unitary religious nature, which favors complementarity and harmony."

What seems clear in Ghannouchi's thought on the scope of the people's constituent power is that designing specific institutional relationships is less important as a mark of the people's freedom to discover its collective will than as part of its obligation to preserve and embody its preexisting shared will and identity. As with certain republican theorists (possibly Rousseau and certain Jacobins), the Islamic political community is primarily a republic of virtue. Its unity around shared purposes and virtues is the ultimate standard by which institutional design is judged, rather than a constitution's ability to manage moral conflict and prevent tyranny.

There is much more that could be said about the theological foundations of this political theory and how he imagines it to advance a vision of human

[24] For all of the subsequent quotations, see Ghannūshī, *Al-ḥurriyyāt al-ʿāmma*, 240–248 (2015 ed., 267–278).

14 ON MUSLIM DEMOCRACY

perfection. But this should suffice to establish the tension between the ideal theory of an Islamic democracy and the theory of pluralist, liberal democracy. Ghannouchi's theory is based not on a people divided over conceptions of the good, but rather on a people that sees itself as God's caliph, His deputy on earth. This "caliphate" is both an individual and collective status. But it is also an aspiration to realize an ideal form of public Islamic deliberative reason. The caliphate is fulfilled collectively when the community of the deputized believers deliberates publicly about the meaning of revealed texts, its genuine interests, the circumstances of the age, and the conditions for applying this or that legal norm.

Thus, for Ghannouchi "there is no contradiction in saying that the people is the source of sovereignty and that the Qur'an and prophetic Sunna are the source of legislation. The people is who understands the Book and Sunna, acts in accordance with them, and reflects on its own conditions and circumstances to see what matters are for application and what matters are for suspension or amendment."[25] The people's sovereign powers are related to all of the actions that relate to bringing God's will into reality. All of the powers of reception, interpretation, judgment, imagination, deliberation, application, and enforcement are held by the people. If we compare this to the "sleeping sovereign" metaphor,[26] on this view God is the sleeping sovereign who has uttered His commands and instructions at one single point in time and then left them to an agent for enforcement. The people here is God's minister, agent, or deputy, holding all powers of interpreting the sovereign's instructions, fitting them to the circumstances, and enforcing them. Barring a new sovereign intervention (which for Sunni Muslims is doctrinally related to the return of the Messiah), the people's authority is thus irrevocable. Since God is not going to intervene directly to correct misguided interpretations of His will, the people can be seen as fully sovereign and all claims to truth or authority in understanding His instructions are struggles within that sovereign body.

It should be clear enough from the preceding that Ghannouchi's pre-2011 ideal theory was of a democracy organized around a shared collective endorsement of a conception of the good and a comprehensive doctrine. It is a vision of a radically egalitarian and democratic perfectionist political order, where the conception of the person is built around the theological anthropology of mankind's universal vicegerency of God. It is tolerant and protects

---

[25] Ghannūshī, *Al-ḥurriyyāt al-ʿāmma*, 120 (2015 ed., 134–135).
[26] Richard Tuck, *The Sleeping Sovereign: The Invention of Modern Democracy* (Cambridge, UK: Cambridge University Press, 2016).

extensive civil and political liberties, but it is not liberal and still less fully secular. Importantly, Ghannouchi's own comprehensive theory was not all he wrote on political matters. This kind of philosophy always coexisted with a different register of thought, more public, thinner, more pragmatic, more immediate, more liberal in some ways. But the ideal theory was never officially abandoned or repudiated.

Pluralism, Consensus, Law: "Muslim Democracy" as Non-Ideal Theory

The idea of a break with political Islam and its replacement by something called "Muslim democracy" did not emerge with the 2011 revolutions. Scholars have been writing about "post-Islamism" and an ideological shift to "Muslim democracy" since the mid-1990s.[27] While it falls somewhat out of the scope of this study, it is important to note that widespread disillusionment in Iran with the project of creating an Islamic state has led to a very rich reformist discourse by religious intellectuals, many of whom were early partisans of the idea of an Islamic republic.[28] It must also be noted that the ideal theory of a "republic of virtue" that harmonizes the demands of divine

---

[27] For example, Asef Bayat, "The Coming of a Post-Islamist Society," *Critique: Journal for Critical Studies of the Middle East* 5, no. 9 (1996): 43–52; Seyyed Vali Reza Nasr, "The Rise of 'Muslim Democracy,'" *Journal of Democracy* 16, no. 2 (2005): 13–27; Robert W. Hefner, ed., *Remaking Muslim Politics: Pluralism, Contestation, Democratization* (Princeton, NJ: Princeton University Press, 2009); Michaelle Browers, *Political Ideology in the Arab World: Accommodation and Transformation* (Cambridge: Cambridge University Press, 2009), esp. ch. 2, "A More Inclusive Islamism? The *Wasatiyya* Trend"; and Jocelyne Cesari, *The Awakening of Muslim Democracy: Religion, Modernity, and the State* (Cambridge, UK: Cambridge University Press, 2014). See, most recently, Ravza Altuntaş Çakır, *A Political Theory of Muslim Democracy* (Edinburgh: Edinburgh University Press, 2022), which is the first book-length study of the ideological and theoretical aspects of Muslim democracy.

[28] These include the well-known figures of Abdolkarim Soroush and Mohsen Kadivar, both living presently in exile in the United States. (See Abdolkarim Soroush, *Reason, Freedom, and Democracy in Islam: Essential Writings of 'Abdolkarim Soroush*, trans. and ed. Mahmoud Sadri and Ahmad Sadri (New York: Oxford University Press, 2000). They also include figures like Muḥammad Mujtahid Shabastarī, Muḥammad Ḥussein Ṭabāṭabā'ī, Mahdī Ḥā'irī Yazdī, and Muṣṭafā Malikīān. See, e.g., H. E. Chehabi, "Society and State in Islamic Liberalism," *State, Culture, and Society* 1, no. 3 (Spring 1985): 85–101; Mahmoud Sadri, "Sacral Defense of Secularism: The Political Theologies of Soroush, Shabestari, and Kadivar," *International Journal of Politics, Culture and Society* 15, no. 2 (Winter 2001): 257–270; Babak Rahimi, "Democratic Authority, Public Islam, and Shi'i Jurisprudence in Iran and Iraq: Hussain Ali Montazeri and Ali Sistani," *International Political Science Review* 33, no. 2 (2012): 193–208; and the excellent book-length studies Tawfiq Alsaif, *Islamic Democracy and Its Limits: The Iranian Experience Since 1979* (London: Saqi, 2007), Meysam Badamchi, *Post-Islamist Political Theory: Iranian Intellectuals and Political Liberalism in Dialogue* (Cham, Switzerland: Springer, 2017), and Eskandar Sadeghi-Boroujerdi, *Revolution and Its Discontents: Political Thought and Reform in Iran* (Cambridge, UK: Cambridge University Press, 2019).

16 ON MUSLIM DEMOCRACY

and popular sovereignty always coexisted not only with deep personal pragmatism and flexibility on Ghannouchi's part but also with less perfectionist and more pluralistic aspects of his theoretical writings, as well as the public statements of the various political formations from the Islamic Tendency Movement to Ennahda. The same text, for example, that denounces Madisonian pluralism and calls for a moral unity in political life explicitly declares toleration for and willingness to collaborate with a full range of political parties (including Communist ones). So we should not picture a clean break between a pre-revolutionary, "utopian perfectionist" political thought in Ghannouchi's writings and a post-2011 "pragmatic, pluralist" political thought. The two have long coexisted, and it is not clear that an unambiguous unity can be established for all of Ghannouchi's theoretical reflections.

Nonetheless, while the pragmatic and radically pluralist elements of Ghannouchi's thought predated 2011 and the long constituent moment of Tunisian politics that culminated in the 2014 constitution, the post-2014 period is important both for some formal and official breaks with the legacy of "political Islam" and for the nature of Ghannouchi's published writings. The single most important official moment is the decision of Ennahda to formally abandon the label "political Islam" and describe itself as a "Muslim democratic" party at its May 20–22, 2016, party congress. The concluding statement of the congress declares that "the Ennahda Party has in practice gone beyond all the justifications that may be used to consider it part of what is called 'political Islam,' and that this common label does not express the essence of its current identity nor reflect the substance of its future vision. Ennahda believes its work to be within an authentic endeavor to form a broad trend of Muslim democrats who reject any contradiction between the values of Islam and those of modernity."[29] As noted by many both within[30]

[29] "Conference Concluding Statement," 2016 (on file with the author).

[30] See the comments of Ennahda party member (and former Tunisian minister of employment and vocational training) Sayida Ounissi two months before the May 2016 party congress in "Ennahda from Within: Islamists or 'Muslim Democrats'?," Islamists on Islamism Today series, Brookings Institution, March 23, 2016, https://www.brookings.edu/research/ennahda-from-within-islamists-or-muslim-democrats-a-conversation/. Longtime Ennahda activist and party leader Said Ferjani also asserted that "Islamism ended once Ennahda entered government and shared responsibility for social and economic provision and became accountable to the electorate and to civil society" (Said Ferjani, "The 'End of Islamism' and the Future of Tunisia," Hudson Institute, April 29, 2016, https://www.hudson.org/research/12349-the-end-of-islamism-and-the-future-of-tunisia). Ferjani has also been quoted as saying that "Islamism is not an ideology for governing. It's a language of opposition" (quoted in Monica Marks, "How Big Were the Changes Tunisia's Ennahda Party Just Made at Its National Congress?," Washington Post, May 25, 2016, https://www.washingtonpost.com/news/mon key-cage/wp/2016/05/25/how-big-were-the-changes-made-at-tunisias-ennahda-just-made-at-its-national-congress/. Ghannouchi himself presented this to a Western audience as "a result of 35 years

FROM ISLAMIC DEMOCRACY TO MUSLIM DEMOCRACY 17

and outside the party, this was less a break than a ratification of long-term elements of the party's ideology and political culture.

However, this more formal and seemingly permanent turn is also a call for more substantive doctrinal reformulation. While elements of the more radical commitment to political pluralism always existed alongside the more ideal, perfectionist elements in Ghannouchi's thought, it must be said that almost none of the elements of perfectionism and "universal caliphate" talk can be discerned in his post-2011 writings and speeches. The shift is less a matter of addition of the pluralist elements than of subtraction. Ghannouchi's post-revolutionary writings and speeches have been gathered in a number of places. One volume, *Irhasat al-thawra* (Premonitions of the revolution),[31] contains essays, articles, and interviews from 1999 to 2014, with the bulk originally published from 2010 on. Most of the essays translated in this volume are taken from this collection. This section will draw on some of his post-revolutionary writings from this collection, particularly those from the crisis year of 2013: "The Implications and Requirements of a Post-Revolutionary Constitution" (translated in this volume), "Human Rights in Islam" (translated in this volume), "The Democratic Transition in Tunisia," "The New View of Tunisia," "From the Founding to the Revolutionary Constitution," "Freedom of Conscience," and "The Tunisian Model Is Confirmed and Verified." Ghannouchi has also published a series of pamphlets on "the grounding of modern conceptualizations" of various core political terms: "democracy," "citizenship," "secularism," and "freedom"[32] (although they often consist of short essays and interviews from before 2011). In

---

of constant self-evaluation and more than two years of intense introspection and discussion at the grass-roots level. At an Ennahda Party congress held in May, more than 80 percent of the delegates voted in favor of this formal shift, which represents not so much a sea change as a ratification of long held beliefs. Our values were already aligned with democratic ideals, and our core convictions have not changed. What has changed, rather, is the environment in which we operate. Tunisia is finally a democracy rather than a dictatorship; that means that Ennahda can finally be a political party focusing on its practical agenda and economic vision rather than a social movement fighting against repression and dictatorship." Ghannouchi, "From Political Islam to Muslim Democracy."

[31] Rāshid al-Ghannūshī, *Irhāṣāt al-thawra* (Tunis: Dār al-mujtahid, 2015). The title of this book is meant to represent Ghannouchi's response to the charge that Islamists sat out the 2011 revolution and were never devoted to a democratic, revolutionary break with the previous regime (personal communication with Ghannouchi, January 1, 2019).

[32] *Al-dimuqrāṭiyya naḥu taʾṣīl li-mafāhīm muʿāṣira* (Tunis: Dār al-Ṣaḥwa, 2015); *Al-muwāṭana naḥu taʾṣīl li-mafāhīm muʿāṣira* (Tunis: Dār al-Ṣaḥwa, 2016); *Al-ʿilmāniyya naḥu taʾṣīl li-mafāhīm muʿāṣira* (Tunis: Dār al-Ṣaḥwa, 2016) *Al-ḥurriyya naḥu taʾṣīl li-mafāhīm muʿāṣira* (Tunis: Dār al-Ṣaḥwa, 2016). Other short pamphlet-style publications include *Ruʾya fī al-ʿamal: al-niqābī wa al-iqtiṣādī* (Tunis: n.p., 2017); *Naḥu afaq jadīd: nuṣūṣ ḥawla al-Islām al-dīmuqrāṭī* (Tunis: n.p., 2018); and *Shurūṭ al-nahḍa ʿinda al-mufakkir Mālik bin Nabī* (Tunis: n.p., 2020).

18   ON MUSLIM DEMOCRACY

addition to these, he has published a number of his Friday sermons (*khutab*) from the post-revolutionary period.[33]

A number of these essays are translated in this volume, and readers can draw their own lessons and conclusions. But, on my reading, the basic outline and distinctive features of Ghannouchi's ideology of Muslim democracy are the following: (1) political and civil freedoms are the necessary precondition for all other social and religious goods, and freedom as a value is affirmed in many aspects of Islamic theology and practice; (2) political life must be seen primarily as a contract to jointly pursue shared worldly and social goals, rather than to advance a specifically Islamic moral community; (3) the existing range of moral and political pluralism in Tunisian society must be treated as a more or less fixed fact about society; (4) Islamic morality requires pursuing political agreement given the existing ideological disagreement that presently exists; and thus (5) the *shari'a* is now an almost generic commitment to the rule of law and limited government, rather than a denser corpus of rules, methods, and principles.

Long before the 2011 revolution and drafting of the 2014 constitution, Ghannouchi wrote numerous essays on the importance, meaning, and priority of both individual and political freedoms in Islam, including two translated and published in this volume ("Basic Freedoms in Islam" and "Freedom First"). These essays are noteworthy because they do not merely reiterate the classic Islamist assertion of a "positive" conception of freedom (as popularized by thinkers such as Abu'l-A'la Mawdudi and Sayyid Qutb) according to which Islam frees us to act according to our innate inclination to monotheism and in line with the ethical prescriptions of the *shari'a*. Of course, Ghannouchi does still retain something of this positive, perfectionist conception of freedom, with all of its attractions and dangers. He writes in "Basic Freedoms in Islam" that "the more humans are subservient to God, the further they advance along the scale of emancipation. They become *more free* because faith and obedience provide them with energy to advance their aspirations, promote their interests, control their needs and desires, mobilize their talents, and strengthen their willpower."

But when Ghannouchi writes of "basic freedoms" and the priority of freedom, he also makes a point to valorize the freedom of the human subject to act and choose without constraint, or what is conventionally referred to as "negative" freedom. This kind of freedom, or freedom of the will in a social

---

[33] Rāshid al-Ghannūshī, *Al-minbar: khuṭab jum'a ba'd al-thawra* (Tunis: Dār al-mujtahid, 2015).

context, is for Ghannouchi "a condition for moral responsibility, which is in itself a fundamental element in the process of piety." Thus, while Ghannouchi does not abandon the conception of freedom as self-mastery or moral perfection, he combines this with a recognition of the political and moral value of more liberal understandings of freedom. For example, in "Freedom First" he writes that "there is no real justification for worrying about the effects that pluralism and freedom in general might have on Islam, because all the misfortunes that have afflicted Islam and Muslims came about when the Islamic world was neither pluralistic nor free. If there is a real danger to Islam that we should fear, it would be intellectual inertia and the despotism of rulers. Freedom is good, a blessing, and one of the major objectives of Islam, and when it is denied, people's humanity is denied and God's religion is exposed to the gravest dangers. How could it be right for Islamists to call on ruling parties, most of which are secular, to recognize freedom, when they are not prepared to offer them reciprocal recognition?"

On my reading, this long-standing interest in freedom and civil society, predating the Jasmine Revolution and the official turn to "Muslim democracy," is the primary starting point and framing for understanding the ideology of Muslim democracy. But the 2011–2014 constituent period was crucial in accelerating certain developments and shifts in emphasis.

One primary shift is the increasing emphasis that Ghannouchi places on the precedent of the Prophet's covenant (Sahifa) of Medina. Throughout his many statements and articles since 2011, Ghannouchi returns time and again to what he sees as the lessons of the Sahifa. Of course, this has long been regarded as the foundational moment of Islamic governance, although not the moment that provided authoritative precedent for jurists and theologians after the death of the Prophet. But what Ghannouchi takes as its example has undergone a remarkable transformation. In *Public Freedoms in the Islamic State* Ghannouchi uses it precisely to argue for a perfectionist vision of politics. The lesson of Medina is that politics is not merely about the (Madisonian) purposes of managing conflict or advancing worldly political goals; rather, its aim is to form a genuine community in which all can participate in forming and pursuing a shared and common will.

Ghannouchi developed a slightly more complex view of the significance of the Sahifa in the years prior to the revolution. In some essays, he views Medina as having created a kind of hybrid form of political community and membership, according to which Muslims achieved the union of moral community and political association, while the latter was offered to

20   ON MUSLIM DEMOCRACY

non-Muslims. In a 2010 article he uses the fact that the Sahifa of Medina involves both a confessional conception of *umma* and a political conception of it to argue that non-Muslims had always enjoyed "citizenship rights" in Islam, and that modern understandings of equal citizenship do not depend on a prior commitment to secularism.[34] In a later article from that same year, he again stresses that Medina was a city of multiple religious communities in which citizenship was based on shared possession of a territory, not shared creed. But at this point he was still eager to stress that this meant that Islam was not merely a private matter but also "the source and reference for law and values for the community that believes in it through the institution of *shura*. The modern mechanisms of democracy can be identified as based on this, which moves it from being a mere source of moral values toward an institution through which the *umma* exercises its authority and power over its rulers, via elected committees that represent public opinion." Within such a system "there need be no fear of Islam on grounds of freedom, since Islam is a comprehensive emancipatory resource, based on the nature [*fitra*] that God has created us with, and is thus not any kind of imposition on it or alienation from it."[35]

But the post-2011 writings go even further in stressing that the lesson of Medina for post-revolutionary Tunisia is that Islamic governance was founded originally in circumstances of radical pluralism, precisely where a shared will or purpose among "citizens" could not be assumed. Ghannouchi writes that the first written constitution in Islam (if not the world), the Sahifa, codified an essentially pluralist political formation, and that "we [Muslims] are lucky that our first state was a pluralist state."[36] In a later essay he reiterates that the founding of Medina provides Muslims with the authoritative example of founding a pluralistic political order, with citizenship (not religion) as the fundamental principle of rights and duties.[37] The authoritative precedent of the Sahifa thus becomes the overarching, legitimating frame for accepting pluralist democracy.

The fundamental mechanism of the political order in this model is contract (*ta'aqud*) rather than moral formation. The Sahifa presents to Muslims the model of the Prophet establishing a state on the basis of contract in a

[34] "Al-Islām wa'l-muwāṭana," in *Al-muwāṭana naḥu ta'ṣīl li-mafāhīm mu'āṣira*, 12.
[35] "Ḥiwār ḥawla al-muwāṭana," in *Al-muwāṭana naḥu ta'ṣīl li-mafāhīm mu'āṣira*, 29.
[36] "Ma'ānī wa mujibāt dustūr mā ba'd al-thawra," in *Irhāṣāt al-thawra*, 227. Translated in this volume as "The Implications and Requirements of a Post-Revolutionary Constitution."
[37] "Ru'ā li-Tūnis al-jadīda," in *Irhāṣāt al-thawra*, 241.

religiously pluralist society, a state that establishes a civilizational model open to all mankind, capable of assimilating and incorporating all creeds, cultures, and races within a contractual and civilizational framework, without expulsion, wars of cleansing, or plans for forced assimilation.[38] In this religiously plural society, religion itself figures as a kind of dignifying (*takrim*) of man with reason and freedom. It is not the role of the state to prove the truth of any one religion or to provide for religious conformity; the state's role is, rather, to recognize members as they are, and to provide for peaceful coexistence, cooperation, and the development of a spirit of commonality based on equality in citizenship.[39] In this model of a political society, the purpose of governance and political life is almost exclusively "secular": protecting persons based on residence and membership (not creed), dispensing justice on the basis of equality, providing for mutual defense, and upholding contracts.

Ghannouchi uses this understanding of Medina not only to argue for a limited conception of politics and to justify political cooperation with non-Islamic parties but also to argue for a broad consensus model of constituent politics. As noted above, while Ghannouchi's Ennahda party quickly emerged as the country's single largest political formation, it was unable to dominate political institutions. (Ghannouchi claims repeatedly that there was no wish to do so even if they had had the numbers.) As a consequence, Islamists were forced to compromise on a number of symbolic issues: forgoing any reference to *shari'a*, dropping the language of gender "complementarity," affirming the universality of human rights, removing the criminalization of blasphemy and offenses against the sacred from the constitution (but not necessarily from ordinary legislation), and adopting a hybrid presidential-parliamentary model of governance rather than the parliamentary model Islamists preferred.

What is interesting is that Ghannouchi does not merely defend these as necessary compromises given the balance of power, or as "the best we could get," or as a distinctly political choice to prioritize stability over partisan goals. Rather, he advances a view of consensus itself as a highest principle of legitimacy, particularly in constituent moments. This is most remarkable in his discussions of why they agreed to drop the *shari'a* clause from the constitution. He claims that the highest commitment in the drafting of the constitution was that it gain the widest possible agreement in Tunisian

[38] "Dustūr Madīna," in *Al-muwāṭana naḥu ta'ṣīl li-mafāhīm mu'āṣira*, 58.
[39] "Dustūr Madīna," in *Al-muwāṭana naḥu ta'ṣīl li-mafāhīm mu'āṣira*, 60.

22   ON MUSLIM DEMOCRACY

society, rather than the consensus sufficient for ratification. The constitution must be seen as the constitution not of a particular party but rather of the whole country, in which the entire range of political, intellectual, and social trends is found. Since it is crucial that the people and the citizens in all their orientations see themselves in it, the constitution could not be promulgated with a bare 51 percent majority but instead must be ratified on a broader consensus.

But here it gets tricky, since a constitution must also guard and reflect the identity of the particular country it is set to govern. In the case of Tunisia, there was a consensus around an Arab, Islamic identity, but the determination of what those terms mean must not be monopolized by any party. Here Ghannouchi's "populist" (quasi-Protestant) theology enters: "In Islam there is no church that monopolizes [*tahtakir*] the interpretation of Islam. Instead, this is a matter left to the community and to ordinary people through their own institutions, which elaborate the meaning of that Arab-Islamic identity. Thus, when the question of the place of *shari'a* law in the constitution was raised, we found that it was a matter of disagreement [*mawdu' ikhtilafi*], and we said that constitutions are not based on what there is deep disagreement on but rather what is a matter of consensus."[40] This, I think, is a crucial passage (perhaps *the* crucial passage) for understanding the move from Islamism to "Muslim democracy." Of course, Ghannouchi always knew that many contemporary Muslims did not wish to enshrine the *shari'a* as the governing law of their society, and yet his entire intellectual project was traditionally an interpretation of what it means for a Muslim community to govern itself by *shari'a*. And, in some of that previous writing, the rejection of *shari'a* itself was not treated at all as a reasonable disagreement. Yet in the constitution-drafting period, the view is that it would be unreasonable or inappropriate to base so foundational a concept of legitimacy and legislative sovereignty on a controversial principle. But why? What makes disagreement about the *shari'a* itself reasonable or worth respecting, rather than mere disagreement on specific points of *shari'a*?

Ghannouchi doesn't elaborate on this question. What he does say is that "the constitution should also be based on a foundation of human values because we are part of humankind, which has refined certain principles such as democracy and human rights. We are also heirs to the principles of reform and consider the reformist school one of the sources of our constitution and

---

[40] "Ma'ānī wa mujibāt dustūr mā ba'd al-thawra," in *Irhāṣāt al-thawra*, 228.

FROM ISLAMIC DEMOCRACY TO MUSLIM DEMOCRACY   23

of our distinctive Tunisian way of thinking. We want to build a civil state in which legitimacy is derived from the people [al-nas], that is, from the populace [sha'b] and the governed. There is no legitimacy for any ruler except from a clear delegation from the people through free, fair, and pluralistic elections."[41] It is not entirely clear what the deeper Islamic or principled foundation for this preference for wide consensus is, except for the repeated insistence that "we need to expand freedoms as much as we can. Justice is one of the ultimate objectives of Islam, as is freedom. . . . Constitutions serve to prevent despotism, not to prevent freedom, and every move toward expanding freedom moves in an Islamic direction."

He makes similar statements on the other points of disagreement. While he thinks that Islamists were unfairly criticized over the term *takamul* to refer to the nature of gender relations (he points out that it literally refers to men and women completing each other, and not that women are *merely* men's complements), he concedes that part of the lesson here is to "avoid terms that arouse suspicion or where people do not agree on what they mean, so we have advised our colleagues to drop the term 'complementarity,' although we believe that complementarity is a form of equality and that the two genders complement each other, not that just one of them complements the other. But as long as there are any misgivings about the term, then we say that constitutions should be consensual and not divisive."[42]

The question of the universality of human rights has a similarly pragmatic implication for Ghannouchi. Of course, this language is sensitive since it raises questions about the universality of Islam and whether Islam has a potentially superior approach to human rights. But "we believe that we Islamists should be happy that humankind agrees that humans have rights regardless of their race or religion, and so we should not be upset about the idea that human rights are universal. This is a guarantee of rights and freedoms, and Islam came to serve the interests of people, so anything that guarantees people's interests and rights is part of Islam, even if it is not specified in any Qur'anic verse or hadith."[43]

In a separate essay, he addresses more directly and substantively the harmony between Islamic and secular conceptions of human rights.[44] This is

---

[41] "Ma'ānī wa mujibāt dustūr mā ba'd al-thawra," in *Irhāṣāt al-thawra*, 228.

[42] "Ma'ānī wa mujibāt dustūr mā ba'd al-thawra," in *Irhāṣāt al-thawra*, 229.

[43] "Ma'ānī wa mujibāt dustūr mā ba'd al-thawra," in *Irhāṣāt al-thawra*, 230.

[44] "Ḥuqūq al-insān fi'l-Islam," in *Irhāṣāt al-thawra*, 231–236. Translated in this volume as "Human Rights in Islam."

24 ON MUSLIM DEMOCRACY

not particularly remarkable at this point for his defense of specific rights like freedom of conscience, freedom of religion, rights to property and to the fruits of one's labor, and the social rights (work, basic income, education, housing, even political participation), all of which he thinks are modern juridical mechanisms for defending interests that Islam also values and which are in their general direction in accord with the precepts of Islam. What is more interesting is the way that the fundamental theological foundation of his perfectionist political philosophy is deployed to defend this replacement of the *shari'a* with "universal" human rights. The doctrine of the universal caliphate of mankind (*istikhlaf*) in this essay now refers to God's dignifying (*takrim*) of all mankind and the fact that Islam seeks the welfare and happiness of all of humanity, not just Muslims. The individual, "negative" freedoms that underpin much modern human rights discourse are seen as squarely within the heritage of Islam since they are the foundation of the quintessential act of faith: the declaration of the *shahada*, which is an expression of the individual's freedom and responsibility before God. If some of the specific articulations of the *shari'a* and human rights appear divergent, this is of little concern, since Islamic law articulates the various interests and goods of mankind in a scaled, gradual way from the fundamental and necessary to details that embellish an overall rights scheme. What matters ultimately is a convergence on the interests themselves, which Ghannouchi sees in modern human rights.

How to Think About Muslim Democracy

How should political theorists (and social scientists) understand the move to an ideology like that described above? By way of conclusion, I would like to suggest three possibilities. The first is that it is purely an ideology of convenience, rhetorical messaging forced upon a movement by political necessity. This does not imply that the ideology is merely window dressing or that it is advanced insincerely; rather, it demonstrates that a party has moved beyond its ideological phase into the realm of post-ideological political competition. Between 2011 and 2021, Ennahda participated in multiple governing coalitions (both formal and informal) with a variety of secular parties. During this period, Ennahda's vote shares in parliamentary elections ranged from 20 percent to 37 percent, with its relative vote share declining in every election from the first democratic election to the National Constituent Assembly in 2011. While the party maintained its socially conservative base, its own campaign rhetoric minimized reference to divisive religious goals, and after elections it maintained a strategy of governing through consensus with other major parties. Its concessions on religious issues eventually caused a faction to splinter off and form a more conservative Islamist bloc (Karama) in the 2019 elections.

Political scientists have traditionally put forward explanations for the moderation of Islamist parties, including (1) electoral incentives, (2) the effect of state repression, (3) interaction with other political parties and movements, and (4) the effect of many party activists living in exile in liberal democracies.[45] To these we might add a variation on the second explanation, the repression-moderation hypothesis. Democratic transitions are always precarious and never guaranteed success. But in the case of Tunisia between 2011 and 2021 there was no guarantee that Ennahda in particular would not be the target of an anti-democratic coup. The case of Egypt in 2013, which essentially destroyed the Muslim Brotherhood as an active force in Egyptian political life, was a constant cautionary tale for Ghannouchi and Ennahda leadership. Indeed, as of April 2023 the Saied government appears determined to formally eradicate all political opposition, especially the Ennahda party. That this kind of counter-revolutionary coup was a possibility all along lay behind Ghannouchi's view that forming coalitions with secular rivals between 2011 and 2021 was a necessary strategy for maintaining the incentive for all political forces to remain committed to the democratic system.

On this view, the turn to an ideology of "Muslim democracy" can be interpreted as a way of signaling to other political parties Ennahda's commitment to democratic transition and that it does not aim at a monopoly of political power or turning Tunisia into an Islamic republic.[46] This is a strategy of reassurance to other forces designed to support democratic transition while also aiming at securing certain reciprocal guarantees to Ennahda that those parties will not seek their exclusion or repression. It is thus part of a broader strategy, along with Ennahda's refusal to seek the exclusion of former Ben Ali officials and to support the controversial 2017 "administrative reconciliation law" that granted impunity to civil servants who were implicated in

---

[45] For a survey of these views, with a defense of the fourth explanation, see Sharan Grewal, "From Islamists to Muslim Democrats: The Case of Tunisia's Ennahda," *American Political Science Review* 114, no. 2 (2020): 519–535.

[46] See, for example, Stathis N. Kalyvas, "Commitment Problems in Emerging Democracies: The Case of Religious Parties," *Comparative Politics* 32, no. 4 (July 2000): 379–398.

26 ON MUSLIM DEMOCRACY

corruption under Ben Ali and allow them to return to government offices. This controversial legislation blocked investigation into the prior corruption and prevented courts from ruling on human rights violations.[47]

This interpretation sees the turn to "Muslim democracy" not in doctrinal or intellectual terms but perhaps as an anti-ideology of political necessity. It lies somewhere between recognizing the fact that most Ennahda leaders and activists had for a variety of reasons adopted a moderate, pluralist political praxis and stressing the strategic dilemmas of a minority Islamist party trying to avoid a counterrevolution and political crackdown. This interpretation, however, does not make much of the ideological and theoretical aspects of "Muslim democracy" as a worldview and conception of politics. I would thus like to consider two other frames of analysis.

A second way of thinking about Muslim democracy is through certain (Rawlsian) liberal concerns with how comprehensive doctrines grapple with the fact of deep moral disagreement when they enter the world of democratic politics. Is the turn to Muslim democracy reflective of a historical intellectual reckoning with the fact of political and moral pluralism in modernity and how the relationship between Islam as a system of truth and Islam as a system of political justice must be rethought? Rawls himself conjectures that "once political groups enter the public forum of political discussion and appeal to other groups that do not share their comprehensive doctrine . . . it is rational for them to move out of the narrower circle of their own views to develop political conceptions in terms of which they can explain and justify their preferred policies to a wider public so as to put together a majority. As they do this they are led to formulate political conceptions of justice. These conceptions provide the common currency of discussion and a deeper basis for explaining the meaning and implications of the principles and policies each group endorses."[48]

Readers of this volume can judge for themselves the strengths and depths of Ghannouchi's argument for moral and metaphysical (in addition to political) pluralism and whether the turn away from the Islamic *shari'a* is deeply enough grounded for a full doctrine that could take the place of the earlier theory of Islamic democracy. It is possible that the present relationship of Islamic doctrine (as understood by Ghannouchi and others) to the 2014

---

[47] See Amna Guellali, "New Reconciliation Law Threatens Tunisia's Democracy," Human Rights Watch, October 2, 2017, https://www.hrw.org/news/2017/10/02/new-reconciliation-law-threatens-tunisias-democracy.

[48] John Rawls, *Political Liberalism* (New York: Columbia University Press, 1993), 165.

FROM ISLAMIC DEMOCRACY TO MUSLIM DEMOCRACY 27

constitution is more akin to a constitutional consensus that Islamists can nonetheless be content with for principled reasons (some of them "Islamic" and some of them "freestanding," derived from political experience), unlike the merely modus vivendi compromises with authoritarianism.[49]

Of course, Rawls's ideas of a "constitutional consensus" and an "overlapping consensus" are ideal types, and his idea of a sequence according to which political groups only begin to defend their policies in public once a roughly democratic constitution is established does not accord with reality. But there are some relevant questions here pertaining to the exact relationship between Islam as a comprehensive doctrine and the 2014 Tunisian constitution.

It should be clear what the core ambiguities are. Whereas Ghannouchi's ideal theory for an Islamic democracy imagines that the Islamic *shari'a* is both the foundation of the political community and the framework for public reason in a functioning political system, the 2014 constitution excludes any reference to *shari'a* at all. Whereas the ideal theory is based on a conception of the person as both individually and collectively God's deputy on earth, the 2014 constitution does speak of an "elevated status of humankind" but is otherwise based on the principle of equal citizenship within a nation-state. Whereas the ideal theory was fundamentally committed to moral unity across all political institutions and between rulers and members of the community, the 2014 constitutions articulates simply the aims of "building a republican, democratic and participatory system, in the framework of a civil state founded on the sovereignty of the people, exercised through the peaceful alternation of power through free elections, and on the principle of the separation and balance of powers, which guarantees the freedom of association in conformity with the principles of pluralism, an impartial administration, and good governance, which are the foundations of political competition, where the state guarantees the supremacy of the law and the respect for freedoms and human rights, the independence of the judiciary,

---

[49] Rawls defines a constitutional consensus in the following way: "The [liberal] principles [of political justice] are accepted simply as principles and not as grounded in certain ideas of society and person of a political conception, much less in a shared public conception. And so the consensus is not deep. . . . While there is agreement on certain basic political rights and liberties—on the right to vote and freedom of speech and association, and whatever else is required for the electoral and legislative procedures of democracy—there is disagreement among those holding liberal principles as to the more exact content and boundaries of these rights and liberties, as well as on what further rights and liberties are to be counted as basic and so merit legal if not constitutional protection. The constitutional consensus is narrow in scope . . . not including the basic structure but only the political procedures of a democratic government." Rawls, *Political Liberalism*, 158–159.

28 ON MUSLIM DEMOCRACY

the equality of rights and duties between all citizens, male and female, and equality between all regions."[50]

It is true that Ghannouchi has given *reasons* for the acceptability of the constitution derived from plausible religious commitments, but his preference is to do so without reference to the prior doctrine. He suggests rather a simple continuity in his views. Even when he acknowledges that the constitution required compromises and concessions, he does not expressly say whether accepting those compromises means revising earlier views on the fundamental basis for political life.

On my reading, there are two questions in particular of interest: Is the idea of *shari'a* permanently limited to this role of limiting government, or is this something future Tunisians might revise in different political circumstances? And are non-Islamic "comprehensive doctrines" themselves reasonable or merely tolerable? While Muslims may have obligations to respect the freedom of conscience of others, should differences around the fundamental acceptance or rejection of Islam be seen as something internal to reason or a failure of it?

Virtually every other principled question follows from the conception of justice and the permanence of pluralism. There are reasons to think that present constitutional compromises may have principles behind them but still be compromises. First, there is no deep account offered of why disagreement about the *shari'a* itself is reasonable or worth respecting. Rather, there is the observation that presently the question of *shari'a* is too divisive and, more intriguingly, that the objections of Tunisians to *shari'a* rest on misunderstandings and the manipulation of radical secularists.

Second, there is reason to believe that Ghannouchi still regards secular comprehensive doctrines as insufficient grounds for a principled moral life. In his 2013 essay "Human Rights in Islam" (translated in this volume) he writes that the general direction of human rights declarations and international covenants is in accord with the precepts of Islam and its objectives of advancing justice, freedom, and equality in the divine dignifying of humanity, but the experience of humanity shows that humans do not live without adopting God in some fashion: "In the human soul there is a hunger that can be sated only by turning to God." In Ghannouchi's view, the basic defect in modern human rights declarations derived in the most part from materialist philosophies is the claim that humanity can be independent of its Creator in

---

[50] From the preamble: https://www.constituteproject.org/constitution/Tunisia_2014.pdf.

FROM ISLAMIC DEMOCRACY TO MUSLIM DEMOCRACY 29

organizing life and attaining happiness. The results of this, despite some partial progress, are the domination of the strong over the weak, the destruction of the environment, and the fracturing of connection and compassion between humans. Whereas when human rights are based on and refer to the Creator, this gives them a kind of sanctity and makes them secure in the hearts of all believers. It also makes their defense a religious duty, with a reward for performance and a punishment for neglect. And it makes them comprehensive and positive, as opposed to the formalism and partialness of secular human rights schemes, since God is the creator of man and is more knowledgeable of the true needs of His creatures. It dignifies the authority of the law that protects these rights with the authority of religious conscience represented in the feelings of the believers with the eternal supervision of God.[51]

One possibility, as theorized by Rawls, is that the practice of politics could make the liberal principles embedded in the 2014 constitution seem attractive and irreplaceable given the permanence of moral pluralism around questions of religion and lifestyle. Over a long enough period of time, the political compromises involved in accepting the constitution will be given some kind of deeper theological justification. (Of course, this possibility would be negated by the permanence of the coup and authoritarian backsliding.) Other possibilities, however, are conceivable, and even suggested by some of my own conversations with Ghannouchi about democracy and reasonable pluralism published in this volume.

Given these ambiguities, I would like to suggest a third way of understanding Muslim democracy, which involves something like a combination of the two preceding ones. Is Muslim democracy reflective of a turn to politics as a semi-autonomous sphere of human life (not merely derived from metaphysics or ethics) that has its own dynamics and imperatives? If so, does it reflect a turn toward beginning with political values (stability, security, welfare) and seeking a minimal moral consensus with rivals so as to avoid war and violence, but without giving up the possibility for struggling within the political realm for specific values and outcomes? This would reflect an abandonment of the "sovereign imaginary" in politics (in which either divine or popular sovereignty, or a combination of both, is seen as the organizing principle of political order) and a turn to a more provisional conception of politics. It would be a shift from a hegemonic conception of Islamic moral truth

---

[51] "Ḥuqūq al-insān fi'l-Islam," in *Irhāṣāt al-thawra*, 236, and in "Human Rights in Islam" in this volume.

30   ON MUSLIM DEMOCRACY

as the grounding commitment of the political community to an agonistic conception of the political community as composed of rival communities each struggling for primacy within a shared constitutional order.

While the turn to "Muslim democracy" has largely been seen through the lens of moderation and consensus, which generates questions about whether it is sincerely affirmed and potentially a stable commitment, it can also be seen through the lens of political agonism. Agonism recognizes that a large aggregation of people in a nation will have conflicting purposes that engender more or less serious conflict and that groups are given to attempts to use political power to further their own purposes and possibly subordinate others, yet sometimes signal that they are willing to limit the use of political power by law and direct it to public purposes. In turn, politics often requires different capacities than "ethics" does: practical judgment, means-end rationality, consequentialist thinking, and the ability to form coalitions. Antagonism and conflict should be seen not only as failures of democratic transition but also as largely constitutive of "the political" in human societies: "politics" refers to the practices and institutions through which we create and maintain order despite the reality of conflict.

Through this lens, we can make sense not only of the flexibility and pragmatism of Ghannouchi and Ennahda between 2011 and 2021 but also of the expectation that a constitutional order allows for the political pursuit of sectarian political aims. The turn to "Muslim democracy" need not be seen as a way station to full secularization or a Rawlsian overlapping consensus whereby there is a principled commitment to not argue for laws on the basis of religious doctrine. It can be seen primarily as a response to the fundamental circumstances of politics (disagreement and conflict) and a preference for a non-violent constitutional settlement within which parties may then struggle for their own views and programs. It differs from traditional Islamist ideal theory in that it does not theorize a comprehensive Islamic political order from the outset but assumes the world of actually existing politics. It also does not forswear the pursuit of religious objectives in politics, but its choice of priorities may be more contextual, ad hoc, and determined by political judgment given changing circumstances. It accepts pluralism as a fact and a constitutional order perhaps as an "incompletely theorized agreement,"[52] but it does thus not feel the need to provide a deep, Islamic

---

[52] Cass R. Sunstein, "Incompletely Theorized Agreements," *Harvard Law Review* 108, no. 7 (1995): 1733–1772.

account of why other doctrines or ways of life are fundamentally reasonable or principled.

This Volume

This volume first presents ten previously untranslated essays, speeches, and interviews by Ghannouchi. Originally published between 2005 and 2013, these chapters pertain broadly to the themes of civil freedom, pluralist democracy, and the variety of inspirations for contemporary Islamic thought. Following this is a series of dialogues between Ghannouchi and myself on a wide-ranging set of topics from his personal biography to the precise relationship between traditional Islamist commitments and the turn to Muslim democracy. It is hoped that this volume will provide English-speaking readers with a valuable primary source for understanding a vital movement in twenty-first-century Islamic political thought.

ESSAYS ON FREEDOM,
DEMOCRACY, AND
CONSTITUTIONALISM
(RACHED GHANNOUCHI)

1
Basic Freedoms in Islam

Anyone considering the question of freedoms in Islam may perceive a contradiction between religion and freedom. Religion is based on worshipping God ("I created the jinn and humankind only that they might worship Me," Qur'an 51:56), whereas freedom appears to mean quite the opposite—emancipation from all constraints. This understanding has led some groups of Muslims to say that there is no such thing as freedom in Islam.

If we look beyond disputes over words and examine the nature and ultimate objectives of Islam, this apparent contradiction readily disappears. Mankind is God's vicegerent [caliph] on Earth[1] and not a god—a relationship that presupposes a master, who is God Almighty, and a subordinate charged with obligations, who is mankind. However, this relationship requires that mankind enjoy two attributes—reason and freedom. These are the bases of the burden of trust with which mankind has been honored and which all other creatures turned down: "We offered the burden of trust to the heavens, the earth, and the mountains, but they refused to take it on and were afraid of it, but man took it on" (Qur'an 33:72).

Freedom is the condition for mankind's moral obligation to obey God's commandments, as the scholars of Islamic moral theology ['ulamā' al-uṣūl] say, and it is one of the effects of God honoring human beings and placing trust in them: "We have honored the sons of Adam" (Qur'an 17:70). This honor and trust mean that human action involves a choice between worshipping God consciously and voluntarily or rebelling against doing so. After explaining to His servants the path of guidance away from wrongdoing, God says, "Those who wish can believe and those who wish can disbelieve" (Qur'an 18:29).

This is a lecture given at a Ramadan gathering in the Muslim Association Centre in Newcastle, England, in August 2005. Published in *Al-Ḥurriyya naḥu ta'ṣīl li-mafāhīm mu'āṣira* (Tunis: Dār al-Ṣaḥwa, 2016), 23–61.

[1] [On the centrality of this claim for modern Islamic political thought, see Andrew F. March, *The Caliphate of Man: Popular Sovereignty in Modern Islamic Thought* (Cambridge, MA: Belknap Press of Harvard University Press, 2019). —Ed.]

On Muslim Democracy. Rached Ghannouchi and Andrew F. March, Oxford University Press.
© Oxford University Press 2023. DOI: 10.1093/oso/9780197666876.003.0002

36 ON MUSLIM DEMOCRACY

When the Prophet Muhammad was saddened that his people were reluctant to believe, God said, "So would you force people to believe?" (Qur'an 10:99). This means that acts of obedience to God lose all value as acts of worship as God's deputies on Earth if they do not stem from a conscious will that is free and responsible. This necessarily refutes any apparent contradiction between religion and freedom. Rather, freedom itself becomes a condition for religiosity in itself.

Real religiosity is reinforced and enhanced by freedom, in such a way that the freedom of a human being is commensurate with his or her subservience to God. Human freedom is different from the freedom of other beings in the sense that it is distinguished by consciousness and choice, which transcend and are not subject to the logic of immediate necessity. It is poised between the necessity of human needs and choice based on responsible commitment that takes guidance from revelation. This gives hope of, and the possibility for, liberation from dependence on matter, instincts, and impulses. In fact, worshipping God enhances the humanity of mankind and enables humankind to assume the duty of developing and cultivating the world ['imarat al-ard][2] through a devotional path that links human needs to seeking God's favor.

So the more humans are subservient to God, the further they advance along the scale of emancipation. They become *more free* because faith and obedience provide them with energy to advance their aspirations, promote their interests, control their needs and desires, mobilize their talents, and strengthen their willpower.

All of God's deeds are wise and just. How could we conceivably expect anything other than wisdom, justice, and mercy to emanate from the Wise One? Ibn Rushd was not mistaken when he gave his epistle the title *The Decisive Treatise Determining the Connection Between Law and Wisdom*.[3]

---

[2] [The theme of civilizing, cultivating, or developing the Earth (*'imarat al-ard*) is a long-standing aspect of Islamic theological anthropology, derived from Q. 11:61 ("He brought you into being out of the earth, and made you thrive [*ista'marakum*] thereon"). "Civilizing the Earth" was held by many classical thinkers to constitute one of the central purposes for which God created mankind, and for certain ethical theorists one of the (Aristotelian) "functions" (*fi'l; érgon*) of the human. For some modern Islamic thinkers, like the twentieth-century Moroccan legal theorist 'Allal al-Fasi, whom Ghannouchi frequently cites, *'imarat al-ard* is treated as one of the objectives of the divine law. —Ed.]

[3] [Ibn Rushd's text *The Decisive Treatise* takes the form of an Islamic religious opinion (a *fatwa*) in which he defends the practice of philosophy in Islamic legal terms. For an English translation see Averroës. *The Book of the Decisive Treatise Determining the Connection Between the Law and Wisdom; &, Epistle Dedicatory*, trans. Charles E. Butterworth (Provo, UT: Brigham Young University Press, 2001). —Ed.]

BASIC FREEDOMS IN ISLAM   37

Is it significant that in record time Islam caused societies that had been underdeveloped, such as the Arabs, Berbers, Turks, Kurds, and Africans, to advance, enabling them to absorb and develop the heritage of earlier civilizations, such as those of the Greeks, Romans, and Persians, by building cities where trade, sciences, and arts flourished and people of all ethnicities mixed? Cities such as Baghdad, Cordoba, Shiraz, and Sarajevo were open cultural spaces to which talented people of all confessions and ethnicities were drawn and which provided the necessary conditions for creativity, such as basic freedoms—especially freedom of belief—at a time when Europe was mired in ignorance and anyone who dared to interact with this heritage was burned alive in the courts of the Inquisition.

Religious Observances Are a Catalyst for Freedom

When we examine the religious observances prescribed by Islam, we find that they are a clear expression and reinforcement of the faculty of the will, because they are a manifestation of freedom, a product of freedom, an auxiliary to freedom, and a witness to freedom. For example, fasting is to abstain voluntarily from eating, drinking, and so on, despite the need for food and drink. A wonderful example of freedom is the sight of a family gathered around a table piled with delicious food but abstaining while they await the time for *iftar*. Despite being extremely hungry and thirsty, they suppress their desires. It is an exemplary human scene, unparalleled in the animal kingdom.

Faith and the desire to obey God and draw closer to Him are what free Muslims from dependence on their desires and impulses. Muslims are not required to suppress or eliminate these desires, or even to despise and shun them, since these desires have been implanted in them to perform functions that are essential to life. They are, however, required to control them and not to be controlled by them, to be their master and not their slave, and satisfying these desires in accordance with Islamic rules becomes in itself an act of religious observance. Prayer in general, and especially the dawn prayer, is an impressive sight that bears witness to freedom. Love and fear of God drive Muslims to leave their beds, perform their ablutions, and seek God's favor in a devotional atmosphere that affords them comfort, security, peace of mind, strength, and happiness, renewing their resolve and enabling them to persevere with the challenges of life.

38   ON MUSLIM DEMOCRACY

This does not make them oblivious to their problems but provides them with new sources of energy, giving them a renewed passion for life, in the belief that God is looking after and guiding them. This gives them enough strength, initiative, and persistence to face difficulties and challenges from any source.

The story of the Prophet Joseph provides us with useful lessons. Joseph is the prototypical pious young man who can curb his impulses and rise above constraints. This is the basic meaning of freedom, which raises us from the level of animals to that of humans through commitment to an ethical code. Joseph had to balance the claims of religion, in the form of commitment to divine commandments, and of society, which pushed him toward deceit and treachery toward someone who had been generous to him. He preferred to lose his social status and be imprisoned over losing himself by submitting to treachery and vice. In his own well-known words, conveyed to us in admiration by the Qur'an: "My Lord, prison is more to my liking than what they call on me to do" (Qur'an 12:33). It is a testament to religion, which frees the human being from reliance on any factor that would usurp his or her free will and take human beings back to the low level of animals, satisfying their sexual needs as an unconscious and involuntary response so that it becomes an instinctive act and not an act of reason. Freedom is meaningless without the capacity to control one's impulses and personal inclinations. The Prophet Muhammad expressed this when he said: "Strength doesn't mean bringing down your enemies: it means controlling yourself when you're angry."

There are those who say that the question of freedom only arises in the Islamic tradition in two contexts: first, in a social context where freedom is defined as the antithesis of slavery—the free as opposed to the slave—and second, in the context of the relationship between human beings and their Lord with respect to the extent of human free will. The subject has been a heated topic for debate between theologians for centuries, between those who affirmed human freedom to the extent that it detracted from God's absolute power (the Mu'tazila) and those (like the Ash'arites) who defended God's absolute freedom of will and denied any real difference between human deeds and the natural movement of other entities. A third party attempted to find a compromise by arguing that human acts are "acquired" [kasb], but this position remained ambiguous and tended to be grouped with the second position. This latter position, the Ash'ari position, is the one that has dominated Islamic theology since the fifth century of the Islamic era. It was one of the

BASIC FREEDOMS IN ISLAM 39

factors behind the decline of Islamic civilization until the appearance of the reform movement approximately two centuries ago.

From its earliest stages, the Islamic reform movement challenged the determinist doctrines that were prevalent because of domination by a gnostic Sufi culture. The reformers asserted that human beings had agency and were responsible for their fate—a revival of the idea of predestination [*qadar*] with which the first generation that founded Islamic civilization and those who have followed in their path throughout history operated. They see fate [*qadar*] in terms of the specific cosmic and normative order that God established for His servants and which, if humans understand and act properly within it, will ensure their happiness in this world and the next. This requires reflecting on this order, discovering its secrets, and taking advantage of them in accordance with the requirements of *shari'a*. Fate is a conscious submission to divine decrees that shape the universe and that are revealed through prophecies. It is this conscious submission that frees the human will.

Much as a correct understanding of the doctrine of predestination has been and remains a great source of strength for believers and the key to their success, it has also been a factor in their weakness and, when misunderstood, a denial of human will. Even as great a reformer as Muhammad Iqbal[4] said, "The weak Muslim uses divine fate and destiny as an excuse, whereas the strong Muslim sees himself as God's fate and destiny."

Although fate is important, it is wrong to claim that the subject of freedom in the Islamic tradition is confined to these two contexts alone. For freedom, as the Tunisian theorist of the objectives of Islamic law [*maqasid al-shari'a*] Muhammad al-Tahir Ibn 'Ashur (1879–1973) has explained, is one of the objectives of the Islamic *shari'a*. He writes that the Muslim community must be free, not partially but generally and in all aspects of life, since all of the obligations of the *shari'a* are void in the absence of freedom. And the Prophetic hadith says: "God has pardoned my *umma* for their mistakes, their forgetfulness, and that which they have been forced to do under duress" (Hadith al-Nawawi, 39).

Freedom, therefore, is a condition for moral responsibility, which is in itself a fundamental element in the process of developing piety.

---

[4] [Muhammad Iqbal (1877–1938) was a South Asian poet and philosopher particularly known in the modern Islamic reformist tradition for *The Reconstruction of Religious Thought in Islam*, a series of lectures published as a book in 1930. —Ed.]

40 ON MUSLIM DEMOCRACY

It is no surprise that Islamic scholars have taken an interest in the question of freedom, especially through the science of the objectives of shari'a (maqasid al-shari'a). While the scholars traditionally identified five·universal necessary objectives that the divine law serves to preserve (religion, life, reason, property, and lineage), the great scholar al-Tahir Ibn 'Ashur added two other objectives, justice and freedom, in his book *The Objectives of Islamic Shari'a*.[5]

In the Qur'an, God Almighty defines His Prophet's mission as being to "command the right and forbid the wrong, to allow them whatever is beneficial and ban whatever is harmful, and to relieve them of their burden and of the chains that bound them" (Qur'an 7:157). Islam came to break the shackles that bind souls, minds, and bodies and that subjugate some humans to fellow humans under any pretext.

Islam, therefore, did not introduce slavery nor command its establishment, although slavery was a common practice throughout the world and the basis of economic production in various societies. Islamic teachings and rulings worked to promote the emancipation of slaves and gradually to dry up the sources of slavery, despite the deviations from the values and objectives of Islam that occurred on this issue, as with others.[6]

Islam is a call to freedom and liberation. The prominent theorists of contemporary Islam Sayyid Qutb and Abu'l-A'la al-Mawdudi were not mistaken when they defined Islam as a comprehensive emancipatory revolution.

It is true that there are still some who commit serious sins and acts of injustice while using the pretext of predestination. However, the verses of the Qur'an bear witness that God rejects abominations, sins, and injustices and has forbidden them, warning those who commit them of the most severe punishment in this life and the next, if they have not repented. "God demands justice, generosity, and giving shelter to relatives. He forbids indecent acts, abominations, and injustice. He warns you, so that you might remember" (Qur'an 16:90). The Prophet Muhammad taught that God's favor cannot be sought by acts of disobedience but must be sought by acts of obedience.

In one of the hadith reports relating divine speech directly (Hadith Qudsi) God says, "My servant does not draw near to Me with anything more beloved

---

[5] [Available in English translation: Muhammad al-Tahir Ibn Ashur, *Treatise on Maqasid al-Shari'ah*, trans. Mohamed El-Tahir El-Mesawi (Herndon, VA: International Institute of Islamic Thought, 2006). —Ed.]

[6] [On the history of Islamic religious thought and practice related to slavery, see Jonathan A. C. Brown, *Slavery and Islam* (Oxford, UK: Oneworld Publications, 2019). —Ed.]

to Me than the religious duties I have obligated upon him. And My servant continues to draw near to Me with supererogatory deeds [*nawafil*] until I love him. If I love him, then I am his hearing, his sight, and his hand." That is a sublime concept of freedom. This means that if people seek to draw near to God, God paves the way for them to do good and to overcome the obstacles that stand in their way. "If someone fears God, God gives them a way out and provides for them in ways they would not expect" (Qur'an 65:2–3).

Seeking God's favor is a voluntary act of choice, because it is not the only choice that God created as a possibility for humankind. "Say the truth from your Lord, and those who wish can believe and those who wish can disbelieve. We have prepared a fire for the unjust" (Qur'an 18:29). If humans choose to obey, they choose the way that will unleash and expand their capacity to act without being dependent on either the circumstance or on others. Thus, freedom must be realized first internal to the self so that it may then manifest outside it, ultimately to such a degree of freedom and devotion that if they make a vow to God (voluntarily), they will surely carry it out.

Such a religion cannot be accused of establishing slavery. The obvious fact is that Islam brought spiritual, social, and political emancipation— emancipation that starts in the depths of the soul, the mind, and the will, and then spreads to every corner of social, economic, and political life, free, positive action, either individual or communal, that is impervious to despair or frustration. "Do not weaken and do not be sad. You shall prevail if you are believers" (Qur'an 3:139). God also tells us, "Only those who do not believe will despair of God's mercy" (Qur'an 12:87), and the Prophet Muhammad said, "Seek God's help and you will not be powerless."

This religion is not based only on acts of worship, interactions with other human beings, and ethics; it is a comprehensive and integrated way of life. Muslims are called on to set up a system that conforms with their beliefs and values and translates them into systems of life that realize their freedoms and basic rights, which are the sole reason the *shari'a* was revealed, and which the scholars of Islamic legal theory have summarized as the major human interests (*al-masalih al-kubra*) that form the objectives of the Islamic *shari'a*: the preservation of religion, human life, reason, kinship (the family), and property. Some modern legal theorists have added to these the attainment of justice and freedom.

These major human interests are pronounced in all contemporary declarations of human rights, such as the Universal Declaration of Human Rights proclaimed by the United Nations in 1948, which was a very

42 ON MUSLIM DEMOCRACY

progressive step toward recognizing that all humankind has a common identity, despite varied ethnicities and religions, and that, as such, they deserve basic rights and freedoms, such as the right to life, the right to freedom of belief, the right to practice their beliefs, the right to family life, the right to take part in public affairs, the right to access justice in fair and independent courts, the right to earn a fair wage, the right to freedom of movement, et cetera.

From an Islamic perspective, these rights as a whole can only bring happiness, since they recognize that humans have equal rights by virtue of their common origin. "He created you from a single soul" (Qur'an 4:1). Islam teaches that doing good deeds is the only means through which human beings can claim superiority. Sadly, a vast gap persists between these fine human rights declarations and realities of injustice, as we see continued discrimination and power imbalances between powerful and weak countries, and inside countries between rulers and their oppressed and humiliated peoples.

Indeed, one of the prerequisites for achieving the objectives set out above is the establishment of a just political system. The (third) caliph 'Uthman said, "God restrains through the ruler what He does not restrain through the Qur'an." Thus, shared institutions are critical to protecting rights and freedoms. The Prophet Muhammad incessantly urged his followers to organize themselves collectively: "You must keep together. Those who deviate from the collective will deviate to the hellfire." The Prophet taught that when embarking on a journey, even if within a group of just three people, the group should choose a leader. However, this human need for order does not justify despotism and autocracy. On the contrary, it means that participation in decision-making, or *shura*, is the right way.

In this sense, a system based on free will, participation, and *shura* is the Islamic system. Anything based on rule by one individual is a Pharaonic system, which the Qur'an repeatedly condemns and warns against: "And Pharaoh led his people astray, and did not guide them" (Qur'an 20:79). In contrast, Islam offers the system of consultation, of participatory decision-making, instead of the autocratic alternative. Islam even praised the Queen of Sheba when she said to her advisors, "Let me have your counsel in this matter. I will take no firm decision without you" (Qur'an 27:32).

Islam is a system of community that is fair and consultative. The Pharaonic system symbolizes every despotic and dictatorial system that gives rise to corruption and arrogance on Earth, as the Qur'an expresses it. Pharaonism is not just a historical event that the Qur'an mentions to remind us of an Egyptian king in bygone times. The Pharaonic system is the antithesis of a state based on justice and the rule of law, since the will of Pharaoh is the law itself. Did he not declare brazenly to his people "I am your supreme lord" (Qur'an 20:12) and "I do not show you except what I see" (Qur'an 40:29)?

In contrast with that, the *shura* system was introduced to affirm that government has no legitimacy unless there is freedom of choice, on the grounds that the people is sovereign [*sahibat al-sulta*], while the ruler is the nation's servant and agent. The nation installs rulers in accordance with the will of the people, monitors them, advises them, and dismisses them whenever it wishes. This requires converting *shura* from a principle of governance and an ethical value into a system of government, regulated by specific devices. Islam left these procedures to the minds and experience of humans to elaborate and improve in accordance with their changing circumstances.

Muslims, however, fell seriously short in this respect, which led to the conferring of legitimacy on authoritarian governments when the rule of the Rightly-Guided Caliphs, a government by consultation, was distorted into rule by rapacious monarchs. This model continued until Western thought, after many bitter experiments, was able to achieve a successful transition from despotism and develop a set of mechanisms and arrangements that could help make the ideal of *shura* and consultative rule a reality, insofar as that is humanly possible.

In fact, Islam paved the way for democracy, as *shura* was among the ideas conveyed to the West as part of the process of cultural exchange that took place between the two civilizations. The West continues to develop and embed it within its own environment and history, cutting it off from its Islamic roots, as it has done with many other concepts, until it reached its present form, which remains open to evolution and change. Government must draw its legitimacy from the will of the people through a real mandate, as we sense in the caliph Abu Bakr's accession speech: "I have been given authority over you although I am not the best among you." Thus, he acknowledged that it was not his personal qualities that were the source of his legitimacy but rather the fact that people had chosen him based on their own free will, and nothing else.

We see this also in the caliph 'Umar ibn al-Khattab's speech when he says, "Obey me as long as I obey God in my dealings with you." This makes clear that the oath of allegiance is a contractual arrangement with conditions, and not a matter of loyalty to an individual or to the ruler. It is an affirmation of the supremacy of the law over the authority of the ruler, as well as an affirmation of the people's right to monitor the ruler and even rebel against his authority if he goes beyond the legal framework (obedience to God and His apostle).

Islam places an emphasis on responsibility, as seen in the saying of the Prophet Muhammad, "Each of you is responsible for his flock." This reinforces the independence of society and gives it a power of supervision [over its government]. Some of the Prophet's Companions were an example of this, such as Bilal ibn Rabah, who was a slave before Islam gave him recognition as a citizen with full rights, imbued with a sense of dignity and responsibility equal to all others, even as regards the caliph 'Umar ibn al-Khattab. Bilal was such a strong critic that 'Umar ibn al-Khattab would supplicate, "O Lord, spare me from Bilal and his friends."

The caliphate began as a system of consultation and peaceful transfer of power similarly via consultation, which is the reason for the use of the term "rightly guided" as applied to government under the Prophet and the first four caliphs. Despite the transformation that occurred with the departure from this model under subsequent rulers, this change did not prevent the existence of political and intellectual diversity. It did not enable governments to dominate society, which retained many independent features: the idea of the supremacy of the authority of the *shari'a*; rulers were denied the authority to interpret the texts of revelation, on the grounds that this was the jurisdiction of the scholars (*'ulama'*); and the mosque remained independent as an institution, which served as a sort of people's parliament where Muslims discussed their most important concerns pertaining to culture, education, society, or politics. The Friday sermon, for example, offered a weekly opportunity to present Islamic positions on the most important recent events in society and in the life of the *umma*, creating a permanent link between fixed religious truths and the changing world of politics, society, and culture.

Very extensive civil society activity also existed throughout Islamic history. For example, it was not rare for the state to follow one school of Islamic law (*madhhab*) while the general public followed a different school with its own institutions. The Hanafi *madhhab*, for example, was the official *madhhab* of the Abbasid, Mamluk, and Ottoman states, while many of the provinces they ruled followed other *madhhabs* in terms of religious opinions (*fatwas*), court judgments, and education, which shows that civil society had wide authority and autonomy from the state. Even within the same province or town, it was common for Muslims to have a multiplicity of legal systems and a multiplicity of courts that applied them—a trace of the spirit of Islam that emphasized freedom, the freedom of the individual to choose: "There shall be no coercion in religion" (Qur'an 2:256).

A people's freedom is in virtue of the fact that it is the source of legitimacy for all authority, and the nation is free to choose the government according to a program, to hold it in check, and even remove it from power. In the Western experience, the principle of *shura*—that is, government by the people—was translated through the creation and development of systems and institutions, such as parliaments elected from rival parties, which allow for peaceful transfers of power between a majority that governs and a minority in opposition; the separation of legislative, judicial, and executive powers; freedom of the press; and respect for the principle of citizenship with equal rights and duties regardless of race or belief.

These procedures and mechanisms, which are still evolving and improving, are the most advanced form of contemporary *shura* and of democracy in its contemporary expression. These are the basic source of the strength and success of the nations that have adopted them, despite the flaws within their ethical and value systems, and although their foreign policies continue to be shaped by hegemonic tendencies that involve plundering the resources of oppressed peoples. The absence or limited existence of such mechanisms at most stages of Islamic history has been one of the main reasons behind the retreat and decline of Islamic civilization, along with external factors such as Western control of maritime and land trade routes, which stifled the Islamic world.

In fact, there is nothing in these mechanisms that goes against the values of Islam, regardless of the broader value framework in which they operate. They can be seen as the soundest way to transform the Islamic principle of *shura* from a principle and value into a system that ensures that the objective of *shura* is achieved—shared decision-making rather than autocratic rule.

It is an extraordinary paradox to see some Islamists, crushed by despotic regimes, shy away from democracy and regard it with a mistrustful eye, clinging to a superficial understanding that sees conflict between democracy and Islam as inevitable. Some incessantly repeat the claim that democracy means rule by the people, whereas in Islam it is God who rules—a revival of the Kharijite objection to the caliph 'Ali. On this basis, the Kharijites rejected the decision to go to arbitration after the Battle of Siffin and declared 'Ali to be an unbeliever. 'Ali responded to their naivety by saying, "It is a truth through which a falsehood is intended," since people need an imam, whether righteous or unrighteous.

It is naive to contrast rule by the people (democracy) with rule by God (Islam). It brings to mind its Kharijite precursor and does injustice to Islam in that it associates Islam with despotism and dictatorship. But genuine Islamic government is not like this; it does not defy the people and impose itself on them by brute force. The essence of Islamic government is that it is consultative, that is, its legitimacy stems from the free choice and consent of the governed. In fact, democratic procedures are the best way to achieve the great objective of consultative government.

The rejectionists conflate democratic procedures, which are neutral, with the ethical, cultural, and philosophical values in the framework in which a system operates. The latter vary from one people to another. The framework might be secular, or it might be Buddhist (in Japan, Thailand, and Sri Lanka), Hindu (in India), Christian, or Jewish. Why then should it not be Islamic? Islam's doctrinal and ethical framework is more receptive to pluralism than other religions, given the absence of a central, clerical authority that monopolizes the interpretation of religious texts. Islam overtly recognizes the right of each Muslim to interpret religious texts according to his or her knowledge, and calls for consensus, the recognition of freedom, and religious and political pluralism ("There shall be no coercion in religion," Qur'an 2:256) from the outset. The so-called constitution of Medina [the Sahifa] was a model for a pluralistic state.[7]

It is also a paradox to see that non-Muslim countries that have adopted democracy are now closer to the Islamic model of *shura* than Muslim countries.

---

[7] [The legacy of the "constitution" (Sahifa) of Medina, a pact between the Prophet Muḥammad and the tribes of Medina (including Jews and other non-Muslims) is a central theme in Ghannouchi's theory of political and moral pluralism in a modern Muslim democracy. For Ghannouchi, "Medina" has come to signify not the fusion of religion and political power (or *dīn wa dawla*, "religion and state") but the original Islamic commitment to pluralism, the rule of law, and limited government based on the pursuit of shared worldly ends. This theme will appear numerous times throughout these essays. For the English-language translations of the Sahifa, see A. Guillaume, *The Life of Muhammad: A Translation of Ibn Isḥāq's* Sīrat Rasūl Allāh (New York: Oxford University Press, 1967). For other translations of the pact of Medina, see W. Montgomery Watt, *Muhammad at Medina* (Oxford: Clarendon Press, 1956); R. B. Serjeant, "The 'Constitution of Medina,'" *Islamic Quarterly* 8 (1964): 3–16; Muhammad Hamidullah, *The First Written Constitution in the World*, 3rd ed. (Lahore: Sh. Muhammad Ashraf, 1975); Michael Lecker, *The "Constitution of Medina": Muḥammad's First Legal Document* (Princeton, NJ: Darwin Press, 2004); Saïd Amir Arjomand, "The Constitution of Medina: A Sociolegal Interpretation of Muhammad's Acts of Foundation of the *Umma*," *International Journal of Middle East Studies* 41, no. 4 (2009): 555–575; and Ovamir Anjum, "The 'Constitution' of Medina: Translation, Commentary, and Meaning Today," Yaqeen Institute for Islamic Research, 2021, https://yaqeeninstitute.org/ovamiranjum/the-constitution-of-medina-translation-commentary-and-meaning-today. —Ed.]

BASIC FREEDOMS IN ISLAM   47

This fact led so great a reformer as Muhammad ʿAbduh to comment after his [1888] visit to Europe, "I went to the West and saw Islam, but no Muslims; I got back to the East and saw Muslims, but not Islam."

There is another aspect that illustrates the meaning of freedom in Islam—the economic aspect. Giving alms [*zakat*] is not only an act of worship, but at the same time a socioeconomic act. It helps to stimulate the economy by promoting transfers of wealth, "so that it does not only circulate between the wealthy among you" (Qurʾan 59:7). It also reduces inequalities between the various groups in society in line with Islamic teaching. Making *zakat* an act of worship adds a very powerful individual incentive, based on faith, which also makes giving alms a voluntary act, born of free will and transcending the desire for material possessions. The institution of *zakat* refines the act of giving—those who give alms simply want to enjoy God's blessings. This is different from taxation, cut off from the devotional aspect of *zakat*, which all Muslims with more than a minimum amount of property are required to pay, whether or not there is a state that demands it, in the same way as other religious obligations such as prayer. Thus, *zakat* is repeatedly mentioned in the Qurʾan in conjunction with prayer, to emphasize its importance and the close link in Islam between the material and the spiritual. In Islam property belongs to God; humans are only God's deputy [*mustakhlaf*] in disposing of property and are accountable for whether they use and spend it well or badly.

The idea that property belongs to God frees humans from becoming slaves to material possessions and encourages them to keep a watchful eye over their own desires, so that they are not enslaved by the logic of profiteering, accumulating, and hoarding wealth. It elevates human beings, giving morality a role in guiding their conduct and that of society, reminding us of the principle that all are equals.

It should come as no surprise that the principles of Islam include elements that simultaneously combine religion, as a way of life, and the worldly, in the sense of material or intangible needs, reflecting the fact that humans are a composite of matter and spirit. Islam is, after all, directed at human beings and takes as its starting point their composite nature and reality.

As such, freedom in this domain extends to allowing freedom of initiative and freedom to own property, so that wealth is not confined to a small minority—a class, a ruling elite, the leaders of a party, or those who enjoy monopolies. On the contrary, Islam recognizes everyone's right to property, and in fact Islamic history sets a unique example for communal ownership, which covers most land, such as tribal land, which enabled all members of

48 ON MUSLIM DEMOCRACY

the tribe to use land to the best of their ability without claiming that it was their personal property. Property could also be collectively owned under religious endowments (*awqaf*), a practical application of the public ownership of resources through society and not through the state, a form of ownership that was outside the domain of the state or of individuals. The endowment (*waqf*) status allows for property to be owned by society and to be used by anyone, without giving any individual the right to dispose of it as the private owner. This lays the basis for a balance of power between society and forces that, by their nature, seek to bypass, repress, or exploit society for their own purposes. The more the balance shifts in favor of society, the greater the chances for freedom and the wider its scope.

The structure of the Islamic economic framework combines moral elements, utilitarian elements, and material elements with psychological, social, and organizational aspects. It protects people from unethical competition, regulates the freedom of the market through moral and religious precepts that give priority to the public interest, and prevents the deification of profit and capital. This saved the historical experience of Muslims, despite its shortcomings, from descending into war profiteering, widespread slavery, genocide in the name of spreading civilization, and the systematic destruction of the environment due to greed and plunder—a factor in the affluence that the great powers enjoy in the world today.

The caliph 'Umar once asked people if he was a king or a caliph, and they replied, "If you raise money lawfully and disburse it lawfully, you are a caliph. If you raise it unlawfully and disburse it unlawfully, you are a king." From another perspective, the balance between the logic of rights and the logic of duties in the thinking of the Prophet's Companions was a model that gave them the strength to entrench a spirit of social liberation by rejecting exclusion, degradation and marginalization. The archetype for that was Abu Dharr al-Ghifari, the venerable Companion of the Prophet who has been described as the first socialist in history, though his condemnation of the beginnings of a wealth gap in the nascent Islamic society was motivated only by Islam, a creed that is accused of encouraging people to be submissive, dependent, and fatalistic. Yet that faith produced a revolutionary like al-Ghifari, who said, "I am amazed when I see someone who cannot find his daily bread and doesn't raise his sword." Throughout history, these convictions have remained the basis for struggles against such inequalities.

Freedom underpins all the pillars of Islam, and the subject of women's rights confirms this. Islam emphasizes women's status as equal human beings.

The basis of this is the view that regards women in light of their humanity before their feminine nature. The Qur'an expresses it thus: "We have dignified the children of Adam"—a dignifying that does not recognize maleness or femaleness, since these are basically physical features of humans, while Islam looks at human beings as a whole, that is, as a composite of the physical and the spiritual, and so to reduce humans to things is to detract from their value and ignore the fact that they are unique and honored by God. Thus, the principle that men and women are equal in human value ("Women are the sisters of men") is the basic, default principle. The world is based on a system of pairs or couples: "Of everything We have created pairs" (Qur'an 51:29), and "O people, fear God who created you from a single soul" (Qur'an 4:1).

One has to distinguish between equality and sameness, since recognition of special characteristics is one of the prerequisites for respecting human beings and one of their most basic human rights. A man cannot replace a woman as a mother, because to be a mother is not just to perform a function but to have the willingness and psychological capacity to fulfill the child's material, emotional, and spiritual needs. Islam elevates motherhood from being merely a question of the social division of labor to the level of an obligation in the doctrinal sense. This transforms the role of motherhood from the level of need to the level of action through the power of faith that it confers on it by associating it with divine reward, as we see in the saying of the Prophet, "Heaven lies under the feet of mothers."

Although this is the spirit of Islam when it comes to honoring women, this is not to say that women have not been the victims of injustices in Islamic history—for example, discrimination between boys and girls in educational opportunities. While ignorance has been widespread among Muslims, women have suffered, and still suffer, from the most onerous share of this ignorance. This went as far as excluding women from mosques, the center of social and religious life in Islamic societies. Bringing women back into mosques and allocating space for them there were among the fruits of the reformist movement, after many centuries of decline.

Women were even defined in terms of "honor" that had to be protected. What is more, they were sometimes known by the name of their reproductive organ [*bud*], despite the fact that God Almighty honored humankind as a whole and addressed his commands to all human beings when he said, "I created the jinn and humankind only that they might worship Me" (Qur'an 51:56). Yet, women were treated as second-class citizens, denied access to the mosque and to participation in the public affairs of Muslims.

50 ON MUSLIM DEMOCRACY

Modern civilization has also weakened society by ignoring gender differences and emphasizing the role of those who are economically productive over the role of those who bring up and educate children, moving away from the family toward free relationships. This is how all civilizations have collapsed: desires and passions rebel against God's commandments in the name of freedom, and people fall into the worship of passions, devils, and unrestrained capitalists who will trade in anything without limits.

Civil Society Is a Way to Break Free

Civil society in Islam is a society distinguished by certain psychological, social, and moral characteristics that enable it to be free from allegiance to anyone but God and thus create within it resistance to hegemony, oppression, and enslavement. This was embodied in Islamic societies before the period of "modernity," in that they saw human beings as individuals and as a society whose message from Islam was "All of you are responsible." Every Muslim is responsible for improving his or her own soul, family, and fellows as far as they are able to do so. They are responsible for upholding the right and combatting injustice, and are responsible for cooperating with their brethren in doing so. In Islam the state is not everything, but rather the individual and society are the basic principle and foundation [of ethical and political action].

In this context, Muslim societies established civic institutions independent of the state or ruler to provide services to students, travelers, soldiers, and the sick, and even to support marriage and encourage chastity. Some of them cared for animals that had been abandoned when they could no longer work, especially beasts of burden.

Islamic history in general was familiar with what we might call a people's army, in contrast with a regime army. Society-based education took the place of government-provided education. Health services and trade associations were among the organizations that exerted a social pressure that constrained the dominance of the state. For this purpose, society used its traditional institutions, such as the tribe, the mosque, and the Sufi lodges (*tekiya* or *zāwiya*). This, together with the scholars' authority to guide society, guaranteed that public affairs were conducted in a way that maintained the relationship between Heaven and Earth, between the historical and the metaphysical, between the individual and the group, and between the state and society.

All governments are naturally prone to seek to dominate and control. They have been formed for the sake of serving the people, but if they hold all the levers of power in society, they will make society serve them. Islam set out this challenge when it urged people not to bring their conflicts to their rulers, particularly through bribery, and to not direct their appeals to the elite. Rather, every Qur'anic address is directed to the entire people (the *umma*) and humanity as a whole ("O people!," "O you who believe!"). In this there is an impetus to collective social agency on the part of the people or the *umma* to preserve its affairs, like basic social unity, which provides for people the capacity to bring about change and freedom while confronting aggression. This allows even non-Muslims to benefit from this and is why Islamic history did not witness religious wars, unlike Europe. Rather, all wars in Islamic history have been expressions of political opposition to the government's conduct, motivated by a desire to change it toward something more like the sound example set by the Prophet, which embodied Islam's justice.

So throughout history it has not been possible to subjugate this *umma*, even if there was no longer a state to protect its territory. It achieved that through its cultural and social structure, and those factors still provide resources for a renaissance and for resistance to invasion and despotism. Freedom is conditional on culture, but also on the ability of civil society to invent institutions that create a balance with all the forces that threaten its existence, whether internal or external.

The Prophet Muhammad based Medinan society on citizenship and not on religious creed. This pluralistic society operated within a framework of freedom and law, through the first document of constitutional law in history—what is termed the Sahifa of Medina, which brought together Muslims, other monotheistic groups, and even the "Hypocrites" [the so-called *munafiqin*, those who pretended to be Muslim but were working to harm and undermine the new Muslim community], and guaranteed rights to all of them.

Islam's message was subject to repression in its Meccan phase. It was under siege and at war in its Medinan phase, since all the first battles took place in Medina or on the outskirts of the city, such as the Battles of Badr, Uhud, and al-Ahzab [also known as the Battle of the Trench, or al-Khandaq], which shows that the Muslims, persecuted in Mecca and forced to emigrate to save

52 ON MUSLIM DEMOCRACY

their lives, did not initiate war but were defending themselves. The war with the Persians and the Byzantines began because they killed the Prophet's messengers and constantly encroached on the edges of the Arabian peninsula and even Medina itself. The idea that might is right dominated relations between countries, in the complete absence of any international law.

The peoples who embraced Islam, whether entire societies or the majority within societies, did so freely, out of conviction, and gradually, so that the process lasted for several centuries, as in the case of Egypt and the Levant, and some countries in the heart of the Islamic world still have Christian majorities, such as Lebanon. They chose Islam after the Islamic jihad freed their will from the domination of theocratic regimes that posed as gods, leaving them free to choose. They chose Islam because they admired the morals of the conquering Muslims and the way they dealt with them. If these peoples had converted to Islam when threatened by the sword, there would now be no one of any other faith in the lands of Islam, as is the case in countries ruled by Christians, such as Andalusia. Islam protected Christians in Andalusia when it was strong, after which Christians wiped out Islam as soon as they had the upper hand. In fact, they tried to annihilate each other as well, Catholics and Protestants, and secularism was imposed as a solution to put an end to grueling religious wars. Islam did not require an equivalent to secularism because it recognized freedom and religious pluralism from the start, and there is no Arab country without long-established non-Muslim minorities.

The oldest churches and synagogues today are in the Islamic world, such as the three-thousand-year-old synagogue on the Tunisian island of Djerba, whereas the oldest mosques in European cities are no more than a century old—a testimony to Islam's tolerance and to the fact that it did not rely on coercion as a method. In Iraq, which was at the center of one of the greatest Islamic states, Islam protected to this day the existence and culture of people who worshipped idols, trees, and devils.

Indeed, the map of current-day Islam shows that Islam arrived in most of these areas through Muslim merchants who settled among these peoples, who in their turn liked them and embraced their religion. A prime example of this is Indonesia, the most populous contemporary Muslim country in the world. The most important cities in Islamic civilization, such as Baghdad and Damascus, to this very day have populations of multiple religious backgrounds, and their history was not marred by genocidal wars fought on ethnic or religious grounds. The Prophet Muhammad never forced people to follow him but instead invited them to dialogue and asserted his right to address his message to people, as when he said, "Don't stand between me and the people."

Throughout its history, Islam has been a victim of violence, but despite this status has refrained from reacting. This allowed it to gain the support and sympathy of people. Thus, even when the Prophet entered Mecca victorious, and some Muslims called for revenge on their enemies who had oppressed them, he suppressed his anger, mastered his feelings, and refused to punish them.

Even the Hypocrites (*munafiqin*), the most dangerous group in Islamic society, were allowed to profess their faith publicly; the Prophet Muhammad never required them to be held to account for their true feelings, and he warned against taking revenge, "lest the Arabs say that Muhammad kills his Companions," and so as not to open the gates to liquidation. Thus, the Prophet's revolution was the first peaceful revolution in history, so much so that credible and impartial historians say that the number of people killed on both sides in the Prophet's military campaigns was no more than a few hundred.

The social system that Islam established was progressive and advanced relative to the systems that prevailed in Europe and other parts of the world at that time, because it heralded a logic of law based on voluntary contractual obligation, the opposite of the religious compulsion of the church, kings, and emperors. Whenever Islam reached any territory, it came to liberate people, as was the case in Egypt, the Levant, Andalusia, and Bosnia, where the Byzantines were persecuting indigenous peoples who belonged to another Christian denomination. Local people saw in Islam a savior that would ensure security, freedom, and justice in regions that had been full of conflict, oppression, and corruption.

The massive corpus of Islamic jurisprudence is evidence that the law was supreme in Muslim societies. This output has helped to inspire contemporary legal systems, although they have sought to conceal this influence. For instance, the French legal code benefited from the special relationship France had established with the Ottoman state in its alliance against the Spanish, the Austrians, and the Hungarians. Islamic culture was not only a source of inspiration for the French Revolution, but also for the English revolution through Roger Bacon, Martin Luther, and other pioneers of the Renaissance and the Reformation, who had been influenced by al-Ghazali and Ibn Rushd.

Despite its shortcomings, wherever it has gone, the Islamic model has established civilization as an alternative to barbarism and chaos, and religious

54 ON MUSLIM DEMOCRACY

and intellectual freedom and justice as an alternative to despotism, arbitrary government, genocidal wars, and civil wars. This gave it an appeal that opened the gates to its expansion.

Today, we need to talk about the growth of Islam in Europe, for example. By the logic of Islam, any territory where basic freedoms are guaranteed, especially religious freedoms, is territory that is open to Muslims to live in.[8] Secularism in Europe can take credit for guaranteeing basic freedoms, including religious freedoms, to all citizens or residents of its territory, including Muslims. Islam entered Europe in recent decades and flourished thanks to these freedoms, with mosques and Islamic centers growing in number and in the quality of their work, whereas in the past European chauvinism, which reduced Europe for many centuries to ignorance and bloody religious wars between Protestants and Catholics and produced the Inquisition courts, prevented Europe from discovering Islam in a peaceful context, as is happening now.

The question of the right to embrace and renounce Islam (the latter being termed "apostasy") still raises questions, since criminalizing apostasy goes against the principle of religious freedom. The incident that initiated this debate took place after the death of the Prophet, when some Arab tribes effectively renounced Islam by refusing to pay the religious tax to Abu Bakr. There was disagreement between Abu Bakr and 'Umar ibn al-Khattab on this issue. Abu Bakr decided to fight those tribes, but 'Umar objected, saying, "How can we fight people who have proclaimed that there is no god but Allah?" Abū Bakr replied, "By God, I will fight those who separate prayer from *zakat* (almsgiving). Will Islam fade away while I'm alive?" 'Umar said that they continued the discussion until Abu Bakr had persuaded him. That shows that the caliph did not use his influence as someone with authority, but rather used the force of argument.

The rejection by the Arab tribes who refused to pay *zakat* cannot automatically be read as a rejection of Islam. Broadly speaking, it was a rebellion against the state that took the form of armed resistance and refusal to pay *zakat*. If any group of people in any modern state refused to pay taxes and took up arms, it would be considered rebellion against the state's authority that called for a decisive response. The incident above that broke out in early Islam was more akin to a political revolt based on nostalgia for tribal

---

[8] [Here Ghannouchi is playing on the shared root of "conquered" and "opened" in Arabic: *fath*, *maftūh*. Whereas classical lands were "opened" by Islam through conquest, today Western lands may be "open" to Muslims because of their guarantee of religious and civil liberties. —Ed.]

BASIC FREEDOMS IN ISLAM 55

authority and rejection of the institutional state that Islam had created and of which most Arabs had no experience. The issue at stake was not primarily a doctrinal one—no one went back to revering the old idols, al-'Uzza, Manat, and Hubal. The refusal to pay *zakat* was a declaration that they rejected the state, though many of them did not reject the declaration of faith or prayer. They rejected the state as a sociopolitical institution, which they saw as consecration of the authority of the Quraysh over the rest of the tribes.

Thus, the more logical conclusion is that "apostasy" in its doctrinal or political sense was a crime to which the ruler had the authority to respond, based on an assessment of how harshly or leniently to deal with it, like other offenses for which the penalty is discretionary [*ta'zir*]. Most religious scholars saw apostasy as an offense with a compulsory penalty [a *hadd* crime]. One reason for the disagreement on this is that, other than the historical incident set out above, the religious texts on the subject are not conclusive and determinate [*qat'i*]. The Qur'an warns those who renounce Islam doctrinally that they will face severe punishment in the afterlife: "Those of you who renounce their religion and die as unbelievers, their deeds will come to nothing in this world and in the hereafter" (Qur'an 2:217). As for the reliable hadiths on the subject, these are open to interpretation, and all were narrated by a single source.[9] They cannot serve as evidence, since one of the precepts of Islamic law is that corporal punishment can only be applied where there is conclusive textual evidence supporting such a penalty.

Islam came as liberator for humankind ("We sent you [Muhammad] only out of compassion for the people of the world" (Qur'an 21:107)), to save human beings from their passions, from Satan, and from being led astray, and to give them strength to resist political tyranny, economic exploitation, and social discrimination.

What we are lacking in the Islamic world today is freedom. That is what Muslims came to Europe and America to seek, fleeing despotism, poverty, and ignorance. It was not at all to escape Islam in order to embrace disbelief, but rather to escape to countries where there is freedom and respect for humanity, just like the early Muslims whom the Prophet advised to move to Ethiopia when their families were being oppressed in Mecca, telling them, "There lives a king under whom people are not mistreated." Thus, Islam made

---

[9] [In Islamic jurisprudence, Prophetic *hadith*-reports were more credible the more independent lines of transmission they had. Reports with only a single chain of transmission were known as "solitary *hadith*," or *hadith ahad*. The latter could sometimes be used for legal purposes but never for theological disputes. —Ed.]

56 ON MUSLIM DEMOCRACY

clear that civilization is founded on justice, even where there is disbelief, but it cannot be based on injustice, even if there is faith. Justice is the order of the universe and the basis of civilization: "We sent down (the Qur'an) with the truth, and it came down with the truth" (Qur'an 17:105).

We call on God to help this *umma* prosper and guide it to all that is good. O Lord, make us into people who listen to what is said and follow the best of it. Praise be to God, Lord of the Worlds.

Peace and mercy be upon you.

2

The Dialectic of Unity, Difference, and Political Pluralism in Islam

The contemporary Islamist literature on politics is growing, compensating for the shortage of such material in our recent past and hopefully helping to establish freedom and the principles of citizenship as the basis for rights and the authority of the people as the sole source of legitimacy. On the one hand, this should open the way for political pluralism, tolerance, public participation in government, and peaceful transfers of power through fair pluralist elections. On the other hand, it should put an end to, or at least clip the wings of, the curse of despotism that has clouded most stages of our political history. It would also thwart all attempts to claim that rulers deserve to rule without consultation, and undermine every justification for setting up secret organizations to plan acts of violence or coups as a means to bring about reform, establish justice, and prevent iniquities.

But, in fact, this literature is usually based on narrow-minded and intemperate ideas. Sometimes the writers denounce those who disagree with them as infidels and say it is legitimate to kill them. This provides the enemies of Islam with a perfect opportunity to misrepresent Islam's image and values and add fuel to the fires of Islamophobia. The plentiful literature in this field still contains not a few defects because of the influence from a heritage of extremism and narrow-minded thinking that emanates from the caves of the remote past on the pretext of making sure that monotheism is stripped of defects and that we are immune from the impurity of learning from infidels.

Under these circumstances the development of Islamic thought sometimes seems to have come to a standstill during the last half century, if not regressed to some extent from the heritage of the reformists—from Rifaʿa al-Tahtawi [d. 1873] to Hasan al-Banna [d. 1949], by way of Sayyid Jamal al-Din

---

Paper submitted to the European Council for Fatwa and Research (ECFR) seminar on political jurisprudence (*fiqh*) for Muslim minorities in Europe, Istanbul, July 3, 2006. Published as a short pamphlet by the European Council for Fatwa and Research and republished as Rāshid al-Ghannūshī, *Jadaliyyat al-wiḥda wa'l-ikhtilāf* (Tunis: n.p., 2016).

On Muslim Democracy. Rached Ghannouchi and Andrew F. March, Oxford University Press.
© Oxford University Press 2023. DOI: 10.1093/oso/9780197666876.003.0003

58   ON MUSLIM DEMOCRACY

al-Afghani [d. 1897], Muhammad 'Abduh [d. 1905], and Khayr al-Din Pasha [d. 1890] in Tunisia. This applies to Islamic thought's receptiveness to useful aspects of the culture of the age, especially with respect to *shura* (consultation) or public participation in politics, through democratic procedures. Most of the Islamist literature that posits pluralism, freedom, citizenship, and popular sovereignty as the basis for rights and state-building also remains marred by a considerable degree of vagueness and reluctance to take the principle of freedom to its logical conclusions as a basis for the relationships that Muslims have and for their religious and worldly responsibilities in all the contracts that they enter into, starting with the contract of faith and ending with the contract of *bay'a* as the sole source of legitimate government.[1]

This means that this literature in general falls short of offering a humanitarian vision with space for everyone, however much they might disagree— space as wide as that promised in God's compassionate discourse: "O people, we have created you male and female. We have made you nations and tribes so that you might come to know one another. The noblest of you in the eyes of God are those who are most pious" (Qur'an 49:13).[2] This also means that, whether they live in a Muslim-majority country or as a minority elsewhere, and whether they are weak or strong, Muslims ask of those who are different from them only for what they would be willing to offer those others if they had the same legal status, according to the adage: "As you owe, you are owed." Islamic political theory seems to remain constantly fixated on addressing Muslims alone ("O you who believe," to use the Qur'anic term), and has never, or not sufficiently, opened up to the parallel divine discourse that addresses people in general ("O people," to use the alternative Qur'anic term).

It has not made an effort to elaborate a political theory that follows the spirit and objectives of the constitution of Medina, which laid the basis for a state and a society that did not exclude any of the existing ethnic or religious components—a state and a society that were also open to accommodating all the people who joined this community—migrants from Mecca, the Muslims of Medina, the Jews, and those who followed them and joined them and fought alongside them. "They are one community, separate from

---

[1] Ḥasan al-Turābī, *Al-Siyāsa wa'l-ḥukm: al-nuẓum al-sulṭāniyya bayna al-uṣū' wa sunan al-wāqi'* (Beirut: Dār al-Sāqī, 2003), 110.
[2] [Ghannouchi quotes approvingly in this context the Iraqi-Lebanese Shi'a cleric Muḥammad Mahdī Shams al-Dīn (d. 2001), who himself draws on the views of the Shi'a scholar al-Sayyid Muḥammad Mahdī Baḥr al-'Ulūm (d. 1797). —Ed.]

DIALECTIC OF UNITY AND POLITICAL PLURALISM   59

other people," as the wording of that constitution holds.[3] Tawfiq al-Shawi comments, saying, "Our noble Prophet did not restrict citizenship to Muslims from Mecca and Medina. He included those who followed them and joined them. Joining the community meant any act or status that implied affiliation with the community's citizens and sharing with them the responsibilities and commitments of citizenship."[4] In this way the constitution of Medina, which accurately reflected the humanitarian spirit of the Qur'an, laid the basis for a pluralism that allowed room for all civilizations, ethnicities, and religions. It offered them all ample space to make their own contributions, and as a result, the civilization of Islam was spared religious wars and ethnic cleansing.

Politically, when it came to translating the principle of *shura* into a system that achieves what is required and does not fall short of it, it offered the possibility that public policy should not be decided by one or several individuals but would be a matter for the whole community, and that the only authority that rulers have would be the authority that the people, the holders of authority, vest in them by means of a valid contract, on the understanding that the ruler serves them and is employed by them and that they have appointed him as their delegate to implement some of the obligations that God has imposed on them after taking counsel with them. The people could also oversee the actions of their ruler and review the contract whenever they want, without him claiming that he is sacrosanct or that his authority is personal property that he can pass on to anyone he wants.

But this promising version of Islamic practice did not last long. The desert winds soon blew it away and covered it with the dust left over from the legacy of the theocratic empires that Islam overthrew. It was as if pure rain fell from the sky, flowed into the valleys, and interacted with the dross that was there to form a mixture that looked less and less like the rain that had fallen from the sky. Eventually the process slowed down and stagnation set in, in the form of despotic regimes that took root and almost stripped *shura* of all substance other than a superficial veneer.

As soon as Muslims woke up, enemy artillery was pounding their strongholds, signaling that the center of civilization had moved to the other side, which had seen a renaissance in its intellectual, industrial, and military structures by taking advantage of the cultural and humanitarian heritage

---

[3] See Muḥammad Ḥamīdullāh, *Majmūʿat al-wathāʾiq al-siyāsiyya fiʾl-ʿahd al-nabawī waʾl-khilāfa al-rāshida* (Cairo: Lajnat al-Taʾlīf waʾl-Tarjama waʾl-Nashr, 1941), 41.

[4] Tawfīq al-Shāwī, *Fiqh al-Shūra waʾl-istishāra* (al-Manṣūra, Egypt: Dar al-Wafaʾ, 1992), 321.

60   ON MUSLIM DEMOCRACY

of the Muslims. In a sense, though theoretically rather than practically, this renaissance was an expression of the humanitarian prospects offered by the Qur'an. It had developed humanitarian philosophical ideals that spoke of human rights, pluralistic democratic systems, and international laws that aspired to embody these prospects, as the German philosopher Immanuel Kant and the philosophers of the Enlightenment had done.

Muslims, even in their more progressive form, as represented by the Islamic middle way (*al-wasatiyya*), still seem to be somewhat frightened of freedom or so lacking in confidence in their own peoples that they are reluctant to trust their judgment. They may also have little confidence in human nature or in its predisposition toward goodness, or confidence that human nature will soon revert to what is good if it is given a chance to discover goodness, for which freedom is an indispensable condition. This raises questions about the status and limits of difference and pluralism in Islamic thinking, especially politically. What are the obstacles along the way? What has been the outcome of the Islamic experience in this respect? What are the implications of all this for Muslim minorities, especially in the West?

I. Unity and Difference in the Structure of Islam

Islam has attached great importance to the doctrine of monotheism, and has built all its structure upon it, so much so that the concept of monotheism has permeated all the behavior of Muslims and every cultural achievement of the Islamic community. Monotheism means countering polytheism in all its theoretical and practical forms. The other side of the doctrine of monotheism, and one of its consequences, is belief in the unity of the community and of the Islamic polity, the caliphate, and warnings against internal strife, dissent, and extremism as threats to unity and obstacles to creating the harmony and consensus that Islam seeks and advocates. But uncompromising advocacy of monotheism and rejection of polytheism and dissent are not intended to challenge the reality that disagreement has always been inherent in human nature.[5] As God has said, "If only, in the generations before you, there had been people with a vestige of good sense to prohibit iniquity on Earth. There were only a few, whom We saved. But those who did wrong pursued their luxurious ways and they were sinners. Your Lord would not destroy

---

[5] Sayyid Quṭb, commentary on Sūrat Hūd (11), *Fī ẓilāl al-Qur'an* (Cairo: Dār al-Shurūq, 1982).

DIALECTIC OF UNITY AND POLITICAL PLURALISM   61

their towns unjustly if the people were righteous. If your Lord had wanted, He would have made all people a single community, and yet they still disagree, except for those toward whom your Lord has shown mercy, and that is why He created them" (Qur'an 11:116–119).

Commenting on the first of these verses, Rashid Rida [d. 1935] said, "This verse appeared after God's revelations about the destruction of nations for their wrongdoing and their iniquities on Earth, to let it be known that if there had been among them groups or factions with a modicum of common sense, virtue, and righteous strength to deter people from wrongdoing, iniquity would not have spread among them and corrupted them, and so they would not have perished."[6] In this way, as [twentieth-century Shi'a scholar] Muhammad al-Tabataba'i [d. 1981] explains it, people were divided into two categories: the sinners and those who survived, spared by God because they denounced injustice and iniquity. Hence God's postscript: "If your Lord had wanted He would have made people a single community, and yet they still disagree, except for those toward whom your Lord has shown mercy."[7] Fakhr al-Din al-Razi [d. 1210] comments on this verse thus: "By injustice, polytheism is intended here: 'Polytheism is a great injustice' (Qur'an 31:13), and the meaning is that God does not destroy towns simply because the inhabitants are polytheists, as long as they are righteous in their dealings with each other. The outcome is that a group of people is not punished by annihilation because they are polytheists or unbelievers, but if they treat each other badly and seek to do harm and are iniquitous. So jurists say that God's rights are based on indulgence and tolerance, while the rights of people are based on constraint and parsimony. There is a traditional saying that kings can survive when they are infidels but they cannot survive when they are unjust. The meaning of the verse is that God does not destroy them simply for being polytheists if they are righteous and treat each other properly."

The evidence for this is that the people of Noah, Hud, Salih, Lot, and Shuaib were punished with annihilation because of what God said about them doing harm and injustice to others.[8] He created them different, although they shared the same nature—different in mental faculties, tastes,

---

[6] Rashīd Riḍā, commentary on Sūrat al-Hūd, *Tafsīr al-manār* (Cairo: Dār al-Manār, [1948–1956]), 244.

[7] Muḥammad Ḥusayn Ṭabāṭabā'ī, *al-Mīzān fī tafsīr al-Qur'an* (Qum: Mu'assasat al-nashr al-Islāmī), 11:60.

[8] Fakhr al-Dīn al-Rāzī, *Tafsīr al-Fakhr al-Rāzī al-mushtahir bi-al-tafsīr al-kabīr wa-mafātīḥ al-ghayb* (Beirut: Dār al-fikr, 1995), 16:80.

62   ON MUSLIM DEMOCRACY

temperaments, colors, physical strength, and skills. And if God had wanted, He could have made them one community, in doctrine, color, strength, and inclinations, but because He wanted them to be free, difference resulted from them being free and rational beings, and it was not a deviation from nature. On the contrary, it was inherent in nature's origin and part of the intention of the wise Creator in His plan to appoint mankind as His vicegerent, or deputy, on Earth.[9] Mankind can be right or wrong, go astray or choose the right way, do good or do evil. Difference is not something incidental that will pass.

As [Tunisian scholar] Muhammad al-Tahir ibn 'Ashur [d. 1973] has said, "Of course God created humankind in such a way that differences between people are likely to arise over various questions, including the question of right and wrong, and they will vary in how far advanced they are. When God says, 'For that He created them,' the word *for* refers to God's motivation. Since He created them all with the same natural disposition, one that leads them to hold different opinions, and since He desired the corollary of that disposition and was aware of it, then difference was a teleological reason for creating them. This is not contradicted by the Qur'anic text that reads: 'I created the jinn and humankind only that they might worship Me' (Qur'an 51:56). The teleological purpose does not need to be exclusive. It suffices that it is the purpose of the act, and there might be other purposes alongside it, as an additional constraint."[10] Many people find it problematic that humankind should have been created to differ and not "as an act of mercy." Ibn Abbas says, "He created them out of mercy," since it would not be permissible to say "He created them to differ," because the demonstrative, *dhalika* ("that") in this case, should preferably refer to the closest noun. Besides, if He created them to be different and wanted them to differ, how could he punish them for being different?

But there is no inherent contradiction between mankind being created to be different and their being created as an act of mercy. The context of the verses is evidence for the conventional belief that God is just and does not punish a group of people when it includes groups or factions that take a stand against iniquity and the iniquitous, that He is willing to overlook His people being averse to His message and that He reassures them that their Lord is able to guide them if He has a mind to do so. But He wanted to create them free,

---

[9] [See the previous essay in this volume ("Basic Freedoms in Islam") for the introduction of the idea that mankind at large, and the Muslim *umma* in particular, has been designated by God as His caliph (deputy, or vicegerent) on Earth. This doctrine, which is a central pillar in twentieth-century Islamic thought, has a complex and manifold set of meanings and implications. —Ed.]

[10] Muḥammad al-Ṭahir ibn 'Āshūr, *Tafsīr al-taḥrīr wa'l-tanwīr* (Tunis: al-Dār al-Tūnisiyya li'l-nashr), 12:180–190.

so some of them are believers and others are infidels, whether righteous or iniquitous, and the differences between them persist until those who live live and those who perish perish "with clear evidence," as the Qur'an expresses it [in 8:42].

Disagreement does no harm as long as it is fair and reasonable and does not involve injustice or aggression. When people disagree in this way—for example, over the fundamentals of true religion—they are treated with mercy. When it comes to details based on speculative reasoning, including over the balance between advantages and disadvantages and so on, then those who speculate, whether they decide rightly or wrongly, shall be judged on the merits of their case. This is the ultimate form of tolerance toward disagreement: in fact, it encourages it. That is because human beings are tested by disagreement because they are both honored and burdened with reason and freedom. As God says, "We have made some of you as a test for others, to see whether you will be patient" (Qur'an 25:20). They are tested as individuals and as members of a group. It is a difficult test, and passing the test is the way to civilization and gaining the divine mercy that is promised. God said, "He who created death and life to test which of you does the best deeds" (Qur'an 67:2). There is no test more difficult than disagreement, to see whether people are as fair toward those who disagree with them as they are toward those who agree, toward friends as much as toward enemies. Does a group of people tested by differences, as they inevitably will be, have enough of the culture of *shura* and the tools for managing it in a civilized manner to protect the blessings of difference, such as enriching and stimulating dialogue, generating new ideas and methods, and opening the community's horizons?

The "fifth rightly-guided caliph" ['Umar II (d. 720), the eighth Umayyad caliph], is quoted as saying that it would not have pleased him if the Prophet Muhammad's Companions had not disagreed. Such disagreement is likely to preserve the unity of the group, as well as increase the chances that it will develop, be receptive to all kinds of new and useful things, and absorb a new input of vital energy. It would be conducive to cultural development that is benign, propitious, and irrelevant to religious obligations, unlike objectionable forms of difference that prejudice the fundamentals of Islam, the close ties of fraternity, and the unity of society, which would be terrible forms of disagreement. This is one of the criteria for judging the state of development of a community and the extent to which it is civilized or backward: how it handles differences, that is, the amount of consultation [*shura*] there is and

64 ON MUSLIM DEMOCRACY

the methods it uses to deal with the differences by which it is tested. Does it condemn it, denounce it as a heretical innovation, as erroneous or appalling? Does it reject disagreement and disown those who disagree, as is the habit of those who are steeped in backwardness and stagnation? Or does it address differences with goodwill, by seeking to understand what lies behind other opinions and what usefulness and truth they might contain, in order to highlight those elements, see what faults they might contain, and explain them objectively and respectfully to those who disagree?

Differences Are a Universal Norm

Differences are a universal norm among God's creatures and evidence of divine creativity. As God says in the Qur'an: "Among His signs are the creation of the heavens and the earth, and your various languages and colors. These are signs for those who know" (Qur'an 30:22). The Qur'anic text makes powerful reference to the law of differences in the universe, which proves the power of the Creator and his unique ability to create in this way. "Have you not seen that God sends water down from the sky, and with the water We have produced fruits of various colors, and in the mountains there are seams of white and red and various colors as well, and some that are jet black. And among men and beasts and livestock likewise, there are various colors. Those of His people who know fear God" (Qur'an 35:27–28). Commenting on this verse, Shaykh Ibn 'Ashur says it is "an explanatory reprise of what God said earlier about the differences in people's inclinations to accept or reject guidance because of the dispositions that they are endowed with, in order to show that differences are an inherent law by which God created the creatures of this mundane world."[11]

The author of *The Qur'anic Interpretation of the Qur'an*, Dr. 'Abd al-Karim al-Khatib,[12] held the view that "differences between people are necessary for their lives to be well-ordered"[13] and quoted the 'Abbasid-era theologian and *littérateur* Al-Jahiz [d. 868] on human difference: "God Almighty gave people different natures in order to make them into a harmonious whole. He did not want to harmonize them in a way that would conflict with their

---

[11] Ibn 'Āshūr, *Tafsīr al-taḥrīr wa'l-tanwīr*, 20:300.

[12] [Abdelkrim al-Khatib (1921–2008) was a cofounder of the Justice and Development Party, a Moroccan Islamist party. —Ed.]

[13] 'Abd al-Karīm al-Khaṭīb, *Al-tafsīr al-Qur'anī li'l-Qurān* (Beirut: Dār al-Fikr), 12:1214.

well-being." In other words, He did not want to create them as exact copies, or in the Qur'anic expression "a single community," like communities of bees or camels (in fact, the rule of differences also applies to them, and none of them, and no tree, for example, is just a copy of another, but the differences between them are limited, in that they are denied free will, reason, and the power to imagine, which means that various generations, however distant they may be, do not add anything new).

Mankind as God's Vicegerent [Caliph] on Earth and Divine Guidance

Setting up humankind as God's vicegerent, or deputy, on Earth, which was the objective of creation when God populated the world with humans, is a test for humankind, which has a dual nature in which tendencies toward good and evil are in contention. God endowed human beings with mental capabilities and the free will to choose, and then sent prophets to assist their powers of reason so that they could find guidance in the light of revelation, saving them from wasting their energy in metaphysical labyrinths where they ought not to venture: such as trying to understand the nature of God and prophecy, issues related to the Day of Resurrection, good and evil, and what is permitted and what is prohibited. Pondering such questions has long cast the human mind beyond time and space, leading humans astray and distracting them from their natural and productive activities within the domain of time and place.

But divine inspiration has concentrated on delineating the general structure of concepts and values that God wants for mankind (doctrines, forms of worship, and moral principles), often leaving it to human reason to work out the details of how they live, depending on what is appropriate to their social circumstances and the levels of their culture and civilization. He created them free and rational and enlightened their minds with revelation and general directives for how to live. Inevitably they have differed, either accepting or rejecting God and revelation, on one hand, and, on the other hand, in how they applied the general principles of revelation to a changeable and diverse reality. The fact that they are committed to the ideal of mutual consultation (*shura*) does not spare them from this difference, since the purpose of *shura* is not to eradicate differences from the lives of humans, but rather to regulate their lives in a way that restores a modicum of voluntary agreement in a world of difference and diversity, in order to prevent enmity and strife from developing inside society, and to undermine any justification for tyranny and intolerance in a way that is overbearing toward the people God has created. The order to establish a system of *shura* is an admission of differences and an attempt to transcend them whenever it comes to taking a decision that is important to the community, since no one should be able to take such decisions unilaterally. But how should the process of *shura* be managed? What are the conditions for being the person who consults the public at large? On which issues should they consult all adult members of society, and on which issues need they consult only people of influence? How can they be accessed in a far-flung community? What does the caliph have to do with this system of *shura*?

All this shows that revelation does not start out by denying the natural disposition to be different, either in humankind or in the very structure of the universe. That is not what one would expect from a religion that is connected to human nature [*fitra*], and the same applies to all the other components of human nature. It recognizes them and tries to refine them and develop them in the direction of meeting human needs and resolving human problems in order to achieve the highest possible level of harmony and compromise between, on the one hand, a free and rational nature that results necessarily from having differences and, on the other hand, God's wish that He be worshipped and recognized as the one God and that the Muslim community should remain united, given that the desire to live in society is also embedded in basic human nature, in parallel with the innate tendency for human beings to focus on themselves and seek their own advantage, or what they consider to be their advantage, even at the expense of other people, which is likely to represent a threat to the unity of society. This calls for varieties of debate, dialogue, and negotiation in search of consensus between these various desires.

So God's instructions related to the details of life came in a form that is general, leaving it to the minds of humans to fill in the gaps through mutual consultation (*shura*), in order to reach a consensus that does not eliminate differences, but moderates them until they are differences of diversity and mercy ("Except for those toward whom your Lord has shown mercy," Qur'an 11:119), differences that enrich life and not differences that lead to antagonism, conflict or antipathy that leads to unrest. "As for those who break up their religion and turn themselves into sects, you have nothing to do with them" (Qur'an 6:159). So the tendency toward difference is a part of human nature that Islam has recognized and sought to mitigate through dialogue, *shura*, and education on brotherliness, love, kindness, tolerance, and rejection of violence and discord, in order to reach a level of agreement that, however far it goes, will never achieve absolute uniformity with no irregularities or asymmetries, since the only absolute unity is God, and everything else is multiple, and unity in the human domain can only be achieved in a relative way that does not completely eliminate the differences that lie within.

Given that the tendencies toward differences and unity are fundamental to human nature, given that the structure of Islam is the intuitive form of religion, and given the principle that Muhammad was the last of the prophets and that his successors are a community that draws its faith from revelation in the absence of any further prophets, the principles of *shura* and *ijtihad* will be indispensable as long as Islam and Muslims exist, as a way to seek some form of consensus. Like *shura*, *ijtihad* is an obligation for all Muslims. All Muslims have something to contribute to *ijtihad* and to *shura*, according to their level of knowledge and understanding, their capabilities, and their responsibilities in society, based on the principle that humans are free, that they are God's vicegerents on Earth, and that Muhammad was the last of the prophets. Because this will inevitably tend to endanger the principle of a united community, as a result of the multiplicity of conflicting opinions, organizing a consultative process is essential. So *shura* is not just an ethical ideal or something that is advocated, but a set of mechanisms, a system of public and private participation in managing public affairs that closes the door on autocracy or chaos. It involves debating opinions that are put forward on public affairs in order to reach a level of consensus on a common position that guides communal action at a particular stage. The field of public opinion is broad enough to allow for pluralism. In fact, public opinion flourishes only in a climate of pluralism. But if it is a question of deciding what to do when there is a pressing need for us to act in unison against others, then "God loves those who fight for His cause in one rank, as if they were a compact structure" (Qur'an 61:4).

II. *Shura* and Pluralism in the Experience of Muslims

Anthropology has disproved the theory that people can exist without differences and pluralism. Muslims had the good fortune that the environment in which the first Islamic social experiment arose and flourished was a pluralistic environment that embraced all of its components and did not

68 ON MUSLIM DEMOCRACY

exclude any of them. Nevertheless, the management of political differences in the experience of Muslims has been, and still is, very problematic, possibly because of dominance by tribal legacies, a culture of despotism, and the burden of geography, in that we live in the center of the world, a crossroads for communications and the site of some of the world's most important material and spiritual resources. This has made us a target for all those who aspire to a world leadership that will not be attained until they get their hands on this region at the heart of the world and who do everything they can to thwart development efforts there, especially if the region is susceptible. And it is certainly susceptible to subjugation, as well as to countless bloody uprisings because of the possibilities of change that objective circumstances permit, uprisings that release pent-up desires and maintain the unity of the community of Muslims, arriving through *shura* at communal decisions that set aside disagreements with respect to action, even if they maintain disagreement as everyone's right in the field of thought, whether they are all Muslims, or mostly Muslim, or whether Muslims are a minority, given that Islamic society since the community of Medina, the first Islamic community to take the form of a state, has been pluralistic, embracing Muslims of various tribes and social strata, along with groups affiliated with other beliefs.

The constitution of Medina, as formulated in the Sahifa, undertook to regulate the rights and duties of citizenship between them, and despite their differences this made them a single community separate from other people, as is stated explicitly in the Sahifa.[14] It was not a community based on dogma but a political community of people who shared the status of citizen in the Medinan state. The constitution of Medina represented a very important precedent for establishing a pluralist society that recognizes citizenship

---

[14] It is surprising how the Sudanese scholar 'Abd al-Wahhāb al-Affendi [whose name is often rendered in his English-language publications as Abdul Wahab Al-Effendi or Abdelwahab El-Affendi; —Ed.] repeatedly emphasizes that "the concept of citizenship is entirely alien to Islam," while the constitution of Medina specifies that the Jews and the Believers are a community, separate from other people. Even if we admit that some differences remain, residing in the territory of the state conferred certain rights, as is stipulated in a verse in chapter 8 (Anfāl) of the Qur'an ("Those who believed, who emigrated and who contributed to God's cause with their wealth and their lives, together with those who gave them shelter and support—those are allies of one another. Those who believe but have not emigrated—you are not obliged to protect them until they emigrate. If they call upon you for help in the name of religion, you are obliged to help, unless it be against another people with whom you have a treaty"; Qur'an 8:72). On the other hand, this protection was given to the Jews on the grounds that they were citizens. See Dr. Jamāl al-Dīn 'Atīya, *Nahwa fiqh jadīd li'l-aqalliyyāt* (Cairo: Dār al-Salām, 2003)), in which Ṭāriq al-Bishrī is quoted as saying that non-Muslim minorities have citizenship in modern Islamic societies on the grounds that they contributed to their liberation (81). The Qur'anic verse cited above also shows that the Jews of Medina were seen as among the members of the lands of Islam.

rights for all components of society, not as individuals, as in contemporary societies, but as groups with ethnic and cultural links. The Sahifa lists sixteen groups, and the constitution of Medina turned all these groups into a union that blended tribal, religious, and political forms of unity, bringing Muslims and Jews together against the pagans of Mecca and their allies. Each of the Muslim tribes was a unit in itself, and then the Muslims as a whole were a unit. Each of the Jewish tribes was a unit, and then the Jews as a whole were a unit. Then the Muslims and the Jews formed a unit, and then the Muslims and Jews together formed the united community. According to the Sahifa, "the Jews . . . are one political community along with the believers."

This very important constitutional document established the principle of citizenship as a basis for governance and provided a precedent that Muslim minorities can benefit from by demanding integration, not as individuals to be treated as fertilizer in the soil of the majority but as a religious-cultural group that should be recognized and whose specificities should be maintained, especially in personal status matters such as family law, inheritance, diet, drink, dress, holidays, places of worship, and educational institutions, as enjoyed by non-Muslim citizens in Medina. The same pattern continued throughout Islamic history in spite of some violations when legal practice fell below the standard established in the constitution of Medina: non-Muslim minorities were treated arbitrarily, prevented from displaying their specificities, or subjected to coercion in disparaging ways, based on an erroneous interpretation of the injunction "until they pay the *jizya* tax willingly, and agree to submit" (Qur'an 9:29)—an interpretation that reduces citizens to the status of warriors whose power must be broken.

As expected, the Prophet remained faithful to the constitution in his dealings with these groups, which were what you might call the "nuclei" of parties in his state. He practiced obligatory *shura*, especially in matters of war and peace, as happened with the decision to fight at Badr and the decision on how to treat the prisoners captured at that battle, and as happened when the early Muslims marched out to Uhud and at the siege of the Trench. He also practiced discretionary consultations with individuals. His Companions distinguished between the Prophet's multiple roles, especially between his role as God's messenger and his political role, where there was more scope for individual points of view and a multiplicity of attitudes. If there was any doubt about anything, they asked.

The nuclei of factions emerged, grew, and soon took shape during the reigns of the first four caliphs, starting with the meeting of the "Portico"

70 ON MUSLIM DEMOCRACY

(Saqifa) in 632 AH, when Abu Bakr was chosen as caliph after the death of the Prophet. This was the second formative event in the foundation of the Islamic state, the first being what is known as the second pledge of 'Aqaba in June 622 CE, when representatives of the "Migrants" (Muhajirun) from Mecca and the "Helpers" (Ansar) from Medina pledged allegiance to the Prophet Muhammad. At the meeting of the "Portico" there clearly emerged a serious desire to preserve the political entity that had taken shape in Medina, based on a profound awareness of the distinction between the prophetic role that had now come to a close and the political authority that was now an established fact and had to be secured in the absence of the person who had exercised that authority, even if he had been a prophet. There was no disagreement or doubt about this awareness among the hard core of Muhajirun and Ansar—the two main parties that were the backbone of the state. The agreement was based on the idea that this was a communal matter and that the Prophet's mission was of concern to them all. They were responsible for the mission, and no party could claim that it had an accepted right to inherit the mission or to be its guardian, even if the Prophet's kin (the Hashimite clan and Ali, their representative) said that they had the strongest claim to govern because of their close ties of kinship with the Prophet.

When representatives of the two main parties met to deliberate, while the Prophet's body was still laid out for burial, each of the two parties—the Ansar and the Muhajirun—made its case that it deserved to succeed the Prophet, as takes place in an advanced parliament. The Ansar had initiated the meeting and were inclined to nominate their most prominent leader, Sa'd ibn 'Ubada [d. 635, the chief of the Medinan Khazraj tribe], but representatives of the Muhajirun arrived and argued against them. In response to the Ansar's argument that they had given shelter to the Muhajirun and supported them, the Muhajirun advanced two powerful arguments—the religious argument that they were the first to support the Prophet, and the social argument, accepted at the time, that they were the Prophet's kinsmen and that the Arabs would not agree to a candidate who was not from the Quraysh, their traditional leaders. It was agreed that they would nominate Abu Bakr and pledge allegiance to him in a *shura* council, to be confirmed by a pledge of allegiance by the wider public in the mosque. The agreement was unanimous or almost unanimous, especially after Ali ibn Abi Talib, the leader of the Hashimite faction, begrudgingly endorsed it later. But Sa'd ibn 'Ubada, who had himself aspired to be caliph, still refused to pledge allegiance to Abu Bakr. He did not take part in communal prayers and he

DIALECTIC OF UNITY AND POLITICAL PLURALISM   71

continued to declare his opposition to the agreement until he died, without being detained or put on trial.

It is noteworthy that when the Ansar faction failed to secure the caliphate for itself, it offered a curious alternative solution—that the Muhajirun and the Ansar should take turns governing. But this proposal failed to win support because its rivals had a strong case and an internal rift in the ranks of the Ansar worked in favor of their rivals.[15] All this shows that the Prophet passed on not merely a religion, but also a state in which the religious and the political remained to a large extent combined. But he did not pass on specific procedures for running this state through specific forms of *shura*, on the grounds that this was a matter for the people and should remain free to evolve in order to accommodate any new and useful experiences within the framework of *shari'a*, which had supreme authority, and of the *umma*, which held authority in place of God and His Prophet in a context of interaction between the invariables of religion and a shifting reality and in the absence of specific procedures for *shura*. Even so, an unusual process did take place, and it was tantamount to a leap forward that transcended the logic of the age and the theocracies and sacred kings that dominated it.

During the reigns of the first few caliphs there was a unique experiment in the peaceful transfer of power from one caliph to the next, through various versions of a genuine pledge of allegiance, although it appears to have been difficult with the third caliph and even more difficult with the fourth. The inherited mechanisms were unable to fulfill the requirements of *shura* because of the geography of the Islamic state, which had expanded with such extraordinary speed that the geography in which Islam had initially emerged and in which the first Islamic model of a state, the Medinan state, had been created, now represented only a very small patch in the middle of a far-flung empire. So the new countries that had become part of the state soon marched on the capital of the state, asserting what they saw as their right to power, wealth, and justice, especially as they could see that people who had been fighting relentlessly against the Prophet until shortly before he died were now marching into positions of power and wealth under a caliph who was advanced in years and whom they considered to be biased against them. So they called on him to retire and there were no mechanisms that allowed that, so they approved his assassination, opening the floodgates to evil that have

---

[15] On this history, see Muḥammad ʿImāra, *Al-Islām wa falsafat al-ḥukm* (Cairo: Dār al-Shurūq, 1989).

72 ON MUSLIM DEMOCRACY

hardly closed since. They speak truly [for example, Abu al-Hasan al-Ash'ari (d. 936)] who say that the first sword drawn in Islam was drawn for the sake of the caliphate—and it is a sword that has still not been put back in the scabbard, because Muslims have not been able to turn *shura* as an ideal into a set of procedures for taking communal decisions to ensure the peaceful management of differences over governance, and this has long fragmented the unity of the *umma* and weakened it. This is something that has been done successfully by other peoples and one suspects that their experience may have been superior.

Muslims split into factions because of the conflict over the caliphate, and those factions soon took on a religious guise because of religion's strong links with worldly matters, including politics in its role of defending people's welfare, which is the purpose of religion. One faction was that of 'Ali, which soon developed a theory, or rather a doctrine, that he was the Prophet's designated successor. This faction carried out a series of armed uprisings under the leadership of the most learned, upright, and militant of the Prophet's descendants, who lost their lives one after another at the hands of a government that claimed the right to speak for the Ahl al-Sunna wa al-Jama'a (Sunni) faction. By then the government had transformed the caliphate into a hereditary monarchy that was clearly closer to the tribal or imperial cultures that prevailed at the time. It imposed itself by force and extracted recognition as a fait accompli in return for concessions imposed upon it—agreeing to rule by *shari'a* and to confine its power to the executive domain. Eventually, when the sword had taken its toll on the Hashimite faction, they developed an idea that kept alive the hope that they could regain the initiative—the idea of occultation, which justified waiting—and they refused to recognize the legitimacy of the existing state.

Not far away, another faction was at work—the Kharijite faction, which was close to the spirit of the desert in its violence and simplicity. The Kharijites and the Umayyad state wore each other down. The extremist Kharijite groups had been annihilated and the only somewhat moderate group that had survived, in the sense that it did not denounce those who disagreed with it as infidels, was the Ibadis. This faction was the opposite of the Shi'a in that it had rejected from the start the idea of hereditary government and the idea that the Quraysh had a right to govern, and even the idea that an imam was needed, if justice could be achieved without one. But the Kharijites and the Shi'a jointly refused to recognize the authority of the largest faction, the Sunni faction. This was one of the fundamental problems of Islamic political theory and prevented it from developing in a safe and reasonable atmosphere. Political theory failed to develop peaceful procedures for opposition, leaving only the options of either accepting the government as a fait accompli and trying to persuade it to make improvements or organizing activity in secret while awaiting a chance to stage an armed uprising, which often created chaos and confusion rather than achieving the change desired. This persuaded the jurists, especially in later times, to recognize that might is right, on the principle that "those who clearly hold power must be obeyed," whereas it should have been possible to develop a culture and literature of peaceful revolutions, or the peaceful jihad that the Qur'an described as the great jihad and which the Prophet extolled, describing it as the best form of jihad, in the manner adopted by Mahatma Gandhi or Ayatollah Khomeini. "So do not obey the infidels, but strive against them strenuously with this Qur'an" (Qur'an 25:52).

Factions Based on a Religious Mission, and Factions Based on Tribe

When it comes to the world of ideas, the factions that arose in Islam can be categorized as missionary factions even if they made use of tribal chauvinism, and tribal factions even if they made use of a religious call.[16] Most of the states that emerged in Islam were a mixture of the two, though in most of them the tribal impulse was dominant, starting with the Umayyad dynasty and to some extent the 'Abbasid dynasty, which began as a mix of the two and therefore lasted longer. The Ottoman state also fell in the tribal category, with some influence from the Byzantine legacy.

In modern times the nationalist factions can be seen as an extension of the tribal model like the Umayyad, while the Islamist parties are ideological parties, some of which are very close to the Kharijites in that they reject the existing state, count on overthrowing it by force, like the violent groups, and scorn any consideration for the balance of power or the practice of politics in the sense of dialogue, negotiation, balancing advantages and disadvantages, gradualism in meeting demands according to priorities, and alliances with political or ideological rivals instead of banking on a confrontational relationship with them. So they end up

---

[16] 'Abd al-'Azīz al-Dūrī, *Muqaddima fī tārīkh ṣadr al-Islām* (Baghdad: Maṭba-at al-Ma-ārif, 1949).

74   ON MUSLIM DEMOCRACY

rejecting democracy and its mechanisms, even refusing to recognize or interact with secular parties, whether they are in power or in opposition. They wave the sword of apostasy in their faces, even if they themselves are in opposition and oppressed. Some of these groups are so extreme that they reject pluralism even in an Islamic framework, on the pretext that "parties" are mentioned in the Qur'an [ahzab] only in a derogatory sense, ignoring the fact that the word appears in a variety of contexts, sometimes in contexts of war and enmity and sometimes in contexts of reform and change, which now include part of a structure of Islamic governance based on consultation or of modern democratic governance on the basis of citizenship rights for everyone and peaceful transfers of power that give the majority the right to govern and the minority the right to oppose and seek power. They sometimes cite hadiths that are weak, fabricated, or open to interpretation, such as the hadith about the Islamic community splitting into seventy-three groups, only one of which will survive.[17] The aim is to deny others a freedom that is still fragile and that faces a variety of internal and external obstacles, in order to deprive advocates of Islam of their right, or rather their duty, to serve their countries according to their beliefs by forming Islamist parties.

These days foreign influence is so strong and Muslim rulers are so weak that the rulers ingratiate themselves with foreign powers and make themselves subservient to them. In many laws in Islamic countries, and even in some constitutions, they have made sure to ban the formation of Islamist parties, and it is ironic that in an Islamic country it may be legal to form parties only on a basis that is contrary to Islam, while the constitutions assert that the state religion is Islam, and even that the shari'a is the basis for the state's constitutional law. Yet one finds some proponents of Islam who try to move the goalposts to their own advantage and seek out weak justifications for suppressing a freedom that does not exist in the first place, such as citing the well-known hadith on "the one group that will survive" and adopting it as one of the fundamentals of constitutional political theory. The same thing can be said about important questions such as the right to take part in

---

[17] Shaykh Yusuf al-Qaradawi has mentioned this hadith in its many versions, saying that many of them are weak. He has discussed the substance of the hadith, proving that it has no value as an argument to challenge the principle of pluralism and tolerance in Islam in favor of calling people infidels, chauvinism, and dismantling Islamic fraternity and the rights and dignity of Muslims. (See Yūsuf al-Qaraḍāwī, Al-ṣahwa al-Islāmiyya bayna al-ikhtilāf al-mashrū' wa'l-tafarruq al-madhmūm: dirāsa fī fiqh al-ikhtilāf fī ḍaw' al-nuṣūṣ wa'l-maqasid al-shar'iyya (Cairo: Dār al-Ṣaḥwa, 1990).)

DIALECTIC OF UNITY AND POLITICAL PLURALISM 75

parliamentary elections or to share power, or the right of women to be politically active as voters or elected officials, based on a problematic hadith that
is also adopted as one of the rules of constitutional theory, depriving half of
society of their right, or rather their duty, to improve society. Or they take the
verses in which the terms "party" or "parties" appear as the basis for banning
pluralism, in a way that would please only tyrants.

When Ibn Taymiyya was asked about the "party of God" that is mentioned
in the Qur'an ("The party of God, are they not the ones who prosper?,"
Qur'an 58:22), he replied that it includes the parties that advocate goodness
and truth and that the party of Satan means the parties that defy God and His
Prophet. Even the Islamist groups that have recognized political pluralism
still have reservations, in principle and in practice, about the right of secular
groups to govern and take part in politics, even if they have joined them in
alliances and common struggles against tyrants. After long and anguished
deliberation, the largest contemporary Islamist movement has, however,
come round to endorsing political pluralism in the framework of an Islamic
constitution. The general trend today in Islamist groups that represent the
mainstream of the Islamist movement is to welcome pluralism in the Islamic
context, and from a practical point of view they even make alliances with
secular movements on general issues such as resisting authoritarianism and
foreign interventions.

After citing the Muslim Brotherhood texts that endorse pluralism,
Professor Mustafa Muhammad says, "If the main Islamist movements,
after long labor pains, have come around and committed themselves to this
sound approach, after a narrow-mindedness that dogged them for a long period, some other movements still fall short of reaching this position. But all
this is no more than a matter of inexperience and narrow-mindedness that
will come to an end one day."[18] The Tunisian Ennahda movement may have
been one of the first Islamic movements that asked to be recognized as a political party from the day it was founded. In the founding charter of its pred-
ecessor, the Islamic Tendency Movement, it announced that it fully accepted
the mechanisms of democracy, including the rejection of violence and secret
activities, and that it was willing to take part in elections and accept competition with all other existing political movements, such as accepting the
results of elections even if they brought the Communists to power, in which

[18] Muṣṭafā Muḥammad al-Ṭaḥḥān, *Taḥaddiyyāt siyāsiyya: tuwājih al-ḥaraka al-Islāmiyya*
(Kuwait: Mu'assasat al-Falāḥ li'l-Tarjama wa'l-Nashr wa-al-Tawzī', 1997), 63.

76 ON MUSLIM DEMOCRACY

case the movement could merely take stock and review its program in order to convince the people of its choices, because even if the people rejected the movement they would not have rejected Islam as a whole but only a particular interpretation of Islam. It would not have been fair or ethical for us to ask the secular parties to recognize us while promising, or rather threatening, that if they let us into the system and we won a majority we would throw away the ladder we had climbed up and ban those who had let us in. At the time this attitude of ours received a fair amount of criticism, with some denouncing it as heretical or misguided or even un-Islamic because it called for a form of pluralism that would not exclude any other movement, whatever its ideological background, as long as it was committed to the exigencies of democracy.

In short, even if the political experience of Islamic civilization is familiar with a theory of *shura*, it has not experienced the application of a recognized political pluralism that represents a constraint on authoritarianism and that achieves peaceful transfers of power and undermines justifications for violence. But that did not deprive Islamic civilization of a very extensive cultural and religious pluralism that prevented the outbreak of religious and ethnic wars that were common until recently in the context of other civilizations, because of the fundamental principles that were deeply rooted in the origins of Islam, such as the principle of freedom of belief, the prohibition of coercion, the principle of promoting virtue and prohibiting vice, the principle of *shura*, and the absence of any religious authority that could monopolize the interpretation of Islamic texts or could grant or withhold passes to Paradise. All of that means Islam is well placed to cultivate a very rich political pluralism and make it flourish—a pluralism that makes use of the procedures of modern democracy, which can work more successfully on Islam's home ground because the Islamic environment can fill serious lacunae in the ideological and ethical structure of Western democracy, such as restoring the teleological purpose of human action, solidarity in human relationships, especially family solidarity and neighborly relations, and the presence of the metaphysical world in the physical world, which would restore the lost connection between Earth and Heaven, between religion and life, between economics and morality, and between might and right. It would also reduce the mania for wrangling over money and possessions, and set ethical constraints on political and economic life, so that it would not be a febrile struggle in which there is no place for the weak. The growing Muslim minorities in the

West could act as a bridge of communication between the two civilizations. While taking part in Western political life, especially in conjunction with humane and progressive movements, they could learn how to operate democratically in practice and in a way regulated by democratic procedures, without succumbing to material and instinctual impulses. God is the patron of success.

3
When Is Islam the Solution?

Introduction

It seems obvious that "political Islam" can now be dismissed only at a very high cost, along with religious and ethical Islam (praying, fasting, wearing the hijab, and giving alms), since interest in it is rising and spreading far and wide, so much so that France, for example, has started to abandon its revolutionary tradition of freedom, driven by a concern to stand up to Islam and take sides with an Islamophobic form of secularism.

There are several aspects to this:

- Islam, unlike all other religions, has been able to absorb the shock of modernity. It has adopted what it wants from modernity on its own terms and according to its own needs, while leaving aside what it wants to leave aside. It sees all projects to secularize or marginalize Islam as failures, and it has developed modern theories and applications in which the principles of Islam are merged with the needs of modern life in various domains such as economics, politics, and social affairs.
- The Islamist project has permeated all sectors of society, and many people have pinned their hopes on its calls for the liberation of Palestine and for reintroducing ethics to a political system that is now so bereft of morality that governments behave like mafia gangs, plundering people's incomes, monopolizing the decision-making process, and hollowing out the electoral process, if there is one, to the point that people no longer have any role in the decision-making process and power never changes hands. The Islamist project, on the other hand, wherever it has obtained space to act, has often found innovative ways to provide services to broad sectors of society that have

July 23, 2009. Published in Rāshid al-Ghannūshī, *Irhāṣāt al-thawra* (Tunis: Dār al-mujtahid, 2015), 71–73.

been left to die in wretched shantytowns where development projects lie in ruins.

- Advocates of the Islamist project succeeded in restoring confidence in the *umma*'s abilities when righteous people managed to mount an effective resistance to the Zionist and American occupation to which Arab states and armies had capitulated.

- It has become clear that the Islamist movement can be excluded from political participation only at an exorbitant price, with calamitous effects that are not confined to the Islamist victims but extend to include all aspects of life. That is because you cannot sideline a social movement without abandoning the law and turning the state and all its agencies into a mafia enterprise and a comprehensive machine for repression, held captive by police and army commanders on the pretext of protecting society from terrorism, as has happened in Algeria, Egypt, and Tunisia.

- This means that the Islamists can be excluded only if you also exclude democracy, the rule of law, the independence of the judiciary, and freedom of information, not to mention killing off any hope of a peaceful transfer of power. This means that the fundamental test for the stability, longevity, and democratic credentials of any regime is the extent to which it has integrated Islamists into the political process.

- Where the Islamists have taken part in elections, those elections have been followed with interest, as has happened in Turkey, Morocco, Egypt, Kuwait, Bahrain, Jordan, and Indonesia, as well as in Iran, where the struggle is restricted to currents within Islam. On the other hand, elections are bland and dreary when the Islamists are driven out of them, as has been the case in Tunisia.

- Islam is the solution. The repeated failure of the regimes that have excluded political Islam has given legitimacy to the growth of the slogan "Islam is the solution." It has prevailed over every competing slogan, and under it the Islamists have waged their political and social electoral battles and achieved considerable amounts of success.

Now that a critical mass of these experiences of participation is available, it is possible to identify a number of lessons to be learned:

1. A clear distinction has been made between Islam as a belief system to which wide sectors of the masses subscribe and as a public good that is

80 ON MUSLIM DEMOCRACY

too big for any one state or group or institution to contain, on the one hand, and what is called political Islam, as represented by this or that organization, on the other.

2. The idea of an Islamist offensive has receded. Consequently, there has been a retreat from the idea of an Islamist wave, which resulted from widespread Islamist participation in politics, as happened in Tunisia in 1989 and in Algeria between 1990 and 1992. Those waves led some people to believe that large numbers of people had fallen under the sway of religious emotion and under the spell of shaykhs, whose image has traditionally been stable, and that these people had lost their ability to discriminate and were unconsciously following the shaykhs for religious motives.

It has become clear that the motives behind the few waves that did take place were not necessarily religious. Other motives that were part of the mix included desire for change, hopes for justice, and rejection of the prevalent authoritarian models of government dominated by old and corrupt rulers.

When the Islamist groups were put to the test, we saw them retreating in some places and advancing in others. This showed that the slogan "Islam is the solution" was of limited efficacy in providing emotional incentives and reliable assets for those who promoted the slogan.

This has forced them to accept that they will be judged, favorably or unfavorably, not simply on the basis that their slogan is religious but also by other criteria. Several Islamist groups have therefore adopted political symbols to be known by, drawn from human values such as justice, development, renaissance, happiness, prosperity, moderation, and reform.[1] This does not diminish in any way their Islamic character, since they recognize Islam as an intellectual, philosophical, and ethical authority that also determines values.

---

[1] [Throughout Ghannouchi's writings, especially his later, post-2011 speeches, the distinction between "human values" and presumably some more particular "Islamic values" appears with some frequency. Ghannouchi uses the former to refer to either universal or widely held values that do not necessarily rely on Islamic truth-claims or perhaps any other metaphysical truth-claims for their authority and validity. This is, of course, a curious move insofar as most Islamic intellectuals (including Ghannouchi in many of his writings) would regard genuinely Islamic values or commitments as the most authentically human ones. Ghannouchi's move here bears some comparison to a Rawlsian distinction between beliefs or values derived from controversial comprehensive doctrines and those that are freestanding or merely "political" and thus eligible as grounds for a possible overlapping consensus between various ethical doctrines. Indeed, as Ghannouchi says in the following sentence, the status of certain values as "human values" "does not diminish in any way their Islamic character, since they recognize Islam as an intellectual, philosophical, and ethical authority that also determines values." —Ed.]

WHEN IS ISLAM THE SOLUTION?   81

Members exist in a domain that is not just a matter of discourse and slogans. It also embraces the effort undertaken to serve ordinary people, defend them, and support their causes.

Regardless of their slogans, all those Islamists competing in the arena have succeeded to the extent that people like them and trust them. It should come as no surprise that people supported a secular leader such as Mustafa Kemal Ataturk because he repelled the invading Western armies from his country's capital at a time when the caliph and shaykh al-Islam had surrendered. The nation cheered for Ataturk and gave him the title "ghazi" (conqueror). "The prince of poets," Ahmad Shawqi of Egypt, wrote: "God is most great, what wonder victory inspires! Khalid of the Turks, renew Khalid of the Arabs."[2]

Tunisians also cheered for Bourguiba when he bore the standard of their country's liberation, although he was not known to be a religious person. Some shaykhs, on the other hand, had behaved in a disappointing manner, and their religious status did them no good. Similarly, people cheered for Gamal Abdel Nasser, even when he persecuted Islamist groups, because they recognized his social reforms, his work overthrowing a rotten and outdated regime, and his promise to liberate Palestine and unite the Arab nation.

The masses might hope for good things from a particular group and give it their votes in an election and then in the next election step back and withdraw that confidence (as happened in Kuwait, for example), while the rise of "faith Islam" (in the form of commitment to the rituals, for example) is a permanent feature. The scope of this functional distinction has grown so much that it is expressed through organizations: the Justice and Development Party in Turkey, as compared with the Unity and Reform Movement in Morocco and its peers in other countries.

Examples of this interaction between Islam and modernity include modern clothing that enables Muslim women to move easily and interact with people, and Islamic banks that are now competing with banks functioning on the basis of Western capitalism.

Through its experiences our *umma* has developed a kind of distinction between religious status and political status—so much so that people will say that they would like someone to pray for them but not to have him as their leader, or that they approve of a particular person in religious matters but not in worldly affairs.

---

[2] [A reference to the military commander during the life of the Prophet and the first Arabs, Khālid ibn al-Walīd (d. 642). —Ed.]

82 ON MUSLIM DEMOCRACY

As leader, the Prophet Muhammad did not hesitate to make sure that some of his closest and best-loved friends did not have positions of command. He told Abu Dharr al-Ghifari, for example: "Don't assume command over anyone. You are a weak man." However, he entrusted leadership positions to men who were recent converts to Islam, such as Khaled ibn al-Walid, Ikrimah bin Abi Jahl, and Amr ibn al-As, doing so because of their military experience.

4

Freedom First

Islamist groups continue to denounce democracy routinely and make a habit of expressing hatred for freedom. They argue that Islam does not offer freedom, but rather requires commitment to the rules of *shariʿa*, thereby creating an odious clash between Islam and freedom. In the meantime, Muslims are living under such despotism that the representative of moderate Islamism, Shaykh Yusuf al-Qaradawi, believes that the demand for freedom should take priority over the demand to implement *shariʿa* law. "The first battle that the Islamic revival and the Islamic movement have to fight in our age is the battle for freedom. Everyone who cares about Islam must stand united in calling for freedom and defending it, because it is indispensable and irreplaceable."[1]

He did not really need anyone to remind him that freedom is one of the objectives of *shariʿa*, since he was already well aware of that, but he was addressing the masses of the Islamist movement, who commonly imagine *shariʿa* to be a set of prohibitions with penalties and limits to freedoms. So he addressed them in a way they would understand. This means that the culture of freedom needs to be deepened and to spread more widely.

1. There are Islamist discourses that are not reassuring and even frightening, but the mainstream of the Islamist movement is rapidly taking democracy on board and is increasingly eager to take part in democratic activities whenever a breach opens in the wall of despotism and allows access to democracy's open spaces. The horrors they experienced under despotic rule may be the main motive for this enthusiasm, and practice may therefore have gone ahead of theory, since theoretical precepts tend to advance at a slower pace.

November 21, 2009. Published in Rāshid al-Ghannūshī, *Irhāṣāt al-thawra* (Tunis: Dār al-mujtahid, 2015), 78–82, and *Al-Ḥurriyya naḥu taʾṣīl li-mafāhīm muʿāṣira* (Tunis: Dār al-Ṣaḥwa, 2016).

[1] Yūsuf al-Qaraḍāwī, *Min fiqh al-dawla fi'l-Islam* (Cairo: Dār al-Shurūq, 1997).

On Muslim Democracy. Rached Ghannouchi and Andrew F. March, Oxford University Press.
© Oxford University Press 2023. DOI: 10.1093/oso/9780197666876.003.0005

84   ON MUSLIM DEMOCRACY

But the problem today lies not in convincing Islamists of the value of democracy, but rather in convincing the despots, which often seems an impossible task. Military rulers who have no roots in society do not hesitate to boast repeatedly that they will not recognize Islamist movements that can fill the streets with followers and that were known to society before those military rulers were even born. This can be explained only as the logic of despotism—an attitude based on the idea that the state and society are someone's private property.

The crucial factor, anyway, is whether the public interest is served, regardless of the ruler's gender. And whether a ruler serves the nation's interests depends not on gender but on the ruler's ability to bring about justice—the crux of all politics based on legitimacy, for where there is justice, God's law is in force. Abu'l-A'la al-Mawdudi, who was not an advocate of women taking part even in parliamentary politics, let alone in presidential politics, once found himself facing a difficult choice between two candidates, one male and one female. He concluded that the female was better suited to the position than the male, so he chose her. As it says in the Qur'an, "And a male is not like a female" (3:36). This was said to console Mary's mother, who was expecting a baby boy and then had a girl. She was upset, and then came the divine reassurance: don't despair, because the female you have been given is better than the male that you hoped for.

This debate reminds me of a relevant incident. I was in Pakistan taking part in a conference of the Jamaat-e-Islami when Benazir Bhutto was in office and Nawaz Sharif was in opposition. Sharif attended the conference as a visitor, and it was not long before a petition started to circulate among the shaykhs, who had been invited from around the Islamic world. They were asked to sign a fatwa saying that women did not have the right to govern, quoting the well-known hadith on the subject. When it reached me I did not pass it on. I thought it was unacceptable that this professional politician should try to trick us by taking advantage of what he knew of our culture. "What are the basic qualities that you want to see in your rulers?" I asked my colleagues. "Isn't it justice toward you in line with the *shari'a*? Once you are certain that your rulers are just and upright, then you can examine other, secondary qualities they might have, such as their gender, their color, and their tribe."

2. When the Muslim Brotherhood floated a party program for consultation, government by non-Muslims was another problem that aroused debate in Islamist circles, especially when it came to relations between

Muslims and their non-Muslim compatriots. The program expressed reservations about non-Muslims serving as president. Although most Arab constitutions already stipulate that the head of state must be Muslim, without anyone objecting or making a fuss, the fact that this program adopted the same position provoked a widespread wave of protest against the Islamists, who were not breaking new ground. On the contrary, they were following a position that was well known in the traditions of Islamic politics. But in my opinion they misjudged the circumstances, especially as the issue was purely hypothetical, because the demographic reality that existed in Egypt made a Coptic presidency extremely unlikely, even if the Brotherhood had called for one. Copts would not have had seats in parliament in Egypt unless the president appointed a certain number of them directly, and even the ruling party would not allow Copts to stand as candidates on its party lists because they had no chance of winning, so how could a Copt hope to win a presidential election? For a start, the presidency was still in the grip of the army, which meant that the debate on the question was of a purely theoretical nature and part of the campaign against the Brotherhood to make people frightened of them and turn people against them. They should not have given this opportunity to those scheming against them. They could have kept their silence on the issue because it was the kind of issue that al-Shatibi considered to be "getting involved in something that is pointless," or they could have committed themselves to having a Muslim head of state without suggesting that it was a constitutional requirement.

Assuming that a prominent Copt had a large popular following and such overwhelming national charisma that he could aspire to this office and win the presidency in free elections, it would not be a national disaster or a religious offense, since the nation can never be misled if people are given the freedom to choose. Egypt has known Coptic leaders who have been highly patriotic and acceptable to the people, such as Makram Ebeid.[2] Some of them were advisors and close associates of Hasan al-Banna.

Syria has had a Christian prime minister, Faris al-Khouri [d. 1962], whose performance was excellent and who had exemplary relations with Islam and

---

[2] [Makram Ebeid Pasha (1889–1961) was a Wafd Party cofounder and secretary-general, Egyptian finance minister, and activist in the 1919 anticolonial Egyptian revolution. —Ed.]

86 ON MUSLIM DEMOCRACY

Islamists. He did not ruin the country; on the contrary, he is remembered with affection. If only all the Muslims who came to power after him through military coups had followed in his path.

So when discussing this and similar questions, why do people focus on the question of gender and the nominal creed of rulers, instead of seeking out what is most appropriate, most effective, and most equitable? As the Prophet Yusuf (Joseph) puts it in the Qur'an, "Put me in charge of the storerooms of the land: I am an experienced custodian" (Qur'an 12:55) and "O father, hire him, for the best you could hire is the man who is strong and honest" (Qur'an 28:26). After all, the agenda of the Islamist movement and the democratic movement in general is to liberate all political entities from the blight of autocracy and despotism, however religious and upright the candidate might be.

The expression "shoot oneself in the foot" rightly applies to those who made this proposal, since they gave their ever-vigilant opponents extra opportunities to discredit them, make people frightened of them, and portray them as attacking the achievements of a modern society and wanting to revert to a theocratic system. Once again, the Brotherhood had no real need to ensure that the laws were in line with a constitution that specified that *shari'a* was a principal source of legislation, since assigning the task to an elected constitutional council or to a council of state that had competent and experienced judges would ensure that the task was handled much better than it would be by Azhari shaykhs in a flawed institution that has been marginalized so decisively that both it and its shaykhs are now seen as laughing stocks.

It would have been more appropriate to take an interest in providing guarantees of freedom, including freedom of the press; in clean elections, which would reduce the chances of despotism; and in developing institutions that are secure from arbitrary interference. There is no reason to fear that Islam might be led astray by elected representatives who reflect the wishes of the nation. The danger comes from either despots or magnates, and one of the Prophet Muhammad's main tasks was to break the shackles holding people back. "And he relieves them of their burden and of the chains that bound them" (Qur'an 7:157).

That may be why the Kharijites preferred government by people who were not from Quraysh, since they would be easier to remove from office. The Muslim generals who ruled Nigeria were more brutal to their people than the Christian civilian who succeeded them through democratic means.

FREEDOM FIRST 87

In former times it was a commonplace of politics from the perspective of Islamic law that God supported governments that ruled justly even if they were not Muslim and did not support unjust governments even if they were Muslim, because the crucial elements in government are justice, competence, serving the public interest, and preventing corrupt practices.[3] When we descend from the morass of argumentation to the field of reality, we discover that it is equally pointless to discuss this question. So let's tackle the real problem and take a stand on the field of battle, rather than somewhere else—and I mean our nation's battle against despotism, fragmentation, and international domination, against the despots and their heirs. So don't abandon the field of battle. Reality bears witness that Muslims are fleeing the land of Islam, which is ruled by unjust Muslims, to the non-Muslim world, which is governed by rulers who reflect the will of their peoples. We have not seen any movement in the other direction, so come to your senses.

The facts we face are very complex and cannot be treated with one-dimensional thinking. Is it not the case that, under the force of reality and in order to preserve the unity of their country, the Islamists in Sudan found themselves compelled to make apparently heavy concessions such as offering southerners the right to self-determination, sharing the country's resources with them, and accepting the principle of citizenship as the basis for rights and assuming official positions, which leads to non-Muslims having the right to assume any office including the presidency? But why should we continue to act only by force of necessity? Why don't we understand the requirements of our world and benefit from them and make use of them, instead of running after them or having them walk on our graves?

3. The *umma* is the guarantor. Because of the reservations that some Islamists have had about democracy, in the sense of accepting the popular will as expressed through the ballot box, an article in the Muslim Brotherhood's draft program proposed a committee of senior religious scholars that would advise parliament on everything related to religion,

---

[3] [Ghannouchi here is referring to the oft-cited maxim "God preserves the just state even if it is unbelieving and does not preserve the oppressive state even if it is Muslim. It is said that the world persists with justice and unbelief and does not persist with oppression and Islam." This is a maxim of governance that can be found in Islamic works of law and governance from the ninth to the nineteenth centuries, particularly in moments where Muslims were ruled by non-Muslims or by unjust, tyrannical Muslim rulers. It can be found, for example, in the works of al-Māwardī (d. 1058), al-Ghazālī (d. 1111, who attributes it to the Prophet), Ibn Taymiyya's (d. 1328) treatise on religiously legitimate governance, and al-Kawākibī's (d. 1902) *Umm al-Qurā*. It was reportedly proclaimed by a conclave of scholars in the wake of the Mongol occupation of Baghdad. —Ed.]

88   ON MUSLIM DEMOCRACY

though without its opinion being binding on parliament. Nevertheless, a propaganda campaign against this program interpreted the proposal in the worst possible way by evoking the example of [Khomeini's doctrine of] *vilayet-e faqih* [the rule of the jurist] in Iran and linking that with the Brotherhood proposal. The distorted way in which it was read overshadowed all the important reform measures that appeared in the program.

The existing regimes and the international powers that support them remain the only obstacle to our *umma*'s longing to be free and to obtain its share of the democratic gains that have extended across all continents except the Arab countries. But aspects of the Islamist discourse of the so-called centrist or moderate [*wasati*] school of thought, which interests us most as the main trend in contemporary Islam on which hopes are pinned, to say nothing of the puritanical trends, are still hesitant about promoting freedom and democracy, about taking them to their logical conclusion, giving believers full and undiminished confidence to associate themselves with the Islamist project and conceding to ordinary people that they are the ones with authority and the only source of authority, instead of being suspicious and condescending toward them and fearful that they will harm the Islamist project.

4. There is a reluctance to take the principle of citizenship to its logical conclusion as the legal basis for assigning rights and duties and for equality before the law regardless of differences of religion, gender, or ideology. In Islamist circles that are seen as part of the centrist *wasati* trend, there is still a reluctance to recognize secular parties in an Islamic state. Although the Brotherhood document on recognizing pluralism was a progressive step, it was silent on this point, although the *umma*'s record and the precedents it provides for accepting religious and ideological pluralism are exceptional compared with those of other communities.

The constitution of Medina does in fact set an important precedent for establishing a state on the principle of citizenship: the Sahifa, the document that lays out that constitution, drew a distinction between religion and citizenship, and considered the recent Muslim arrivals from Mecca, the Muslims of Medina, and whoever might join them later to be "one community, separate from other people," a community based on ideology. Then it treated

Jews from the various tribes as "a community separate from others," again a community based on ideology. Then it brought all these groups together and again described them as "a community separate from others," that is, a political community based on shared citizenship. On top of that, the historical model for the Islamic state, which was based on legitimacy of conquest, has collapsed and been replaced by regional states based on citizenship that is shared equally.

There is no real justification for worrying about the effects that pluralism and freedom in general might have on Islam, because all the misfortunes that have afflicted Islam and Muslims came about when the Islamic world was neither pluralistic nor free. If there is a real danger to Islam that we should fear, it would be intellectual inertia and the despotism of rulers. Freedom is good, a blessing, and one of the major objectives of Islam, and when it is denied, people's humanity is denied and God's religion is exposed to the gravest dangers. How could it be right for Islamists to call on ruling parties, most of which are secular, to recognize freedom when they are not prepared to offer them reciprocal recognition?

This double standard is completely unjustifiable. How long will those who hold power in our *umma* go on denying and repressing instead of sharing recognition and authority? No one has yet proved that the Medinan state excluded any group because of religious differences or, a fortiori, because of political differences, and that stems from the important Islamic principle that there should be no compulsion in religion and, again a fortiori, no compulsion in politics. And so parties of various inclinations can emerge in an Islamic state as long as they are loyal to the state, are committed to peaceful methods, and work to encourage interaction between peoples, nations, and religions ("O people, we have created you male and female. We have made you nations and tribes so that you might come to know one another. The noblest of you in the eyes of God are those who are most pious," Qur'an 49:13).

5. We now come to the question of women holding political power. It is widely believed that the Islamic ban on women holding political power is an immutable and definitive ruling of Islam, whereas in fact, like most questions of politics and governance, this is a matter of discerning what is in the public interest (*maslaha*), which is open to discussion and deliberation. In restricting the rights of women, some people have gone so far as to deprive society and the Islamist movement of women's participation in political life as voters and as candidates. It was not long

90 ON MUSLIM DEMOCRACY

ago that Kuwaiti women were fighting for the right to take part in politics and the Islamist movement opposed their participation. The situation was saved only by a decree from the emir of Kuwait that gave them the right to take part, although the umbrella Islamist movement, the Muslim Brotherhood, had already approved of women taking part in politics at all levels and in all offices other than that of head of state, in line with traditional Islamic jurisprudence, which prevents women holding the highest political office, that is, the office of head of state, based on the hadith "A nation governed by a woman shall not prosper." This hadith does not, however, mean definitively what they would like it to mean. As Shaykh Muhammad al-Ghazali has explained, the hadith can be interpreted either as a legislative ruling or as a comment on the lack of success of the Persians in their conflict with the early Muslims and a prediction of success for the Muslims, in that it refers to the fact that a daughter of the Persian king Khosrow held the throne at the time.[4] But how can it be admissible to adopt this as a ruling in constitutional jurisprudence when it deprives half the members of society of their right, or rather their duty, to take part in political life, a ruling that allows only restricted applicability to definitive texts that affirm the principle of equality, such as the texts on responsibility to promote virtue and prevent vice ("The believers, men and women, are each other's guardians: they enjoin what is just, and forbid what is evil," Qur'an 9:71, and other similar texts)?

But even if it is admitted that the hadith mentioned above is definitive evidence that women cannot hold the highest political office, there is no longer one such office that dominates all others. It has been replaced by regionally bounded presidencies or emirates, especially as the state in our times has evolved into an institution governed by laws and arrangements that prevent anyone from monopolizing the decision-making process. The presidency has become almost a symbolic institution, and by law decisions are taken, after deliberation, by a majority of the decision-making body.

---

[4] [On the controversy surrounding this hadith report, see Mohammad Fadel, "Is Historicism a Viable Strategy for Islamic Law Reform? The Case of 'Never Shall a Folk Prosper Who Have Appointed a Woman to Rule Them,'" *Islamic Law and Society* 18, no. 2 (2011): 131–176. —Ed.]

5

Between Sayyid Qutb and Malek Bennabi

Ten Points

At every stage in the history of a nation, stars appear in the sky as a guide to the perplexed. They can light up the sky even in broad daylight if there are many of them and if they cast strong light that penetrates time and space, like renewable and inexhaustible energy. It is our belief that Sayyid Qutb,[1] the author of *In the Shade of the Qur'an*, and Malek Bennabi,[2] the reviver of Khaldunian thought, may they rest in peace, fall in this category.

1. The late Malek Bennabi may be the legitimate successor to the great scholar 'Abd al-Rahman Ibn Khaldun [d. 1406], although Bennabi

---

February 1, 2010. Published in Rāshid al-Ghannūshī, *Irhāṣāt al-thawra* (Tunis: Dār al-mujtahid, 2015), 107–112.

[1] [Sayyid Quṭb (1906–1966) was one of the leading Islamist ideologues of the twentieth century. Until roughly 1948, he was active in the secular literary movement in Egypt as a poet, literary critic, and essayist. His Islamist writings include *Social Justice in Islam*, *The Islamic Concept and Its Characteristics*, *Universal Peace and Islam*, *Milestones*, and the Qur'an commentary *In the Shade of the Qur'an*. In the 1950s and '60s he was a prominent spokesperson and leading ideologue of the Egyptian Muslim Brotherhood, for which he spent extended periods in prison before his execution in 1966. He is known not only as a preeminent systematizer of modern Islamist doctrine, but also as a prime source and authority for some of the more radical Islamist views. For example, the ideas that every facet of the world can be divided neatly into "Islam" or "pagan ignorance" (*jahiliyya*) and that to not govern purely by laws and commands revealed by God renders a ruler, state, or entire society in open war and rebellion against Islam are associated with Quṭb's writings. Later Islamists, especially those adopting the "centrist" or "moderate" (*wasati*) label, often define themselves by distancing themselves from Quṭb's more radical and uncompromising views, which have been taken up by militant groups from the Egyptian Islamic Group to al-Qā'ida and Islamic State. For a scholarly biography of Quṭb, see John Calvert, *Sayyid Qutb and the Origins of Radical Islamism* (London: Hurst, 2010). —Ed.]

[2] [Malik Bennabi (Mālik bin Nabī, 1905–1973) was an Algerian-born scholar who spent significant periods of his life in France and Egypt. He is regarded as one of the most significant intellectuals in modern Islamic history: he influenced contemporary Islamism, but he is a more independent and unclassifiable thinker than Quṭb. He claimed a wide variety of intellectual influences, notably the great fourteenth-century North African historian Ibn Khaldūn (d. 1406), the Algerian reformer 'Abd al-Hamid bin Badis (d. 1940), Friedrich Nietzsche, and Arnold Toynbee. Among his important works are his commentary on the Qur'an, *Le phénomène coranique: essai d'une théorie sur le Coran*; *Conditions de la renaissance: problème d'une civilisation*; and *Les grands thèmes de la civilisation, de la culture, de l'idéologie, de la démocratie en islam, de l'orientalisme*. English translations of his books include *The Question of Ideas in the Muslim World* and *Islam in History and Society*. —Ed.]

On Muslim Democracy. Rached Ghannouchi and Andrew F. March, Oxford University Press.
© Oxford University Press 2023. DOI: 10.1093/oso/9780197666876.003.0006

was not a historian. But they have in common the fact that both of them were philosophers of history, and especially Islamic history. You might say that both of them were historians of civilization who wielded pickaxes to excavate the foundations on which Islamic civilization was based and through which it flourished and bore fruit, and then tried to explain the stasis that brought Islamic civilization to a halt.

Although Ibn Khaldun showed more interest in the political, social, and religious factors that lead to the rise of states, are responsible for their strength, and make them grow weak and collapse, Bennabi deployed his intellect on a perspective wider than any particular Islamic state. He looked at the phenomenon of culture and devoted his life to the subject. This gave him a unique place in contemporary Islamic thought, which showed more interest in examining Islam itself, as he sought to answer the unsettling question of the Arab Nahda or renaissance period—why Muslims had fallen behind while others made progress.

The reason is that Muslims distanced themselves from the truths of Islam and held a distorted view of them. This calls for a critique of the state of religiosity among Muslims, which might end in many reformers accusing them of introducing heretical innovations or even, in the view of hard-liners, of being infidels, as a prelude to calling on them to return to monotheism, as is evident to some extent in the perspective of some Salafis and in the thinking of Sayyid Qutb in his second phase. Malek Bennabi, on the other hand, was interested in the life and history of Muslims, which he scoured to uncover sources of "backwardness," in contrast to how "civilized" they should be. So from this perspective Muslims can be either backward or civilized. They can be just and rational in their use of time and of their material resources, as Islam wants them to be. But even if they perform their religious rites, they can be unjust and wasteful with their time, their money, and all the resources available to them.

According to the Qur'an and in reality, "some of them are unjust to themselves, some take a middle course, and some are foremost in doing good deeds" [Qur'an 35:32]. On the other hand, non-believers can be just and rational in making good use of their time and material resources, in which case they are civilized, just as they can be backward, unjust, and negligent. So judicious scholars have concluded that governance—or what you might call civilization—can be based only on justice, even without religious faith, but it cannot be based on injustice, even with faith.

Faith is a matter to be judged in the next world, though it has an effect in this world, where deeds are judged according to customary norms—whether good, bad, just, unjust, competent, negligent, diligent, lazy, consensual, or despotic, regardless of intentions. As the Qur'an says, "Those who desire the life of this world and all its finery shall be repaid in full for their deeds in this life and they will not be underpaid" (Qur'an 11:15).

2. I never had the honor of meeting the late author of *In the Shade of the Qur'an,* but I read all his writings when I first made the ideological transformation from nationalism to Islam. I was deeply influenced by him and by his brother Muhammad, and I came across a passage in which Sayyid Qutb criticized "a writer" he described only as Algerian. The point of his criticism was that the Algerian writer drew a distinction between Islam and civilization in a way that implied that Muslims could be either civilized or backward.

Qutb was extremely critical of this distinction because in his view Muslims are necessarily civilized, since Islam is by definition civilization and so there could be no civilization outside Islam. After reading the works of Bennabi I was confused and riddled with doubts. My confusion was dissipated only when I went to Algeria in 1969 on my way back from France by way of Spain, where the remains of our Andalusian ancestors left a deep impression on me. This was my first visit to Algeria and I had no purpose other than to meet Malek, most of whose works I had read.

He lived in a modest house, open to visitors. Conversation with him was difficult because he imposed extreme mental rigor on you. He would ask you to stop, insisting that you be coherent in your presentation and not ramble on, to think and think again before daring to frame a sentence in his presence.

I asked him about the issue that had been puzzling me—the issue of Islam and civilization. He gave a lengthy explanation until he had cleared up every uncertainty or ambiguity about the question for which I had journeyed to visit him. I came out of his house convinced that this issue was pivotal to the man's thinking and not an incidental detail, as it was with many people. It was part of an overall vision that embraced Islamic civilization, the real life of Muslims, and the international scene. It opened wide vistas for us to think and explain, and put in our hands a key to many abstruse questions and problems about history and the world as we know it.

94 ON MUSLIM DEMOCRACY

3. After much thought and uncertainty and after a tug-of-war inside me between the ideas of the two men, the prestige and standing of the two great men dawned on me. I realized that if I wanted an interpretation of any verse from the Qur'an, especially an illustrative interpretation or a comprehensive perspective on how the verses are linked together and cohere and how they are constantly immanent in reality as a force that changes reality and not just as a diagnosis, then no one was better placed than Sayyid Qutb to help me achieve my objective. I could not do without him, but I didn't want to confine myself to him either.

If I wanted to analyze and deconstruct the phenomena of backwardness and civilization and examine the driving forces behind them in our history and our lives, there was nothing in contemporary thought to help me and throw light on the path to reality and to the Qur'an that was better than Malek Bennabi, the author of a number of books on the problems of civilization. If the conversation was about civilization, then no one should cast judgment as long as Bennabi was still around.

The answer to the renaissance question—why did Muslims fall behind and non-Muslims make progress?—was perfectly clear to Sayyid Qutb: the question was wrong in the first place. Muslims fell behind because they abandoned Islam, and so they needed to be reconverted. We have to teach them what "There is no god but God" means as an entire way of life. As for non-Muslims, they did not progress: they are in a state of complete pagan ignorance [*jahiliyya*], because Islam itself *is* civilization.

For Bennabi, that is not the case: Islam is not civilization. Islam is a revelation sent down from heaven, whereas civilization does not come down from heaven but is made by humans when they make good use of their talents while interacting with the time and place they find themselves in. Islam does not create civilization in itself, but through men when they understand it properly, undertake serious engagement with it, and mix it with the natural resources available and with time and place. They make a civilization out of all that. Islamic civilization is this serious interaction between mankind, resources, and revelation.

Muslims might succeed with this interaction and create civilization, or they might fail, and others, that is, non-Muslims, might succeed and produce a civilization with non-Islamic values and objectives, because they have worked in conjunction with the divine laws of nature, making good use of their minds, time, and resources.

4. Bennabi was very interested in the phenomenon of colonialism, which could not have spread in the Muslim world were it not for the backwardness that made Muslims susceptible to subjugation. Bennabi is unusual in contemporary Islamic thought for his analysis of colonialism, which makes him a landmark figure among Third World thinkers, along with Frantz Fanon and Ali Shariati of Iran. He incorporated the struggle of the Muslim world into the broader struggle of colonized peoples, foresaw a Third World liberated from the hegemonic powers of East and West, provided a theoretical basis for Third World institutions such as the Afro-Asian movement and the Bandung conference, and defended the revolutionaries of Asia, Africa, and Latin America against Western colonialism, whether or not they were Muslims.

Bennabi's thinking has a depth that is absent in that of well-known Islamist writers, who qualify as members of conservative schools of thought that see international conflicts almost exclusively from an ideological point of view. This limits the possibility of them meeting and having a dialogue with others, let alone cooperating and forming alliances on the basis of a shared and inclusive vision as oppressed people opposed to their common imperial oppressors and their proxies.

5. This shows another aspect of Bennabi's importance—the fact that he introduced movements in contemporary Islamic thought to liberation forces that have rebelled against international injustice, such as the forces opposed to the economic, cultural, and military tentacles of globalization, as well as forces that defend the environment. But his ideas are a mine that has not been exploited and a resource that has remained neglected.

In his first phase Sayyid Qutb had ideas that converged completely with those of Bennabi—ideas of "social justice" and "Islam's conflict with capitalism" and many other revolutionary dictums. He was even seen as one of the ideologues of the 1952 revolution in Egypt, but the course of events that followed the revolution and Sayyid Qutb's own circumstances almost closed those doors and meant that the only struggle that Qutb could promote was an ideological or political struggle, while the role of the social struggle between the oppressors and the oppressed dwindled until it almost disappeared.

96 ON MUSLIM DEMOCRACY

This struggle was later promoted by the Islamic revolution in Iran, which took advantage of Bennabi's ideas, as well as Qutb's ideas in his first phase. With Islam as its starting point, the revolution offered a vision of international struggle between the oppressed and "the forces of arrogance," drawing inspiration from a magnificent verse in the Qur'an: "We want to bestow favors on those who have been oppressed on Earth and make them leaders and inheritors" (Qur'an 28:5).

"And we shall empower them on Earth and through them make Pharaoh, Haman, and their troops see whatever it is that they feared" (Qur'an 28:6).

6. Some people therefore have good reason to be fearful when they see the Qutb school of thought returning to preeminence in the Muslim Brotherhood. They are frightened that the conflict might be too focused on the domains of doctrine and education, while social and political issues might lose priority—the issues of justice, freedom, and openness to other forces, which would restrict the possibility of forming alliances with the non-Muslim forces that are opposed to despotism, social injustice, and international domination of the Muslim world, although the discourse of the new leader of the Brotherhood,[3] which is receptive to Qutb's way of thinking, is a harbinger of openness to the other forces, since he calls for cooperation with them for the good of the Muslim community on the basis of the concept of citizenship.

Although he has gone a long way toward giving reassuring answers on the fears that have been raised about him, the social issue is the poverty that has ravaged the tens of millions of people who have been crammed into slums and shantytowns, their earnings plundered day and night by gangs with power and money, and who have not received their share of attention from a Brotherhood leader who was affiliated with Qutbism and who focused on questions of education and doctrine. Although those issues are important, everyone—first and foremost the leader of the Brotherhood—knows that the first leader and founder of the organization, of which he is the eighth leader, emerged from among the workers and the unemployed who thronged the

---

[3] [Writing in February 2010, Ghannouchi is referring to Muhammad Badi' (Badie), who was the general guide of the Muslim Brotherhood from January 16, 2010, until this writing (March 2021). He has been in prison since August 2013, following the Egyptian military coup of July 2013 against the elected government of Muhammad Morsi, and the Brotherhood has been led by acting guides since that time (presently Ibrahim Munir). —Ed.]

coffee shops of Ismailia. Over time and under various pressures, the organization moved away from them, the many, partially toward the social elite and the educated middle classes, leaving behind the millions who had been Sayyid Qutb's concern in his first phase.

7. The concept of an "ordeal" [*mihna*] set the tone for the work produced in the second phase of Sayyid Qutb's life. It was excellent material for galvanizing a generation of militants threatened with physical and psychological annihilation by the secular forces on the rise across the world. But this made it an ideology of alienation and did not necessarily serve as nourishment for the Islamist school of thought. The message spread far and wide, so much so that advocates of secularism, especially those who believed in eliminating Islamists, took refuge in the lizard's hole,[4] clinging to instruments of repression and bullying their peoples, who were "Muslim up to the neck," as our friend the late Professor Louis Cantori [1935–2008] said when describing the state of Egypt, meaning that only their heads were not Muslim. A survey on the Brotherhood website IslamOnline posed the following question: Is the purpose of the security wall (along the Egypt-Gaza border) to contain Hamas or to protect Egyptian national security? Only 3.5 percent of respondents chose the second option. If that is how detached those in power are from the Muslim community, is it right for a movement that has managed to spread so wide to cling to a literature of "ordeal"?

8. At a time when imperialist hegemony is still gaining ground in our region, Islamists urgently need to brush the dust off the classic writings of the first stage, especially Qutb's ideas and the ideas of Bennabi, who is still unfamiliar in the Islamist center that is being swept by waves of extreme Salafism. This form of Salafism advocates a narrow doctrinal perspective that can in no way restore the consensus needed by a Muslim community targeted by the forces of international hegemony.

The Muslim community is in serious need of consensus thinking to confront the enemies arrayed against it. At the end of the day extremist thinking

---

[4] [This is an oblique reference to the hadith report that "the Messenger of God, peace and blessings be upon him, said, 'Verily, you will follow the path of those before you, step by step and inch by inch; if they entered the hole of a lizard, you would follow.' We said, 'O Messenger of God, do you mean the Jews and Christians?' The Prophet said, 'Who else?'" (reported in Ṣaḥīḥ al-Bukhārī (3269) and Ṣaḥīḥ Muslim (2669)). Yet here Ghannouchi seems to be repurposing it to refer to the cowardice at the heart of political repression. —Ed.]

98 ON MUSLIM DEMOCRACY

presages only warfare between Muslims and has shown it cannot bring Sunni Muslims together, as is evident in Iraq and other places, let alone bring together all the sects in the Muslim community to confront the common enemy.

Wherever it goes, this extremist thinking plants the idea that other Muslims are infidels or heretics. It sows division between Sufis and Salafis, between Salafis and Ash'aris, and between those who follow a particular *madhhab* and those who do not. But how can non-Sunni *madhhabs* and their followers be excluded from the theater of conflict, not to speak of the non-Muslim sects that have been part of the Muslim *umma* and its civilization throughout history?

9. Under Salafist pressure, the existing visions within the Islamist movement are growing increasingly narrow, which leads to internal strife, as has happened across the Islamic world. Algeria, for example, has had an ample share of it, as if Bennabi had never lived there, and I believe that his influence on the Tunisian and Moroccan Islamist movements has been greater than on Algerian Islam.

10. The ideas of Malek Bennabi converge completely with those of Sayyid Qutb in the first phase of his social struggle. Educators and those responsible for cultural guidance in the Muslim world should understand the double danger to the Muslim community—the danger from the culture of globalization and disengagement from what Sayyid Qutb, in a masterly article he wrote in his first Islamist stage, called the "processions of emptiness" (*mawakib al-faraghat*). In his article, a football match becomes a matter of life and death: embassies are withdrawn and armies almost go on the march, while Jerusalem is lost, Gaza is strangled, and resources are plundered. On the other hand, and more dangerously, in extremist and *takfiri* thinking Qutb's concept of an "ordeal" converges with extremist Salafism in a dogmatic and idealistic attitude toward the problems of Muslims, and in the view that the only way to reform and the only way to enforce conformity is to gather around the palm trees of dogmas and work on them with the finest sieves in line with the most extreme of visions—in other words, to carry out subtractions, multiplications, and divisions in dealing with the differences between Muslims, instead of carrying out additions and looking for common ground, as Fahmi Huwaydi[5]

---

[5] [An Egyptian writer (1937–) with moderate Islamist sympathies. —Ed.]

puts it, instead of judging people and movements by criteria other than faith: by whether they are unjust or just, whether they are friends or enemies, or whether they are peace-loving or belligerent.

Muslims are not necessarily truthful, just, or peace-loving, and non-Muslims do not necessarily always fall in the opposite categories. That's why the Qur'an sorted believers into categories: "Some of them are unjust to themselves, some follow a middle course, and others take the lead in doing good deeds" (Qur'an 35:32). The Qur'an also sorted non-believers into friends, who must be treated kindly and with whom one must cooperate and form alliances, and enemies, of whom one should be wary: "God does not tell you to avoid those who have not made war against you on account of religion and have not driven you out of your homes. You should treat them kindly and deal with them justly. God loves those who are just" (Qur'an 60:8).

6

Islam and Citizenship

Citizenship is one of the fundamental concepts in modern political thinking, as the basis for allocating rights and duties in the state, so what is the position of Islamic political thought toward it?

1. The concept of citizenship, as it has been elaborated in modern political thinking, is associated with the nation-state, on one hand, and with democracy, on the other. The evolution of those two features is generally associated with secularism because in the societies that existed before nation-states, when Europe was dominated by empires that included several ethnicities or nationalities, it was the religious bond that held people together. When those empires fell apart and nation-states took shape on the ruins, they sought other sources of legitimacy. This took place after a succession of intellectual developments and vicious religious wars between the European states, which ended in the Treaty of Westphalia in the middle of the seventeenth century. The eventual outcome was nation-states that are accepted as democratic and secular, where all inhabitants, regardless of religion or ethnicity, enjoy equal rights as citizens and whose rights stem not from sharing a doctrine, but from living in the same territory.

But citizenship did not always mean equal rights regardless of wealth or gender. The right to vote remained confined to landowners and aristocrats, and women did not achieve full rights such as the right to vote, even in theory, until later. In practice women have remained victims of discrimination in pay until the present day.

The important question is whether this link between the nation-state, secularism, and democracy, on the one hand, and citizenship, on the other hand, is an essential conceptual link, as some people claim. Or is it just a historical

July 3, 2010. Published in Rāshid al-Ghannūshī, *Irhāṣāt al-thawra* (Tunis: Dār al-mujtahid, 2015), 135–140, and *Al-Muwāṭana naḥu taʾṣīl li-mafāhīm muʿāṣira* (Tunis: Dār al-Ṣaḥwa, 2016), 19–32.

On Muslim Democracy. Rached Ghannouchi and Andrew F. March, Oxford University Press.
© Oxford University Press 2023. DOI: 10.1093/oso/9780197666876.003.0007

fact that does not justify any attempt to prejudge the future, because something that happened in the past, even if repeated, does not provide conclusive proof that the future will be similar, even if one assumes that the past was always like that, which is itself a dubious assumption?

2. It is our assessment that this link, even if it exists, does not provide any conclusive proof, but is just a feature of the history of the West. When studying social phenomena, the West habitually starts from the premise that the West holds a central place in the world, and hence it believes that what is true of its history and its societies is necessarily true of mankind in the past, present, and future.

We have already seen that the link between democracy and secularism is of this type—that is, just a fact and not a necessary social law. The same is true of the relationship between citizenship and secularism or citizenship and the nation-state. The world, including Europe, has known secular nation-states that do not recognize a right of equality for all their citizens. In fact, they might persecute them to the point of genocide, as the Nazis and fascists did. Blacks in the United States, although it was a secular nation-state, gained citizenship rights only in the 1960s, and even then only theoretically. Muslims and people of other ethnicities and religions are subjected to horrendous forms of discrimination and repression in many secular nation-states. This confirms that this link offers no proof that transcends history, but is just incidental. On the other hand, in both the West and the East there have been democratic governments based on citizenship that have not been secular but have had an official religion, such as the United Kingdom, where the head of state combines religious and political authority, and other Western and Eastern governments.

3. In the Islamic context members of different religious and ethnic communities have enjoyed the rights of citizenship, or at least many of them, under Islamic governments throughout Islamic history, and the Islamic world has been spared wars of genocide or religious or ethnic persecution, starting with the Medinan state, which was based on a written constitution that recognized citizenship rights for all the religious and ethnic components of the population by considering them *umma min dun al-nas* ("a community separate from other people"), according to the term used in the Medinan constitution, which was

102 ON MUSLIM DEMOCRACY

known as the Sahifa (see Ibn Hisham's biography of the Prophet Muhammad).[1] The document specifies that "the Jews are a community and the Muslims are a community" (i.e., doctrinal communities) and that "the Muslims and the Jews are a community" (i.e., a political community with citizenship, to use the modern expression—in other words, partners in a single political system that grants them equal rights as People of the Book and *ahl al-dhimma*, i.e., non-Muslims enjoying the protection of the Muslim state). One of the greatest imams in Islam, the fourth of the rightly guided caliphs, Ali ibn Abi Talib, said of them, "They have been given protection so that they shall have the same rights as us, and the same obligations."

4. The non-Muslim residents of Medina enjoyed citizenship rights, including the right to protection by the state, in return for fulfilling their obligation to defend the state. But some of the Jews of Medina failed to fulfill this obligation and made a secret alliance with the Qurayshi enemy that invaded Medina in an attempt to finish off the fledgling polity, and this was the justification for declaring war on them and deporting them from Medina. It was not because of their religion. Under various Muslim governments throughout Islamic history non-Muslims enjoyed rights that even Muslims envied. Unfortunately, some of them repaid Muslims by conspiring against them even more than their forebears had done. What the Zionists among them have done and are doing in Palestine bears witness to that. They beat the drums of war against Muslims more enthusiastically than anyone else in the world, and this will inevitably bring them to the same fate.

5. All ethnicities and followers of all religions who reside in the territory of the state have enjoyed citizenship rights, including the

---

[1] [As noted in the earlier essay "Basic Freedoms in Islam," Ghannouchi centralizes his interpretation of the Prophet's contract with the tribes of Medina as creating a pluralist political order based on citizenship and shared worldly interests for his justification of Muslim democracy. Again, see the English-language translation by A. Guillaume, *The Life of Muhammad: A Translation of Ibn Isḥāq's Sirat Rasūl Allāh* (New York: Oxford University Press, 1967). For other translations of the pact of Medina, see W. Montgomery Watt, *Muhammad at Medina* (Oxford, UK: Clarendon Press, 1956); R. B. Serjeant, "The 'Constitution of Medina,'" *Islamic Quarterly* 8 (1964): 3–16; Muhammad Hamidullah, *The First Written Constitution in the World*, 3rd ed. (Lahore: Sh. Muhammad Ashraf, 1975); Michael Lecker, *The "Constitution of Medina": Muḥammad's First Legal Document* (Princeton, NJ: Darwin Press, 2004); Saïd Amir Arjomand, "The Constitution of Medina: A Sociolegal Interpretation of Muhammad's Acts of Foundation of the *Umma*," *International Journal of Middle East Studies* 41, no. 4 (2009): 555–575; and Ovamir Anjum, "The 'Constitution' of Medina: Translation, Commentary, and Meaning Today," Yaqeen Institute for Islamic Research, 2021, https://yaqeeninstitute.org/ovamiran jum/the-constitution-of-medina-translation-commentary-and-meaning-today. —Ed.]

right to the nationality of the Islamic state and the right to have the state support them and protect them from every enemy that targets them, whereas Muslims who were not affiliated with the territory of the Islamic state, which was the extent of its jurisdiction, did not enjoy this right at all. In fact, the Islamic state recognized the right of Muslims to provide mutual assistance to each other only within the limits set by the state's supreme interests and by international covenants. This is laid out in chapter 8 (*Anfal*: The Spoils [of War]) of the Qur'an, which clearly privileges Muslims who belong to the territory of the Islamic state and its area of jurisdiction, who enjoy complete support and protection, whereas others [living outside, regardless of religion] do not.

The text of the relevant verse is: "Those who believed, who emigrated and who contributed to God's cause with their wealth and their lives, together with those who gave them shelter and support—those are allies of one another. Those who believe but have not emigrated—you are not obliged to protect them until they emigrate. If they call upon you for help in the name of religion, you are obliged to help, unless it be against another people with whom you have a treaty. God sees what you are doing" (Qur'an 8:72). This means that Sayyid Qutb's famous saying, "A believer's nationality is his doctrine," is disproved, because the nationality of the Islamic state (i.e., citizenship) is established only by residence in the territory of the state, whether the resident is a Muslim or a non-Muslim *dhimmi*.

6. Although the concept of *dhimma* status is flawed in ways that have been exploited to distort it, it is still a prominent feature of the tolerance and sophistication of Islamic civilization, which is based on the principle that "there shall be no compulsion in matters of religion" (Qur'an 2:256) and "you have your religion and I have mine" (Qur'an 109:6). The concept is not, however, an obligatory *shari'a* term, so if it has come to demean some non-Muslim citizens of the state it can be replaced with some other concept to avoid ambiguity, such as the concept of citizenship, on the principle that "they have the same rights as us, and the same obligations." The rightly guided caliph 'Umar ibn al-Khattab agreed to let the Arab Christian tribe of Taghlib pay taxes under the rubric of *zakat* (alms) and not *jizya*, which helped to standardize the criteria for tax collection. Major modern experts on Islamic

104   ON MUSLIM DEMOCRACY

law, such as Yusuf al-Qaradawi and Abdul Karim Zaidan,[2] have agreed to consider the *jizya* as the equivalent of military service, and if military service became part of a citizen's obligations, regardless of religion, then *jizya* would no longer have a place, especially as modern Islamic states are based on citizenship, that is, on the idea that the country is the common property of all the population regardless of their religion, since they all took part in liberating the country from occupation. Legitimacy by liberation is one of the fundamental principles of modern Islamic societies, rather than legitimacy by conquest, on which our societies were based in the pre-colonial period. This established a common basis for rights and duties for all citizens, whatever their opinions or beliefs.

7. No one impartial student of the Qur'an and the Sunna, the sayings and doings of the Prophet Muhammad and his Companions, will have any significant difficulty in recognizing the central importance that human beings hold in the structure of Islam, or in seeing that humans of every color, sect, ethnicity, and economic or social status are descended from one family, and all of them enjoy divine respect ("We have honored the descendants of Adam," Qur'an 17:70), that they are all "God's dependents, of whom He loves most those who best serve His dependents," and that "anyone who kills someone, other than for manslaughter or for spreading corruption on earth, it is as though he has killed all mankind. And anyone who saves a life it is as though he saved all mankind" (Qur'an 5:32), on the grounds that every person per se represents all of humanity, and so to assault any one person is to assault everyone, and to be of service to any one person is to be of service to all of humankind.

The Prophet Muhammad demonstrated the meaning of the Qur'anic verses through a practical example: when a Jewish funeral procession happened to be passing, he stood up for it, to the surprise of his Companions. The two main hadith compilers, al-Bukhari and Muslim, say the Prophet stood up to honor the dead man, and his Companions said, "Prophet of God, it is the funeral of a Jew and not of a Muslim." The Prophet replied, "Is he not a human soul?" This encourages Muslims to welcome anything that is likely

---

[2] ['Abd al-Karīm Zaydān (1917–2014) was an Iraqi-born scholar of Islamic law. Here Ghannouchi is referring to his work on non-Muslims in Islamic law, *Aḥkām al-dhimmiyyīn wa'l-musta'minīn fī Dār al-Islām* (Baghdād: Maṭba'at al-Burhān, 1963). —Ed.]

to enhance the status of the honored beings for whose sake the universe was created, to protect their rights, to defend them against all forms of aggression, and to establish divine justice on Earth, since He sent prophets for that purpose.

As noted by [Tunisian scholar of Islamic law] Shaykh Ibn ʿAshur [d. 1973], the most obvious implication of justice is equality, which makes achieving this ideal in relations between humans one of the sublime objectives of Islam. This means that Muslims should be the first to welcome every human rights charter that stands up for their dignity. If citizenship of this kind has occurred in the Western experience in the context of the secular national state, that is incidental and not a causal corollary, because it had already occurred in one way or another in the context of the Islamic experience, as far as the level of human development permitted.

8. Since most aspects of managing human affairs are worldly matters and since God has equipped the human mind to regulate such things, especially if they pay heed to the light of inspiration, it will do no harm if Muslims borrow knowledge that has enriched all forms of human experience and that has proved useful and appropriate, because such things can fulfill one or more of the objectives of our *shariʿa*, including justice, freedom, equality, and the defense of religions, human life, reason, honor, and property, in a way that leaves ample scope to influence, and be influenced by, all civilizations and also to make corrective adjustments.

9. It is our assessment that, just as secularism in all its forms and in all the ways it is associated with Christianity (sometimes it even looks like Christianity in disguise, as the German philosopher Carl Schmitt said) represents the path that took Western peoples to modernity and to the scientific and political benefits of modernity, such as citizenship and democracy, the path that will take Muslims there is Islam and nothing else, because it combines in one coherent system the conscience of humanity and a social system for humanity, including the material, the spiritual, the worldly, and the eschatological, and because its values are deeply embedded in emotional life and culture. This explains why the marginalization of Islam by the secular elites that have ruled the region was the principal factor in the failure of development experiments in every field—scientifically, technologically, politically, or economically, including the failure to resolve the

106   ON MUSLIM DEMOCRACY

Palestinian question. How could development in any field be expected when the spirit that brought the masses together and the fuel that motivated them were excluded?

The fact that the resistance in Palestine, Lebanon, Iraq, and Afghanistan has managed to redress the balance of power, through the standard-bearers of Islam and their allies, after most secular forces had capitulated, bears testimony to the human resources that Islam could provide if they were deployed in construction and development, rather than in terrorism and destruction. As was evident from the freedom ships that tried to break the blockade of Gaza, intelligent altruistic initiatives by peace activists represent a model for the energies that Islam can mobilize as a form of civil jihad [akin to civil disobedience], rather than in the arenas of armed jihad.

10. We also have full confidence in Islam's developmental capabilities with respect to instilling the idea of citizenship in our culture, democratic life, and civil society. We believe that peace must be the default principle for relations with non-Muslims and that jihad was not meant as a means to proselytize for Islam, impose Islam on its opponents, or eradicate non-Muslim beliefs from the world. All of that is contrary to the letter, spirit, and objectives of a system of religious law that came to enhance human freedoms and, after making its case, to grant humans responsibility for their fate. "So that those who perished might perish in full awareness of the truth, and that those who survived might live in full awareness of the truth" (Qur'an 8:42) and "So that, after the Messengers, people shall have no argument against God" (Qur'an 4:165). But jihad is instead a way to fend off aggression and allow people freedom of choice and of worship, safe from any strife or coercion, and God shall be their judge (see *Fiqh al-Jihad*, the large and important work by Shaykh Yusuf al-Qaradawi).[3]
11. We are not unaware that, as a reaction to international policies that are hostile toward Islam and Muslims and to governments that the West has imposed on the Islamic community, and as a result of ignorance about Islam, there have arisen from within Islam itself some schools of thought that are opposed to the highest values of humanity,

---

[3] [Yūsuf al-Qaraḍāwī, *Fiqh al-jihād: dirāsa muqārana li-aḥkāmih wa-falsafatih fī daw' al-Qur'an wa'l-Sunna*, 2 vols. (Cairo: Maktabat Wahbah, 2009). —Ed.]

that are seriously damaging to Islam, and that add fuel to the fire that Islam's enemies have ignited about Islam's values in order to associate it with terrorism and with hostility toward everything that humanity has struggled to achieve in the way of freedoms, rights, justice, the fine arts, rights for women and minorities, and international relations governed by peace, rather than war or force, as the basis for Islam's relationship with non-Muslims. But if Islam is God's final message to His creation and His blessing to them, then it will not lead them astray, especially at a time when there is a revolution in information and human communications, when facts rapidly come to light, and when there is an urgent need for certainties, because established truths have been shaken and uncertainty is rife.

12. The basic antidote to error is commitment to the guiding principles of *shari'a*—principles that do not restrict reason or limit its activity. On the contrary, they set it free, providing reason with light to guide it, with objectives that protect it from error and with certainties that fill the heart and spare it uncertainty: "Those who follow my guidance will not go astray and will not suffer" (Qur'an 20:123). They will not follow any satanic delusion that entices them to go their own way and try to live without a reason for living or without their benefactor. They will not fall into that disaster that occurs when the intellect is so proud of its own achievements that it claims it can regulate life and attain happiness without any need for God its Creator and His messengers. That would be to pose as a god, or rather to declare that God is dead. Or rather, that would be to kill oneself, lose one's compass, and enter into the wilderness, a dark chaos that may even threaten life as a whole and destroy the family until "evil appeared on the land and the sea" (Qur'an 30:41).

13. All this confirms the public benefit of citizenship as a practical measure and as a principle, if only in a minimal sense—that is, recognition, if only theoretically, that all the inhabitants of a country have equal rights to possess the country; in other words, recognition that they legitimately have equal rights and opportunities and equal obligations under a just legal system based on equality and not on favoritism, while recognizing the great universal certainty that this universe has a Creator who commands and is just and merciful. "And He laid out the Earth for His creatures" (Qur'an 55:10) and "Alike for all who ask" (Qur'an 41:10).

7

The Problems of Contemporary
Islamist Discourse

Although growing wheat, combating disease, taming tyrants until they submit to the will of their peoples, forcing enemies into ignominious retreat, and other such feats can be achieved only through hard, methodical work and massive sacrifices that should be more than enough to change the course of history, honest talk directed toward good deeds still has a role in changing the course of history, given that humans are rational beings.

Since the Islamist discourse is now widespread and has a wide audience, those who adhere to it and those on the inside are better placed than anyone else to examine its problematic aspects, as a way to develop it in accordance with the old adage "Hold yourselves to account before others hold you to account."

When we talk about the problematic aspects of contemporary Islamist discourse, we have to take into account the two following points: (1) At this point we are interested only in talking about the ways in which this discourse is flawed or deficient, not about the positive and successful aspects that ensure that this discourse appeals powerfully to people's hearts and minds and reflects most effectively the concerns of the widest cross section of the masses and their longings for justice, freedom, dignity, unity, independence, the restoration of shattered pride, and the liberation of Palestine, Iraq, and every occupied inch of the Muslim world. (2) We are equally not interested in talking about all the gradations in this discourse. We are only interested in talking about one category of Islamist discourse—the discourse of the centrist [*wasati*] school of thought in the Islamist movement, which is the main school of thought. So, what are the most important ways in which the discourse of this centrist trend in the Islamic movement is flawed?

October 31, 2010. Published in Rāshid al-Ghannūshī, *Irhāṣāt al-thawra* (Tunis: Dār al-mujtahid, 2015), 161–168.

THE PROBLEMS OF CONTEMPORARY ISLAMIST DISCOURSE 109

1. It is a discourse that is dominated by the national interests of the governments of the various countries into which foreign occupiers divided our community. These national interests began as a fait accompli imposed on the Islamic world by steel and fire, but national governments have turned them into an accepted culture that has adopted attitudes that have had an increasingly deep and wide-ranging effect on how we think and feel, so much so that Islamist circles might see a repetition of what happened in Arab nationalist circles when the Ba'ath Party came to power in two neighboring countries—Iraq and Syria. Far from being a shortcut to unity between the two countries, this led to the outbreak of deadly hostilities and a complete rift that was overcome only after the fall of the Iraqi Baathists at the hands of occupation forces. The two countries were then able to exchange ambassadors for the first time in decades.

It is by no means inevitable that the dispute between Morocco and Algeria over the Western Sahara, for example, would be resolved if Islamists came to power in both countries, or the dispute between Egypt and Sudan over the Halayeb Triangle on the Red Sea. It is not improbable that Indian Islamists would take a position on the Kashmir dispute that is different from that of Pakistani Islamists, and in Jordan it is obvious that Palestinians in general have attitudes that are distinct from those of people from the East Bank of the river Jordan. There is nothing to prove that the deep rift caused by a football match between Algeria and Egypt had no effect of any kind on Islamists in the two countries. There are many such examples, and thinkers and educators in the Islamist movement must therefore be alert to the danger that the cancer of narrow national interests might infiltrate contemporary Islamist culture, undermining one of the great principles of Islam—the principle that the community should remain united, which is the social and political counterpart to monotheism. "This community of yours is a single community, and I am your Lord, so worship Me" (Qur'an 21:92).

It also poses a threat to the strategic interests of Islam and the Islamic community at a time when there is a shift toward multinational groupings and overcoming narrow national circumstances, which are no longer able to meet the requirements for the national security of any Muslim country on its own. The countries that exported to us, or rather imposed on us, these powerless and minuscule states have therefore set about diluting the sanctity of state sovereignty in favor of enrollment in larger groupings.

Instead of developing the Arab League system and the Organization of the Islamic Conference system in the direction of creating blocs with shared

110 ON MUSLIM DEMOCRACY

economic and defense interests, we have moved backward. No one speaks any longer about conferences of Arab, Muslim, or North African defense or economy ministers. The existing institutions of union have been stripped of all unionist content, and all that remains of them is their misleading titles, like cats that puff themselves up to look like lions but count for nothing in either war or peace. Even when Arab states negotiate with the Israeli enemy they negotiate individually, and abject surrender has been one bitter fruit produced by the division of the Arab world into separate states.

2. It is a discourse in which the doctrinal and educational element is exaggerated, in isolation or almost in isolation from the associated social and political components. Since doctrine and education are so important in the structure of Islam, their effect must spread further, not just to cover the individual behavior of Muslims but also to color all their social and political attitudes. Otherwise, we would fall into the kind of secularism, insincerity, and schizophrenia that tends to dissociate Islam from the important objectives that it came to establish on Earth in the fields of justice, unity, and shared decision-making.

It is true that, in response to the subversive Kharijite view that Muslims can be declared infidels and outlaws en masse because of their sins, theologians concluded that faith and deeds should be treated separately, such that no deed of any kind could justify declaring as infidel someone who has proclaimed the *shahada*, or declaration of faith. But where faith is mentioned in the Qur'an, it is defined in association with deeds, starting from Quran 2:3–5,[1] 8:2–3,[2] 22:34–35,[3] 49:15,[4] and 70:19–35.[5]

---

[1] ["This is the Book in which there is no doubt, a guidance for the reverent, who believe in the Unseen and perform the prayer and spend from that which We have provided them, and who believe in what was sent down unto thee, and what was sent down before thee, and who are certain of the Hereafter. It is they who act upon guidance from their Lord, and it is they who shall prosper" (*The Study Quran: A New Translation with Notes and Commentary*, ed. Seyyed Hossein Nasr (San Francisco, CA: HarperOne, 2015). —Ed.]

[2] ["Only they are believers whose hearts quake with fear when God is mentioned, and when His signs are recited unto them, they increase them in faith, and they trust in their Lord, who perform the prayer and spend from that which We have provided them" (*The Study Quran*). —Ed.]

[3] ["Your God is one God; so submit unto Him, and give glad tidings to the humble, whose hearts quiver when God is mentioned, and who bear patiently what befalls them, who perform the prayer, and who spend of that which We have provided them" (*The Study Quran*). —Ed.]

[4] ["Only they are believers who believe in God and His Messenger, then do not doubt, and who strive with their wealth and their selves in the way of God; it is they who are the truthful" (*The Study Quran*). —Ed.]

[5] ["Truly man was created anxious; when evil befalls him, fretful; and when good befalls him, begrudging, save those who perform prayer, who are constant in their prayers, and in whose

THE PROBLEMS OF CONTEMPORARY ISLAMIST DISCOURSE   111

From start to finish the Qur'an attacks the Pharaonic model of governance, which combines the doctrine that the ruler is a god with political despotism and economic exploitation in alliance with the rich. It also attacks the extortion practiced by those in power and men of religion. The aim is to promote a form of faith that is coupled with freedom and justice. This appears as clearly as possible in the short chapters of the Qur'an, which are easily accessible to everyone.

Read, for example, Suras 104 ("The Slanderer") and 107 ("Small Kindnesses"), where religion is defined in a social sense, where those who reject religion are not only those who do not believe in God and the Day of Judgment, which is the doctrinal, theological definition, but also those who are contemptuous of orphans and indifferent to the poor, and who refrain from providing assistance to the needy. Ostentatious praying will do such people no good.

In summary, faith is mentioned in the Qur'an only in conjunction with good deeds, and the same is true of the *sunna* in general. But various machinations have stripped faith of its sociopolitical and especially economic content, and in the best of cases good deeds have been reduced to individual acts of piety, whereas the Qur'anic discourse in general is directed at a community and an *umma*, represented by a state. Islam cannot do its work in the world unless the community and the *umma* exist, and so the Prophet Muhammad continued to call for social cohesion until his last days, and warned against any reversion to a state of *jahiliyya*: "Someone who dies without owing allegiance has died a *jahili* death."[6]

It is this social aspect of Islam that started to dwindle on the day the Prophet Muhammad died. Those Arab tribes who renounced Islam in general did so not in order to go back to worshipping idols or even to reject the individual spiritual aspect of Islam, as symbolized by ritual prayer, but in order to reject the social aspect as represented by the system of governance and its duty to collect *zakat*, which threw many Companions of the Prophet

---

wealth is an acknowledged due for the beggar and the deprived, those who affirm the Day of Judgment, and who are wary of the punishment of their Lord—truly there is no security from the punishment of their Lord, those who guard their private parts, save from their spouses or those whom their right hands possess, for then they are not blameworthy; but whosoever seeks beyond that, they are the transgressors; those who abide by their trusts and their pact, who uphold their testimony, and who are mindful of their prayers, those shall be in Gardens, honored" (*The Study Quran*). —Ed.]

[6] [Left unclarified is the full implication of this hadith report, which refers to anyone who dies without pledging allegiance to a caliph of the entire Muslim community. —Ed.]

112 ON MUSLIM DEMOCRACY

into uncertainly and confusion, in contrast with the caliph Abu Bakr, who decided to launch an all-out war against this reversion to worldly *jahili* practices. The caliph declared that he would fight anyone who dared to divide Islam by adhering to the individual spiritual aspect of Islam while rejecting the sociopolitical and economic aspects that were an inseparable counterpart. It was the first war in history waged to defend the rights of the poor.

Although the seven armies that the caliph deployed one after another against the apostates succeeded in suppressing this armed rebellion, and although Islam was saved from a plan to finish it off early, the powerful winds of history soon blew a dark pall of dust over Islam's promise of revolutionary liberation. The Umayyad coup d'état put an end to a state based on *shura*, shared decision-making, and a state for the poor, and the gap between dogma and politics began to widen. It took more than ten centuries for the rift to become complete and obvious, a process that took public form only with the fall of the last version of the Islamic state—the Ottoman caliphate. Islamic movements across the Muslim world then arose, calling for the connection to be restored and using the slogan "Islam is a religion and a state, a religion and a civilization."

Although this impassioned Islamic culture based on community has expanded constantly, a piecemeal and decadent culture remains embedded in the collective consciousness, which sees virtue as tied to individual piety, and even in many cases to mysticism. However much the Islamist movement has freed itself from this legacy of decadence, it remains a product of its environment, however much it claims the opposite, especially when sociopolitical awareness among Islamists is still superficial, which opens the field for Islamist groups to pursue policies that are completely contradictory. This was obvious in Algeria after the coup against democracy and Islam by a military junta, supported by forces that do not disguise their hostility toward Islam. Some Islamist groups declared jihad, while others allied themselves with the junta and others restricted their activities to political opposition. What happened in Iraq in the face of occupation was even more dangerous and disastrous: some Islamist groups were brought in on the backs of the occupying force's tanks, others sought to obtain a share of the spoils, and others declared jihad.

The evidence for this is clear in the claim by one Islamist thinker, Dr. Hakim al-Mutairi,[7] that the culture of Islamists does not include political doctrines,

---

[7] [Hakim al-Mutairi (al-Muṭayrī, b. 1964) is a Salafi Islamist thinker and the founding leader from 2005 of Kuwait's Umma Party. However, among "movement Salafis" (associated with Muḥammad

THE PROBLEMS OF CONTEMPORARY ISLAMIST DISCOURSE   113

which means that their political programs can take almost any form. It means that it is an apologetic and self-justifying culture from which the most contradictory positions can be deduced. This is serious and shameful.

One example of how the doctrinal aspects of Islam have been emphasized in isolation from its social implications and public objectives is that governments, in order to qualify as Islamic, merely embellish their constitutions with Islam and make sure that men in turbans attend public events. After that their status as Islamic is not undermined by any betrayal they commit against the national security of the Islamic world: they can safely make friends with its enemies, take part in conspiracies against Muslim peoples, impose blockades on them, torture people to death, massively plunder the nation's resources, prey on the livelihoods of ordinary people, or send their daughters to dance at receptions for generals from the occupying forces.

3. It is a discourse dominated by prohibitions and penalties. This divests Islam of its social content (justice, unity, and *shura*), leaves the *shari'a* with hardly any meaning other than being a penal system (carrying out the penalties prescribed in the religious texts), and ignores the fact that these penalties are in fact just a small part of *shari'a*, to be resorted to only in exceptional cases, after equitable governance and educational systems have provided every citizen with a decent life and a good education. If unscrupulous people then commit acts of aggression, they must be deterred, and deterrence here is the basic function of these penalties ("And in retribution there is life for you, O people of understanding," Qur'an 2:179). So the aim of *shari'a* is not to impose these penalties, but rather to prevent them from being carried out on the basis of mere suspicion. As the hadith says: "Avoid the *hudud* on the basis of any doubt."[8] That can be done by creating the conditions for prosperity, probity, and godliness that are offered by the *shari'a* of justice.

Surūr, and thus often known as "Surūris"), he is noteworthy for his pro-democratic leanings, arguing that Muslims have the right to choose their rulers. See, for example, his *Al-Ḥurriyya aw al-Ṭawfān* (Freedom or the flood) (Beirut: al-Mu'assasa al-'Arabiyya li'l-Dirasāt wa'l-Nashr, 2008). —Ed.]

[8] [On this maxim and its implications for Islamic penal law, see Intisar A. Rabb, *Doubt in Islamic Law: A History of Legal Maxims, Interpretation, and Islamic Criminal Law* (Cambridge, UK: Cambridge University Press, 2015) and Intisar A. Rabb, "Islamic Legal Maxims as Substantive Canons of Construction: Hudūd-Avoidance in Cases of Doubt," *Islamic Law and Society* 17, no. 1 (2010): 63–125. —Ed.]

114   ON MUSLIM DEMOCRACY

When all the mechanisms of Islam were at work during the lifetime of the Prophet and under the first four caliphs, we did not see piles of amputated hands and feet, people being flogged, or gallows set up in every district in the country. Prosecutions almost ceased because there was no need for them, and even the penalties stipulated in the religious texts were enforced only very rarely, when those who were liable to them repeatedly and insistently asked to be punished, out of a desire for atonement or self-purification, as happened in the cases of the Prophet's Companions Ma'iz [Ibn Malik of the tribe of Aslam] and a woman from the Ghamid clan [al-Ghamidiya],[9] who was praised by the Prophet. "She has repented with a repentance that, if shared out among the people of Medina, would be big enough for all of them," the Prophet said of her, showing that before all else the Islamic project was a social and educational project, rather than a project based on power— an educational project aimed at people and relationships, to improve them by persuasion, by the divine presence, by setting a good example, and by providing people's basic needs and a healthy climate that was conducive to probity.

Believers and a strong, cohesive community have priority over power and governance, unlike in modernization projects that depend for reform on the state and its agencies, that is, on repression and power. And because the Islamist project has been and still is a victim of domination by the secular state that was imposed on Muslims by steel and fire, it should come as no surprise that the role of the state has been exaggerated in contemporary Islamist culture, especially when prominent narratives, even from within Islam as a result of foreign influence, deny the role of the state in Islam and assert that Islam, like other religions, is just a spiritual message, that the Prophet Muhammad is merely God's messenger and that the state is not an essential part of this message, but rather a recently invented appendage.

In reaction to this view, discourse about the state has been overemphasized in the thinking of contemporary Islamists, especially that of Sayyid Qutb and Mawdudi. As an effect of this emphasis, the Islamists have focused on *shari'a* and reduced it to the rules for imposing the canonical penalties, whereas

---

[9] [This refers to two cases in which the Prophet imposed the punishment of stoning for fornication during his lifetime. In both cases, the culprit confessed freely, voluntarily, and repeatedly to the Prophet. As the Prophet first preferred to ignore the confessions until the third or fourth time, these cases represent a certain legal trope that rulers prefer to avoid imposing the punishment of stoning whenever possible, do not go out looking for fornicators to stone, and do not stone for anything less than repeated voluntary confession of intercourse on the part of married persons. —Ed.]

shari'a is in fact another aspect of Islam. It includes doctrine, rituals, morals, and all kinds of rules about how to live and worship. It is this reductionism that made the Sudanese Islamists, whose project was dominated by a legalism based on *shari'a*, tie themselves in knots when faced with a difficult choice—between their commitment to *shari'a* in this sense and commitment to the unity of Sudan, since the southerners refused to stay within a state ruled by *shari'a*. In this way a hasty understanding of *shari'a* led to the partition of a state that was united until the Islamists took power, both when Sudan was under occupation and after it became independent. At their hands the country was torn apart because *shari'a* was misconstrued as a package of penalties and as the antithesis of unity, although unity is not just a part of *shari'a* but one of its principal objectives.

4. It is a discourse that gives priority to superficialities and minutiae. This flawed sense of *shari'a* as penalties and prohibitions means that:

a. The discourse tries to restrict individual and collective freedoms as much as possible, so much so that some Islamists deny that a concept of Islamic law that includes freedoms can be Islamic. Like Hizb al-Tahrir, they adopt the horrendous slogan that there is "no freedom in Islam," but only adherence to the *shari'a*. In this way they posit Islam as the opposite of freedom, at a time when people are rising up against the forces of despotism and hegemony and when Islam and Muslims are the main victims of despotism and have so much to gain from freedom that they are fleeing Islamic countries in search of refuge in countries that are not originally Islamic but that believe in secular democracy.

Because of the historical association between democracy and secularism in Western circles, although that association is neither necessary nor inevitable, some Islamists have disowned democracy, ignoring the fact that Islam is by nature a rebellion against oppressive rulers and wealthy magnates and that the Prophet Muhammad reluctantly abandoned the city he loved most because people there were repressive, rejected his message, and denied him free access to the people of the city. They ignore the fact that Islam flourishes when freedom flourishes and that its message is muted under conditions of despotism. This makes freedom not only an essential demand of its message, but also one of the objectives of Islamic law, as asserted by scholars of the objectives of Islam, such as Ibn 'Ashur.

116   ON MUSLIM DEMOCRACY

b. The focus on appearances and details instead of overall objectives has put battles over the issues of the hijab, niqab, beards, clothing, and alcohol at center stage for a broad cross section of Islamists. As soon as they come to power in any country they start enforcing this formulaic program of theirs, imposing the hijab and niqab on women and closing bars and clubs. They can be so puritanical that they close down hairdressing salons and cinemas, and even throw women out of the workplace.

In societies that apply *shari'a* in this formalistic and repressive sense we have seen how women evade these restrictions en masse as soon as they take off on a plane to Europe and how conflict rages between the morality police and vigilante groups, on the one hand, and, on the other hand, communities uncomfortable with these restrictions, which do not come to people from the inside, as a result of their free choice, but rather from the outside, by means of repression and intimidation, ignoring the fact that people are naturally inclined toward freedom and hate anything to be imposed on them, however beneficial it might be, and that if the state were the key to Islam living and surviving, then Islam would come to an end and there would be no demand for it in the marketplace. Power has generally ended up in the hands of Islam's opponents, so how can one explain the growing demand for Islam and Islam's expansion across the world despite the resistance it faces from its opponents? The details *of shari'a*, such as matters of dress and appearances, are a part of *shari'a*, but its attitude toward them is analogous to the relationship between a house and its décor rather than the foundations, the pillars, or the roof.

As the scholar Shaykh Qaradawi says, it is very important that the culture of contemporary Muslims should adopt a "legal theory of priorities,"[10] so that Muslims are not confused by the various registers of *shari'a* and give the trivial precedence over the serious, the less important precedence over the important, or the esoteric precedence over the exoteric. The Qur'an is explicit about pointing to this distinction: "Do you treat those who give water to pilgrims and maintain the sacred mosque as equal to those who believe

---

[10] [This is a reference to Qaradawi's so-called *fiqh al-awlawiyyat* or *fiqh al-muwazanāt* (the jurisprudence of balancing), which calls for a jurisprudential practice of weighing the priority of goods and Islamic legal rules based on the urgency of the benefit (*maṣlaḥa*) achieved by them. This is reflective of Qaradawi's general pragmatic attitude toward modern Islamic legal reinterpretation, which emphasizes balancing the costs and benefits to certain actions, given a certain textual and traditional background to rules. See, for example, Yūsuf al-Qaraḍāwī, *Fī fiqh al-awlawiyyāt: Dirāsa jadīda fī ḍaw' al-Qur'an wa'l-sunna* (Beirut: Mu'assasat al-Risāla, 1999). —Ed.]

in God and the Day of Judgment and who have made jihad in God's cause?" (Qur'an 9:19).

5. It is a defensive, eulogistic, and moralizing discourse. In reaction to critics of Islam, most products of contemporary Islamist culture tend to be defensive about Islam or to glorify Islam and its history. Although that was understandable at a time when foreign culture was on the offensive, infiltrating the minds of many young people and the world of the elite, and when the Islamic movement was in retreat, that is, until the last quarter of the twentieth century, it is no longer desirable when the influx of Western ideas is in retreat and a wave of Islam is on the rise. It is not desirable to regurgitate literature that praises Islam and glorifies its history without including references to the work of the pioneers in the generation of the Pan-Islamic League and the subsequent generation.

Critical thought is an alien concept and area studies of conditions in the Islamic world are very sparse, confined mostly to repetitive accounts of Islamic doctrines, women in Islam, economics in Islam, governance in Islam, education in Islam, and the environment in Islam. But when it comes to area studies of the economy of a particular country, or educational, political, legal, or social conditions in that country, its history, its international relations, its young people, women, or culture, et cetera, then there are few such studies, maybe because the elite in the Islamic world—doctors, engineers, technicians, civil servants, and teachers—are mostly drawn to technical and scientific disciplines. That has been at the expense of disciplines in the human sciences, literature, and the arts, and it threatens to make Islamist discourse superficial and repetitive. It may also have helped to discourage generations of Muslims from serious reading. Instead, they have made do with the material pumped out by the modern media, so much so that the bookcases in their homes are just decorative pieces of furniture. There is heated debate between the various schools of thought in the Islamic revival because simplification and glorification are dominant, and for the same reason the dialogue between those schools of thought has been difficult, because of the tendency toward simplification and superficiality.

6. The discourse has also been severe and blunt, although the miracle of Islam, the Qur'an, is first and foremost of an aesthetic and expressive

118   ON MUSLIM DEMOCRACY

nature and storytelling has a special place in it. Although books of Qur'anic interpretation try to highlight features of this miracle of rhetoric, writings on religious law account for the greatest part of Islamic culture, while in fact, out of the more than six thousand verses in the Qur'an, no more than six hundred refer to matters of law.

It is true that, besides scholarly works on religious law, the amount of material on cosmology, history, travel literature and collections of poetry has also grown, but few of these works have drawn their images from the Qur'an and its values, rather than from the images, values and objectives of pre-Islamic poetry. Islamist discourse is still basically direct and moralizing, while the Islamists' output in drama, music, poetry, and painting is still weak and meager, maybe because of obstacles such as the association between some arts and the secular or decadent groups that have embraced them, which has given righteous people an aversion to them. They try hard to avoid them and are severely critical of those who work in the arts or patronize them. This deprives the Islamic revival and Islam in general of many opportunities to do good work and spread their message.

No fair-minded person could be unaware of the important role that the film *The Message* [1977, by director Moustapha Al Akkad, starring Anthony Quinn] played in promoting Islam. But Islamic art in this field—what might be called Islamic cinema or Islamic drama—should not be confined to telling stories from Islamic history, because Islamic art, as explained by Professor Muhammad Qutb in his book *The Method of Islamic Art*,[11] is not necessarily art that addresses Islam and Islamic themes. It is every art that is based on Islamic values such as faith, promoting truth, justice, and good deeds, and opposing evil, corruption, and injustice.

Although fatwas by prominent scholars of Islamic jurisprudence such as Shaykh Qaradawi have drawn a distinction between permissible forms of music, visual representation, and female participation in the field of the arts, which are the rule, and reprehensible activities that can accompany such things and that diverge from the rule, there is still a considerable amount of disapproval in Islamist circles toward the arts, while there is an increasing conviction that an Islamic alternative must be offered to the hostile use of the arts by the enemies of Islam.

---

[11] [Muhammad Qutb (1919–2014) was the younger brother of Sayyid Qutb, and spent most of his life after his brother's 1966 execution teaching and writing in Saudi Arabia. The present reference is to his pre-exile book *Manhaj al-fann al-Islāmī* (Cairo: Dār al-Qalam, 1963?). —Ed.]

THE PROBLEMS OF CONTEMPORARY ISLAMIST DISCOURSE   119

Islamic songwriting has grown, including the use of instruments; some daring people have ventured into the field of drama, as happened last Ramadan with the television serial *Al-Qa'qa'*;[12] a group of people has decided to make a serial about the caliph 'Umar ibn al-Khattab;[13] and others plan to make an international film about the life of the Prophet Muhammad.[14] These are important steps toward developing a contemporary Islamist discourse that can fill the dangerous vacuum in contemporary Islamic culture and meet the requirements for overall progress and the promises by God and His Prophet to spread the justice and compassion of Islam among the peoples of the world. "God will cast His light in full, even if the non-believers do not like it" (Qur'an 61:8).

---

[12] [Al-Qa'qa' ibn 'Amr ibn Malik al-Tamimi was a prominent military commander during the early Muslim conquests, taking part in the Battle of Yarmouk against the Byzantine Empire and the Battle of al-Qadisiyyah against the Sassanian Empire. He was the subject of a 2010 television series. —Ed.]

[13] [A thirty-one-episode series on the second caliph, 'Umar, co-produced by the Saudi MBC1 and Qatar TV, aired during Ramadan 2012. —Ed.]

[14] [A possible reference to the 2015 film *Muhammad: The Messenger of God*, by Iranian writer-director Majid Majidi. —Ed.]

8

Secularism and the Relation Between Religion and the State from the Perspective of the Ennahda Party

In the name of God, prayers and peace be upon His Messenger, his household, Companions, and supporters.

Ladies and gentlemen, brothers and sisters, may God's peace and blessings be upon you.

I thank the Center for the Study of Islam and Democracy for giving me the opportunity this evening to speak to this distinguished group of Tunisian men and women and those coming from abroad. I am not here to teach you anything, since the subject we are here to discuss has no set instructions to be delivered but rather only points of view to be deepened and efforts to reach a common ground that would enable our elite, in the period we are now going through, to reach a consensus or something approaching a consensus.

Our topic is quite problematic, as it deals with the relationship between Islam and secularism. Is this relationship one of conflict and complete alienation, or one with some overlap? Related to this question are issues such as Islam's relationship to governance and law, which are all contentious matters. It seems that when we speak of secularism and Islam it is as though we are talking about evident and clear concepts. However, a non-negligible amount of ambiguity and a multiplicity of understandings surround these concepts, in that we are not talking about a single secularism but rather many secularisms, as is the case with Islam, since based on what is presented in public we are faced with more than one Islam, that is, more than one understanding.

Lecture delivered at the Center for Islam and Democracy (CSID) in Tunis on March 2, 2012. Original Arabic text published in Rāshid al-Ghannūshī, *Irhāṣāt al-thawra* (Tunis: Dār al-mujtahid, 2015), 200–208. Translation for CSID by Brahim Rouabah, revised by Andrew F. March. Published with the permission of CSID.

On Muslim Democracy. Rached Ghannouchi and Andrew F. March, Oxford University Press.
© Oxford University Press 2023. DOI: 10.1093/oso/9780197666876.003.0009

RELATION BETWEEN RELIGION AND THE STATE   121

Secularism might appear as if it is a philosophy and the fruit of philosophical reflections which came to confront and fight idealist and religious worldviews. But this is not the case. Secularism appeared, evolved, and crystallized in the West as a set of procedural solutions, and not as a philosophy or theory of existence, to problems that had been posed in the European context. Most of these problems emerged following the Protestant split in the West, which tore apart the consensus that had been dominant in the Catholic Church, and imposed the religious wars in the sixteenth and seventeenth centuries. It was thus that secularism began.[1]

Thus, secularism emerged to provide procedural arrangements to try to facilitate the consensus that was shattered during the religious conflicts. Our question thus emerges here: are we in need of secularism in its procedural aspect? Perhaps the most important idea in all of these procedures is the idea of the state's neutrality, that is, that the state should be neutral toward religions and not interfere in people's consciences. The state's sphere is the "public," whereas religion's sphere is the "private." This is where all of these procedures ended up, despite some of their differences in their precise treatment of religion. In the United States religious interference in the public sphere is evident. Despite the differentiation that exists, there remains a significant religious influence. Their leaders' speeches are laden with religious content and references, and religion is debated in all electoral campaigns, where it manifests itself in issues such as prayer in schools and abortion. This is due to the fact that America was founded by Protestant pilgrims fleeing with their religion from the Catholic Church's persecution in Europe. It is for this reason that the U.S. is looked at as the promised land, the land of dreams mentioned in the Torah and Gospels, despite its secularism. As the Franco-American thinker Tocqueville once remarked, the church is the most powerful party in the United States. This is by virtue of the huge influence that it enjoys, unlike in Europe. Whereas the number of those who can lead prayer in the U.S. exceeds 50 percent, in Europe it does not reach 5 percent.

In the European context, also, there are differences in the state's relationship with religion between the French heritage and Anglo-Saxon one, whereby in the U.K. the queen combines the temporal and the religious powers. The complete separation is the one that is associated with the French

---

[1] [Ghannouchi here adds a linguistic comment, noting that there is disagreement about whether the Arabic word for secularism is derived from the concept of "science" or that of "the world," as both share the same trilateral root in Arabic: '-l-m. —Ed.]

122 ON MUSLIM DEMOCRACY

experience, which resulted from the clashes that took place in French history between the state established by the revolutionaries and the Catholic Church. Even in Europe, therefore, we are not dealing with one experience in secularism, relevant for our purposes, since our elite is influenced by the particular French perspective (unique even for Europeans) where religion is totally excluded from the public sphere and the state considers itself as the sole guardian of national identity. This exclusion of the religious and its symbols from the public domain is what led France to be the only country that would not accept Muslim women covering their heads, whereas we don't see such a crisis in any other European country over the issue of headscarves. This is exclusively due to the particular nature of the relationship between state and religion in France, which was the result of a particular historical experience.

We in turn are not faced with one understanding. Perhaps the most important procedure invented by the secular worldview on this level is the idea of state neutrality, that is, that the state is the guarantor of all religious and political freedoms and should not interfere in favor of this or that party. We pose the following question now: is Islam in need of such a mechanism, that is, the state's neutrality toward various religions?

Islam, since its inception, has always combined religion and politics, religion and state. The Prophet (peace be upon him) was the founder of the religion as well as the state. The first pledge of allegiance made by the group of Medinans who came to Mecca was a religious pledge to believe in God and His Messenger. But the second pledge was to protect the Muslims, even by sword, should Medina be attacked. Medina, and this expression is of the utmost importance, used to be called Yathrib before becoming Medina ["The City"], which implies that Islam is not merely a religion but also carries a civilizational meaning. It is a transferring of people from a nomadic to an urban, that is, civilizational, level of existence. This is why a return to a nomadic lifestyle was considered a great sin once urbanization had been achieved. And it is also no wonder that wherever Islam went it established first garrison towns and then cities, and our country hosts the oldest city built by Arab conquerors in North Africa. Thus, "The City" (Medina) founded by the Prophet is a clear indication that Islam is a religion of civilization, rather than nomadism, whereby it shifted those warring tribes from a nomadic level to a civilized one and united them around a state.

The Prophet was an imam in the religious sense, as he led prayers in mosques, and at the same time a political imam who judged among the people, led armies, entered into treaties, and was responsible for all political procedures. Of relevance to us is the fact that upon his arrival in Medina he established a mosque and put in place a constitution that was called the Sahifa. You have precedents here, Mustapha! [*Pointing to Mustapha Ben Ja'far, president of the Constituent Assembly, who was present in the audience.*] This Sahifa, which is perhaps one of the oldest constitutions in the world, contained a collection of covenants regulating the relations between Meccan immigrants and the "Helpers" of Medina in their various tribes, as they were considered to be a single community, and the Jewish tribes of Medina, who were also considered a community. The Sahifa formed them all into one community distinct from others, but in this sense not a religious community but a political one. The most important concept put forward in modern Islamic political thought, by such modern scholars as Muhammad Salim al-'Awwa and Muhammad 'Umar, is the distinction between the religious and the political as corresponding to the separation between state and religion.

The distinction between that which is political and that which is religious is clear in the Sahifa in that Muslims and Jews are each a distinct religious community, but the combination of the two plus other polytheists constituted a distinct community in the political sense. This distinction can be witnessed clearly in the Prophet's actions, even if the boundaries were not always clear between the religious, in the form of observance and obligation, and the political, which is the sphere of judgment [*ijtihad*]. At times the issue also confused the Companions of the Prophet, and they would ask the Prophet whether something he said was binding revelation or his own opinion and a matter of consultation. If the statement was revelation he would say so, and if it was political he would say that it is open to opinion and consultation, and at times the Companions would disagree with him and offer alternatives. On more than one occasion the Companions differed with the Prophet in his capacity as the head of state, and Shaykh Tahir bin 'Ashur has dealt in detail with the topic of what he called "the statuses of the Prophet." If something pertained to his status as prophet of God, then this was a matter for acceptance and obedience, but if it was in his status as head of the army or political administration and he chose a certain position but a Companion came with a different opinion, then often the Prophet would abandon his own opinion for that of his Companion.

One day the Prophet passed by a group in Medina cross-pollinating palm trees and (coming from Mecca with no experience in agriculture) said: "I do not see the benefit of doing so." The Medinan people thought that that was divine revelation and stopped treating their trees, which made their

124   ON MUSLIM DEMOCRACY

harvest that year of a lesser quality. They asked him why he ordered them to do so, and he replied: "You are more knowledgeable in your worldly affairs." Therefore, it is not the duty of religion to teach us agricultural, industrial, or even governing techniques, because reason is qualified to reach these truths through the accumulation of experiences. The role of religion, however, is to answer the big questions for us, those relating to our existence, origins, destiny, and the purpose for which we were created, and to provide us with a system of values and principles that would guide our thinking, behavior, and the state institutions to which we aspire.

So, Islam since its inception and throughout its history has not known this separation between state and religion in the sense of excluding religion from public life. And since the time of the Prophet until today, Muslims have been influenced by Islam and inspired by its teachings and guidance in their civic life, with the distinction remaining clear. This distinction between the religious and the political is also clear in the thought of Islamic jurists. The jurists have distinguished between the system of social relations (*mu'amalat*) and that of worship (*'ibadat*). The latter is the domain of restrictions and fixed rulings, and reason is not competent to reach truth in the area of creed and worship (i.e., why do we pray five times a day, and why do some have three prostrations whereas others have four?). But the realm of social relations is the domain of searching for the public interest (*maslaha*), for Islam came to realize people's interests, as confirmed by great jurists from al-Shatibi to Ibn 'Ashur. These scholars have agreed that the highest objective of all divine messages is to establish justice and realize people's interests, and this is done through the use of reason in light of the guidelines, objectives, values, and principles provided by religion. Thus, there is a domain of social relations that is constantly evolving and represents the sphere of variables, and there is the domain of creed, values, and virtues, which represents the sphere of constants.

Throughout Islamic history, the state has always been influenced by Islam in one way or another in its practices, and its laws were legislated for in light of the Islamic values as understood at that particular time and place. Despite this, states remained Islamic not in the sense that their laws, actions, and procedures were divinely revealed, but that they were human endeavors and judgments amendable to both agreement and disagreement. States have also practiced a degree of neutrality, and when they tried to interfere and impose one understanding on Muslims, as happened in the 'Abbasid state, it provoked a reaction. It is recorded that the 'Abbasid caliph al-Mansur [r. 754–775] called Imam Malik [b. Anas, d. 795] to him and told him that

RELATION BETWEEN RELIGION AND THE STATE   125

disagreements and interpretations from the One Religion have proliferated to the point that he feared for disintegration of the *umma*, and asked him to amalgamate all these into one viewpoint. Imam Malik produced his famous book of law, *Al-Muwatta'*, with which al-Mansur was greatly pleased to the point that he wanted to adopt it as the obligatory legal code for the entire *umma*. This horrified Imam Malik, who said, "Do not do this, Commander of the Faithful! The Prophet's Companions have dispersed to many lands and have brought with them much knowledge, so allow people to choose what they see fit." This is why we see that one school of thought is dominant in the Islamic West, while another in Egypt, and yet another in the Levant.

It is due to the absence of a church in Islam that what remains is the freedom of thought and interpretation. This will naturally lead to a plurality of interpretations and doctrines, and there is no harm in that except when we need to legislate in the shadow of this diversity, at which time we are in need of a mechanism for choosing among various interpretations. The best mechanism that mankind has come up with until now is the electoral and democratic one, which produces representatives of the nation and makes these interpretations a collective as opposed to individual effort. In the absence of a church representing the sacred on earth, there is no one who speaks in the name of the Qur'an and the divine will. The divine will is only manifested in the *umma*, which expresses it through its interactions and not the monopoly of any party or state.

This is why Imam Ahmad ibn Hanbal engaged in his famous revolt during the time of al-Ma'mun ['Abbasid caliph, r. 813–833, who instigated the famous *mihna*, or "inquisition"], a greatly educated and cultivated ruler who wanted to unite the *umma* around a single view. He was influenced by the Mu'tazili school, who, despite being well known for being rationalists, are often misled by their minds and seek to impose the products of their minds on others. Thus al-Ma'mun decided to impose a particular interpretation of the Qur'an [that it was created by God rather than coeval with Him] and a particular understanding of Islamic creed on the people. Imam Ahmed ibn Hanbal's revolt was to refuse the state's domination over religion. He was persecuted and tortured, but in the end he managed to turn public opinion against the state and force al-Ma'mun to cede, and thus the Islamic world remains until today a world in which no church dominates religious inquiry[2]

---

[2] [In reality, the *mihna* continued during the reign of two caliphs after al-Ma'mun, until roughly 848, when al-Mutawakkil (r. 847–861) reversed course and decreed the profession of the Mu'tazilite view of a created Qur'ān punishable by death. —Ed.]

126   ON MUSLIM DEMOCRACY

and various regions follow this or that school of thought without ever surrendering to the state authority over religion.

While the problem in the West revolved around ways of liberating the state from religion, which led to great revolutions toward this objective, in our context the problem is one of liberating religion from the state and preventing it from dominating religion, and keeping the latter in the societal realm, open to all Muslims to read the Qur'an and understand it in the manner that they deem appropriate, and that there is no harm in the plurality that brings a great measure of tolerance. But should Muslims be in need of laws, the democratic mechanism is the best embodiment of the value of *shura* in Islam, as long as it is not monopolized by an individual but is engaged in collectively by the representatives of the people.

It is of the utmost importance that our heritage is devoid of a church. Maybe only our Shi'a brothers have the idea of a religious institution, but in the Sunni world there is no such thing save for organizations of scholars, but they by their nature disagree and hold different views. Thus we need a mechanism for establishing laws, but for this we need not a single scholar but rather a community of scholars and intellectuals to debate and study our issues in a climate of freedom and accept that the legislative institution is the only one entrusted with the authority to give law by virtue of it being elected.

There is a debate that is currently ongoing in our country between secular currents that may be described as extremist and Islamist ones that may be described in like manner. One would like to impose their understanding of Islam from above using state tools and apparatuses and the other aspires to strip the state, educational curricula, and national culture of all Islamic influences, all the more strange since our society does not aim at any kind of religious confinement. This is at a time when the whole world, including the Islamic world, is witnessing a religious awakening, and having seen the role played by the Catholic Church in the development of Eastern Europe, starting with the efforts of the Polish Pope John Paul II, and also the role of the Russian Orthodox Church in the success of Putin's presidential campaign. At such a junction in time, it is unreasonable to object to any and all religious influence on the state's cultural and educational policies. In fact, we do not need to impose Islam because it is the religion of the people and not of the elite, and Islam has endured for so long not because of the influence of the state, but rather due to the wide acceptance it enjoys among its adherents. In fact, the state has often been a burden on religion. As I said, many of those who belong to the Islamist current and others seek religion's emancipation

RELATION BETWEEN RELIGION AND THE STATE 127

from the state and for it to be left as a societal matter. Why does the state train imams? Why does it control mosques?

The issue of the state's neutrality involves a great deal of risk. If what is meant by the separation between religion and state is that the state is a human product and religion a divine revelation (such a distinction was clear for the early Muslims between what is revelation and what is politics), then this is acceptable. But if what is meant is the separation in the French sense or in accordance with the Marxist experience, then we may engage in a dangerous enterprise that may harm both religion and state. The total emancipation of the state from religion entails the transformation of the state into a mafia, and the world economic system into looting and plundering, and politics into deception and hypocrisy. And this is exactly what happened in the Western experience, despite there being some positive aspects. International politics became the preserve of a few financial brokers owning the biggest share of capital and by extension the media, through which they ultimately control politicians.

The need of people for religion is a deep need because mankind is in need of spiritual and moral guidance, which would enable them to distinguish between the permissible and the impermissible. And in the absence of a church that monopolizes the definition of the permissible and the impermissible, this task is left to be debated by the people, both the few and the many, through intellectuals and the media.

When religion is entirely emancipated from politics and the state, this also carries some risks whereby things would break down, get out of order, and lose social harmony. The proper approach is to find a balance that would guarantee people's freedom and rights, because religion came precisely for the sake of people's rights and freedoms. To achieve this balance, we need to go back to the issue of distinguishing between religion and politics and determine what is constant in religion and what is variable. We need our legislators to be steeped in religious values, so that when they are legislating they do not require instructions from the Ministry of Religious Endowments or from religious scholars. The same goes for ordinary politicians, who are motivated not by religious coercion, but by authentic conviction, because there is no value to any religious practice that emerges from coercion. It is of no use to turn those who are disobedient to God into hypocrites through the state's coercive tools, for God Almighty created people free, and while it is possible to have control over their external behavior, it is impossible to do so over their inner selves.

128   ON MUSLIM DEMOCRACY

This is exactly why we saw two models in dealing with the issue of the head-scarf: one in which the hijab is imposed by the state and another in which it is forbidden by it. Once I was in a Muslim country and as long as we were in the airport all the women were covered, but as soon as the plane took off the veils flew away with it. This is a clear failure of that country's educational system, which was unable to guarantee people's religiosity except through coercive tools. In other countries, like the one we used to live in, women were forbidden by the state in an equally coercive manner from expressing themselves in whatever appearance they saw fit. Each approach is a failure.

The primary orbit for religion is not the state's apparatuses, but rather individual convictions. The state's duty, however, is to provide services to people before anything else, to create job opportunities, and to provide good health and education. But people's hearts and religiosity belong to God. For this reason, I have opposed the coercion of people in all its forms and manifestations and have dealt with such controversial topics as apostasy and stated that the role of the state is to protect people's freedom of conscience. Since the Qur'anic principle of "no coercion in religion" is agreed upon, I have defended the principle of freedom in two directions: the freedom of people to either enter or leave religion, because there is no meaning to religiosity if it is based on coercion, and the Muslim nation has no need for hypocrites who manifest belief and conceal disbelief. Freedom is the primary value through which a person enters Islam, and the pronouncement of the dual declaration of faith ["I bear witness that there is no god but God, and that Muhammad is the Messenger of God"] expresses a voluntary individual choice based on conscious intention. In this manner, the state is Islamic insofar as it ensures its actions are in accordance with Islamic values without being subjected to the tutelage of any religious institution, for there is no such thing in Islam. Rather, there is a people and a nation who decide through their institutions what is religion, and the greatest value in Islam is the value of freedom.

When the Meccan people objected to Muhammad's religion, he asked them not to interfere with his preaching activities and to allow him the freedom to communicate his message to the people. Had they done this, the Prophet would not have had to migrate and leave his homeland. But because his message was so powerful, they could not offer an alternative to counteract it. This is why Muslims consider Islam's proofs to be so powerful that there is no need to coerce people, and when the voice of Islam proclaims, "Bring your proof if you are truthful," this challenge is issued in the heart of intellectual and political conflict.

RELATION BETWEEN RELIGION AND THE STATE   129

Thus, a great deal of the debate taking place nowadays in our country reflects a confused understanding of the concepts around secularism and Islam at the same time. We demonstrated that secularism is not an atheist philosophy but merely a set of procedural arrangements designed to safeguard the freedom of belief and thought, as [the Egyptian academic] 'Abd al-Wahhab al-Messiri distinguished, in his writings, between partial and total secularisms. An example of the latter would be the Jacobin model in French history. The Jacobins waged war on the clergy and raised the slogan "Strangle the last king with the entrails of the last priest."[3] This is a French specificity and not secularism in the sense of a set of procedural mechanisms for safeguarding freedom in society. There is also an ambiguity regarding Islam, for there are those who believe that Islam can only be victorious by confiscating people's freedom and imposing prayers, fasting, and the veil through force. But this would be failure and not success, for God Almighty considered hypocrisy to be the greatest crime, and the hellfire to be the eternal abode of hypocrites, the worst party of humanity.

As our revolution has succeeded in toppling a dictator, we must accept the principle of citizenship, and that this country does not belong to one man or one party or another but rather to all of its citizens regardless of their religion, sex, or any other consideration. Islam has bestowed on them the right to be citizens enjoying equal rights, and to believe in whatever they wish within the framework of mutual respect and observance of the law that is legislated by their representatives in parliament.

This is my understanding of things, and my view with regard to Islam's relation to secularism. I hope that I have touched on the main issues, and I thank you profusely for your attention.

---

[3] [A statement commonly attributed to both Voltaire (1694–1778) and Denis Diderot (1713–1784), it was actually first written by French priest Jean Meslier (1664–1729). —Ed.]

9

The Implications and Requirements of a Post-Revolutionary Constitution

In the Name of God, the Merciful, the Compassionate.[1]

I would like to thank the Democracy and Islam Forum for arranging this conference—the Conference for Dialogue on the Constitution—and I welcome the distinguished academics and members of the Constituent Assembly. I welcome you all, ladies and gentlemen, brothers and sisters. Peace be upon you, and the mercy and blessings of God Almighty.

You have already dealt with this subject. I do not intend to provide a summary, and I am not contributing a paper. I am merely outlining some general ideas, which you have no doubt already discussed extensively.

The constitution is an important subject because a constitution limits the discretion of the ruler and subjects those in power to the rule of law.

The Islamic *shari'a* was only revealed by God for the same purpose—to restrict the powers of the ruler and subject them to law. The first constitution in Islamic history, and maybe in the world, was the constitution of Medina, known as the Sahifa—a very important document devised by the Prophet Muhammad when he arrived in Medina, where the population was ethnically and tribally diverse and where there was religious pluralism, with Jewish and Christian tribes living alongside pagans. From all these a state was to be formed, and we Muslims are lucky that the first state in our history was a pluralist state. So the question of pluralism within the state is not recent: it

---

February 23, 2013, at the Democracy and Islam Forum during the national dialogue on the constitution, held in the Mechtel Hotel, Tunis. Published in Rāshid al-Ghannūshī, *Irhāṣāt al-thawra* (Tunis: Dār al-mujtahid, 2015), 227–230.

[1] [In this important lecture, Ghannouchi discusses a number of the most controversial aspects of the post-revolutionary constitution from an ideological perspective. For a general overview of Ennahda's role in drafting the constitution and how a number of the most important controversies, discussed below, played out, see Monica L. Marks, "Convince, Coerce, or Compromise: Ennahda's Approach to Tunisia's Constitution," Brookings Doha Center Analysis Paper No. 10, February 2014, https://www.brookings.edu/wp-content/uploads/2016/06/Ennahda-Approach-Tunisia-Constitution-English.pdf. —Ed.]

On Muslim Democracy. Rached Ghannouchi and Andrew F. March, Oxford University Press.
© Oxford University Press 2023. DOI: 10.1093/oso/9780197666876.003.0010

A POST-REVOLUTIONARY CONSTITUTION 131

goes back to the foundations of Islam. Political structures in Islamic civilization began in a pluralist form, and this has had repercussions throughout Islamic history. Islamic cities never witnessed religious persecution, and the principles of "no compulsion in religion" and freedom of conscience were constant features. Islamic cities celebrated a pluralism that was not confined to the "People of the Book" but extended even to pagan religions. Iraq, for example, one of the oldest cultural spaces in Islamic civilization, is still rich in religious diversity. Some Iraqis belong to revealed religions and others to pagan religions, such as the Sabeans,[2] the Yazidis,[3] and others who worship trees and other material things.

We Tunisians also have reason to be proud of our history in the nineteenth century, when Muslims became aware of the West's ascendancy, their own backwardness, and the gap between the two civilizations. They pointed the finger of blame not at Islam, but at distorted interpretations of Islam that justified governance by tyrants and corrupt, despotic systems of government. A special relationship emerged between the Zaytuna mosque and government administrators, and a rich dialogue began that led to the first constitution in the Islamic world. A parliament was elected, and this experiment might have evolved had it not been aborted by the French invasion of 1881.[4] Otherwise, we would not have needed to wait more than a century for another constitution.

One of the most important advantages of that first experiment was that it combined Islamic thought, the values of justice and consultation that Islam offered, and the pluralism, democracy, and rule of law that modern thought provided. After that we needed to make many sacrifices, much blood was spilled, and many Tunisians went to Heaven calling for a Tunisian parliament.

[2] [A very small community of Sabeans, or Mandeans, exists in Iraq, and in exile, until today. They practice a dualist and gnostic form of monotheism that reveres many of the biblical prophets (especially John the Baptist) and are possibly the Sabeans referred to in the Qur'an. Ironically, given the comments here, the Sabean-Mandeans have suffered extreme persecution since the American invasion of Iraq in 2003 and have seen their numbers in Iraq depleted. —Ed.]

[3] [The Yazidis, of course, came to global attention a little more than a year after Ghannouchi gave this lecture, as a result of their slaughter and even enslavement at the hands of the Islamic State group. Unlike the Sabeans, they do not fit neatly into the scheme of the revealed monotheistic religions "of the Book." They are a religious sect found in parts of Iraq, Turkey, Syria, Armenia, the Caucasus, and Iran and follow a religion that is a syncretism of Zoroastrian, Manichaean, Jewish, Nestorian Christian, and Islamic elements. Yazidism is a post-prophetic religion (like Baha'ism, for example) and thus not eligible for toleration or *dhimma* status, according to some strict juridical doctrines. They suffered persecution under Sunni regimes from the thirteenth century onward, and this was the basis for Islamic State's claim that they, unlike other religious minorities or political enemies, could be enslaved. —Ed.]

[4] [It is worth noting that the Tunisian constitution of 1861 was actually suspended in 1864 in response to a local revolt. —Ed.]

132 ON MUSLIM DEMOCRACY

God wants this generation to see the first Tunisian parliament and a constitution enacted by Tunisians through their chosen representatives.

What matters to us in the constitution is that it should not be a constitution for one party, but a constitution for the whole country, reflecting all shades of the political, ideological, and social spectrum—in other words, a constitution in which the country can find itself. So the constitution should not be passed with a 51 percent majority: it should seek to obtain consensus approval, meaning at least two-thirds, because it should be a constitution in which citizens of all inclinations can see themselves, and not just a bare majority. Moreover, this constitution should be drafted through participation that is as wide as possible, and not just by a narrow faction.

The constitution should also respect the country's identity: we are an Arab Islamic country, but no one has a monopoly right to interpret that identity.[5] In Islam there is no church that monopolizes the interpretation of Islam. Instead, this is a matter left to the community and to ordinary people through their own institutions, which elaborate the meaning of that Arab-Islamic identity. Thus, when the question of the place of *shari'a* law in the constitution was raised,[6] we found that it was a matter of disagreement, and we said that constitutions are not based on what there is deep disagreement on but rather what is a matter of consensus. So we withdrew this subject from discussion.

The constitution should also be based on a foundation of human values because we are part of humankind, which has refined certain principles such as democracy and human rights. We are also heirs to the principles of reform

---

[5] [Article 1 of the 2014 constitution, declared by the constitution to be unamendable, reads, "Tunisia is a free, independent, sovereign state; its religion is Islam, its language Arabic, and its system is republican." Article 6 reads, "The state is the guardian of religion. It guarantees freedom of conscience and belief, the free exercise of religious practices and the neutrality of mosques and places of worship from all partisan instrumentalisation. The state undertakes to disseminate the values of moderation and tolerance and the protection of the sacred, and the prohibition of all violations thereof. It undertakes equally to prohibit and fight against calls for Takfir and the incitement of violence and hatred." See the English-language translation of the 2014 constitution at https://www.constituteproject.org/constitution/Tunisia_2014.pdf. —Ed.]

[6] [Some more conservative members of the Ennahda Shura Council (namely, Sadok Chorou and Habib Ellouze) argued for a push to include a reference to the *shari'a* in the constitution, as is found in the constitutions of a number of modern Muslim-majority states, such as Egypt, Pakistan, Iraq, and Afghanistan. This led to a vibrant debate within Ennahda, which resulted in a vote against pushing to introduce a reference to the *shari'a* in the constituent assembly. See Tom Heneghan, "Tunisia's Constitution Will Make No Place for Faith; Ennahda Leader Rejects Laws to Enforce Religion," *Al-Arabiya*, November 4, 2011, https://www.alarabiya.net/articles/2011/11/04/175488. See also an interview with conservative Ennahda member Habib Ellouze: Shadi Hamid and William McCants, "Islamists on Islamism Today: An Interview with Habib Ellouze of Tunisia's Ennahda Party," *Markaz* (blog), Brookings Institution, May 25, 2017, https://www.brookings.edu/blog/markaz/2017/05/25/islamists-on-islamism-today-an-interview-with-habib-ellouze-of-tunisias-ennahda-party/. —Ed.]

A POST-REVOLUTIONARY CONSTITUTION   133

and consider the reformist school one of the sources of our constitution and of our distinctive Tunisian way of thinking.[7]

We want to build a civil state [*dawla madaniyya*] in which legitimacy is derived from the people, that is, from the populace and the governed.[8] There is no legitimacy for any ruler except from a clear delegation from the people through free, fair, and pluralistic elections.

We need to expand freedoms as much as we can. Justice is one of the ultimate objectives of Islam, as is freedom, so we should not be afraid of freedom, but rather of despotism. Constitutions serve to prevent despotism, not to prevent freedom, and every move toward expanding freedom moves in an Islamic direction.

Of course, torture in any form and under any circumstances should be outlawed, and there is a thesis in Islamic jurisprudence that provides a foundation for banning and criminalizing torture.[9] The Prophet Muhammad said, "A woman went to Hell because of a cat. She had locked it up and she neither fed it nor allowed it to eat the vermin on the ground." Another woman, on the other hand, went to Heaven because of a dog. She went down a well, filled her water bag, gave water to the dog, and went to Heaven. Torture is a crime that has absolutely no basis in Islam.

Freedom of belief is a fixed principle, as are the freedoms to publish and to create, the right to form unions, the right to access information, academic freedom, and the freedom to do scientific research—all this is part of the principle of freedom. We believe it is appropriate that our constitution should move toward decentralization because the closer the state is to the people the better.[10] Our country is the Arab country that has the greatest

---

[7] [It is common to refer to a distinct "Tunisian reformist" tradition from thinkers associated with the constitutional reforms of the 1860s (like Khayr al-Din Pasha (sometimes referred to as Khayr al-Din al-Tunisi) and Ahmad bin Diyaf to modern theologians and Qur'an commentators like Ibn 'Ashur. Ghannouchi and others will sometimes refer to a "Tunisian exceptionalism" or particularity [*al-khususiyya al-Tunisiyya*].) —Ed.]

[8] [The term "civil state" is frequently used by Sunni Islamists to distinguish their vision of a legitimate constitutional order from both a theocracy (attributed by them to both Shi'ism and medieval Europe) and a secular state with no religious reference. This was frequently remarked upon during the Arab Spring, but the reference to even the Islamic caliphate as a "civil" (*madani*) form of rule was used as early as the 1920s in the writings of Rashid Rida. (See Andrew F. March, *The Caliphate of Man: Popular Sovereignty in Modern Islamic Thought* (Cambridge, MA: Belknap Press, 2019), 47.) —Ed.]

[9] [Article 23 of the 2014 Constitution reads: "The state protects human dignity and physical integrity, and prohibits mental and physical torture. Crimes of torture are not subject to any statute of limitations." —Ed.]

[10] [Article 14: "The state commits to strengthening decentralization and to apply it throughout the country, within the framework of the unity of the state." —Ed.]

134 ON MUSLIM DEMOCRACY

internal harmony, unthreatened by any fault lines or any advocates for secession by any part of the country, so why should we insist on centralized government, which is a feature of dictatorships that has no justification in our country? What we need to do is spread power as widely as possible without having everything depend on the center.

There are still some issues on which there is disagreement—for example, in the discussions that have taken place on gender equality and the language of "complementarity" and "equality."[11] We think it would be preferable to avoid terms that arouse suspicion or where people do not agree on what they mean, so we have advised our colleagues to drop the term "complementarity," although we believe that complementarity is a form of equality and that the two genders complement each other, not that just one of them complements the other. But as long as there are any misgivings about the term, then we say that constitutions should be consensual and not divisive.

On the universality of human rights,[12] we believe that we Islamists should be happy that humankind agrees that humans have rights regardless of their race or religion, and so we should not be upset about the idea that human rights are universal. This is a guarantee of rights and freedom, and Islam came to serve the interests of people, so anything that guarantees people's interests and rights is part of Islam, even if it is not specified in any Qur'anic verse or hadith.

There are subjects, such as criminalizing the normalization of relations with Israel, where we do not disagree on the content but on whether the constitution is the right place for such things.[13] We think it would be best to put this in legislation rather than include it in the constitution. Similarly with

[11] [This was one of the most noteworthy controversies of the constituent process, with an early draft of what became Article 21 of the 2014 constitution proposed by the Ennahda bloc employing the term *takamul*, or "complementarity." The final text reads: "All citizens, male and female, have equal rights and duties, and are equal before the law without any discrimination. The state guarantees freedoms and individual and collective rights to all citizens, and provides all citizens the conditions for a dignified life." —Ed.]

[12] [The preamble of the 2014 constitution includes, in part, the clause "Expressing our people's commitment to the teachings of Islam and its aims characterized by openness and moderation, and to the human values and the highest principles of universal human rights . . ." Referring to human rights as understood in international law as "universal" raises certain issues as to the universal claims of Islamic norms and rights. It is the language of "universality" as much as the substance of any individual rights that raised a controversy for the Islamist bloc during the constitution-drafting process. —Ed.]

[13] [During the constituent assembly, five Tunisian nationalist and leftist parties, affiliated with the popular 14th of January Front, called for the criminalization of normalization with Israel to be inserted into the constitution itself. (See "Tajrīm al-taṭbīʿ maʿ Isrāʾīl yuqassim al-sāḥa al-siyāsiyya al-Tūnisiyya," *Al-Bayān*, March 22, 2012, https://www.albayan.ae/one-world/arabs/2012-03-22-1.1616 260.) —Ed.]

A POST-REVOLUTIONARY CONSTITUTION   135

blasphemy: if there is no agreement on this, then it can be left out of the constitution and be included in statutory legislation.[14]

When it comes to the nature of the political system and whether it should be parliamentary and centralized or presidential or a mixture of the two, compromise to resolve disagreement is the easiest practice, and in Arabic the term *wasat* [the middle] implies benevolence.[15] The Qur'anic verse "And thus we made you a nation of the middle-path [*wasat*]" implies a benevolent nation, so the *wasat* is what is best and it does not refer to the geometric mid-point.

Finding a compromise between the parliamentary system of government and the presidential system does not mean it would be best if everyone made minor concessions on their current position. That way we might arrive at an ineffective system or a system where some parts obstruct others. We tried that approach in the interim arrangements now in force, but when we applied them in practice it created a number of difficulties that almost caused a crisis, because when two separate authorities have to address a single issue simultaneously, which of them has executive power?

We think that a parliamentary system is more democratic because it is closer to the people and disperses power on a wider scale. In any case, in our

[14] [This was one of the most contentious issues within the constituent assembly. Ennahda members of the Rights and Liberties Committee pushed for language that would criminalize blasphemy in the first constitutional draft, which stated that "the state guarantees freedom of religious belief and practice and criminalizes all attacks on that which is sacred," specifically defining the three Abrahamic faiths (Islam, Judaism, and Christianity) as faiths that would be protected from blasphemous attacks. After significant opposition from other parties, domestic civil society groups, international NGOs, and foreign governments, Ennahda reluctantly agreed to remove this language from the final draft of the constitution. This occurred during two noteworthy disputes over free speech in Tunisia: the airing of the film *Persepolis* with Tunisian Arabic subtitles, and a controversial art exhibit in the Abdeliya Palace of Tunis, which was broken into by Salafi Islamists, who destroyed a number of the offending artworks. There was also rioting, which led to city-wide curfews. As noted earlier, the final language of Article 6 reads: "The state is the guardian of religion. It guarantees freedom of conscience and belief, the free exercise of religious practices and the neutrality of mosques and places of worship from all partisan instrumentalisation. The state undertakes to disseminate the values of moderation and tolerance and the protection of the sacred, and the prohibition of all violations thereof. It undertakes equally to prohibit and fight against calls for Takfir and the incitement of violence and hatred." —Ed.]

[15] [Ennahda preferred a more strictly parliamentary system, seeing it as a stronger guarantee against seizure of power by a future strongman, and possibly also more confident of its long-term electoral prospects under such a system. Based on her extensive interviews with party leadership and local activists throughout the country, Monica Marks reports that "Ennahda representatives in the NCA and figures in the party's Shura Council said that debate over the political system was the thorniest, most difficult constitutional issue that Ennahda dealt with during the drafting process" (Monica Marks, "Convince, Coerce, or Compromise? Ennahda's Approach to Tunisia's Constitution," Brookings Doha Center Analysis Paper No. 10, February 2014," 27). Eventually, Ennahda made perhaps its largest compromise in this area, agreeing to a mixed presidential-parliamentary system. —Ed.]

136 ON MUSLIM DEMOCRACY

quest for consensus, we have started to make concessions and have agreed that the president of the republic could be elected by popular vote and, like parliament, should derive legitimacy from the source: that is, the people.

We are prepared to come to agreements in order to avoid endless debates and accept that the president of the republic should have amendment and arbitration powers, as in the Portuguese constitution and other constitutions. Maybe in that way we could bring an end to the discussions and we would not have much further to go. In fact, we must proceed as fast as possible toward drafting the constitution.

The constituent assembly is in the hands of our colleagues, the deputies. It is they who can speed up the process or slow it down, but the leadership of the country is in their hands and we call on our colleagues and on the Islamic bloc and all the other blocs to proceed as fast as possible to bring about stability in the country by drafting a constitution and resolving the issues of the electoral law and the electoral commission and the judicial committee and make other amendments so that we can fulfill for Tunisia an aspiration that originated in the nineteenth century, in a constitution that combines the values of Islam and the values of modernity.

Peace be upon you, and the mercy and blessings of God.

10

Human Rights in Islam

Is there a concept of human rights in Islam? If so, what are its philosophical premises? How is it related to modern declarations of human rights?

In modern times human rights usually refer to the rights embodied in the Universal Declaration of Human Rights adopted by the United Nations in December 1948, in the International Convention on Civil and Political Rights and the International Covenant on Economic, Social and Cultural Rights, both adopted in 1966, and in the subsequent international conventions against forms of discrimination. These are the principal criteria by which countries, societies, and religious groups are judged as to whether they are making progress or falling behind, civilized or "backward," based on whether they respect or violate these instruments.

The United Nations itself then proceeded to set up an institution to monitor the commitment of member states to respect their obligations. International and local networks of organizations have also arisen that specialize in publishing reports on how governments and societies behave with respect to these declarations and conventions. Regional tribunals such as the European Court of Human Rights have been set up to rule on allegations that European states have violated human rights. There are also international tribunals with a mandate that extends to heads of state—a commendable development in itself.

This development shows that people have grown more contrite about attacks on the humanity of weak communities, which in some cases have gone as far as genocide. But there are elements of hypocrisy involved, in that even the most dictatorial regimes and groups compete to raise the banner of human rights and take refuge under it in order to hide their own crimes against basic human rights. There is also a double standard that allows weak countries such as Sudan to be prosecuted while the world turns a blind eye to the strong, such as the Americans and Israelis.

May 29, 2013. Published in Rāshid al-Ghannūshī, *Irhāṣāt al-thawra* (Tunis: Dār al-mujtahid, 2015), 231–236.

On Muslim Democracy. Rached Ghannouchi and Andrew F. March, Oxford University Press.
© Oxford University Press 2023. DOI: 10.1093/oso/9780197666876.003.0011

138   ON MUSLIM DEMOCRACY

From the viewpoint of Islam, however, this development remains commendable, if only because it recognizes that everyone's identity is human and, in that capacity, they deserve equal rights regardless of race, color, religion, or class.

How could it not be so when Islam came with a declaration of divine respect for humanity ("We have honored the descendants of Adam," Qur'an 17:70) and the word "people" [rather than "believers"] occurs five times in the last and shortest chapter of the Qur'an? The farewell sermon of the Prophet Muhammad was a public declaration of human rights. In his concluding message he affirmed the central value of humanity and human rights, and the value of equality between people. He called for women to be well treated, eliminated all distinctions of race or color, and denied there could be any justification for anyone exploiting the needs of their fellow humans.[1]

In Islam people are God's deputies [caliphs] on Earth, and the covenant of delegation—the Islamic *shari'a*—includes all their rights and duties.

In Islam individual rights and the public interest [*maslaha*] have been reconciled, because every individual right includes a right that is God's, that is, the community's [*umma's*], with community rights taking priority whenever the rights are in conflict.

And since the injunctions of *shari'a* are intended to serve the interests of people in this world and in the next, rights that range from the essential [*daruri*] to those that improve upon essential interests [*tahsini*] to those that perfect them in their details and application [*kamali*], it is natural that these interests should be seen as the overall framework within which the conduct of individuals is ordered and private and public freedoms are exercised.

The analysis of the ultimate objectives of the *shari'a* [*maqasid al-shari'a*] successfully devised by the Andalusian scholar Abu Ishaq al-Shatibi [d. 1388] in his masterpiece *Al-Muwafaqat*[2] has therefore won the approval of contemporary Islamic scholars as a basis and framework for a theory of public and private rights and freedoms from an Islamic perspective.

Freedom in Islam and in the experience of Islamic civilization, despite flaws, has been a basic and authentic principle as a prerequisite for a valid

---

[1] [This is a reference to the following passage of the Farewell Sermon: "You know that every Muslim is the brother of another Muslim. All mankind is from Adam and Eve, an Arab has no superiority over a non-Arab nor a non-Arab has any superiority over an Arab; also a white has no superiority over a black nor a black has any superiority over a white—except by piety and good action." —Ed.]

[2] [For a contemporary academic study of Shāṭibī and his theory of the objectives of the *shari'a*, see Aḥmad Raysūnī, *Imam Al-Shatibi's Theory of the Higher Objectives and Intents of Islamic Law* (Washington, DC: International Institute of Islamic Thought, 2005). —Ed.]

declaration of belief in Islam. When it comes to Islamic doctrines and the basis of rights and obligations, before believers confirm that they accept the existence of God and the truthfulness of the Prophet Muhammad, they affirm *themselves* as rational, free beings. In a free and conscious state, the self, the "I," declares: "I bear witness that there is no god but God and that Muhammad is the Messenger of God."

Freedom requires constant exertion and a daily struggle to embody the highest ideals, as reflected in the ninety-nine names of God, in the world at large, and inside ourselves. Human beings, as some modern philosophers have noted, are not free: they become free to the extent that they struggle against the forces of oppression inside them and outside them, and to the extent that they fulfill the highest ideals of the code of ethics derived from the attributes of God.

The human rights that are guaranteed in Islam include freedom of belief. Verses of the Qur'an confirm this repeatedly, and this was reflected in the constitution of Medina [the Sahifa], which recognized the rights and freedoms of all the religious and ethnic communities in the town. The history of Islam has been spared wars of religion or ethnic cleansing because Islam decisively asserts the principle "There can be no compulsion in religion" (Qur'an 2:255). This is the greatest principle in Islam and a solid basis for rights and freedoms. This principle overrules anything that contradicts it. According to the Tunisian scholar Muhammad al-Tahir ibn 'Ashur (in his Qur'anic exegesis *al-Tahrir wa'l-Tanwir* [Verification and enlightenment]), any texts that contradict this were abrogated or are open to interpretation.

From freedom of belief stems a package of rights, including equality as the basis for interaction in the Islamic community. In the Islamic community no one receives preferential treatment on the basis of color, race, or belief. Individuals are equal before the law. Speaking about the rights of non-Muslims under his governance, Imam 'Ali said, "If they are given protection"—that is, nationality as we would say today—"they should have the same rights as us and the same obligations." There can be exceptions to equality between citizens only within narrow limits related to the requirements of public order, the identity of the community, and the distribution of labor in the family and in society, such as the differences in some shares of inheritances.

It is worth noting that although there is nothing reprehensible or shameful about the term *ahl al-dhimma* or *dhimmis* (that is, non-Muslims "protected" by the state), it is not a fixed *shari'a* expression that has to be used in Islamic political thought regardless of how well-integrated citizens are and regardless

140 ON MUSLIM DEMOCRACY

of the extent to which the state is based on citizenship, that is, on equality in rights and duties.

Islam has guaranteed those of all faiths the right to set up places of worship and perform their religious rites in them, putting into practice the basic concept of religious freedom and the principle of no compulsion.

The caliphs gave commanders and military men strict instructions to let people be and not to interfere in the religious commitments they had made. Under strong Islamic rule all religions coexisted. But when the balance of power shifted to the disadvantage of Muslims, they and their mosques usually faced the prospect of mistreatment and even extermination, in both ancient and modern times. The wars of ethnic and religious cleansing to which the Muslims of Andalusia, Bosnia, Kosovo, and Chechnya have been subjected bear witness to that.

Similarly, Islamophobia has spread because of the refusal to recognize Islam and the right to religious freedom and pluralism, whereas Islam recognized freedom of belief right from its beginnings ("You have your religion and I have mine" [Qur'an 109:6]). It repeatedly called for amicable debate and consensus on shared values such as monotheism and combating injustice ("Say, 'People of the Book, come to an agreement between us and you—that we shall worship only God, that we shall consider none His equal in any way, and that we shall not treat each other as masters in place of God'"; Qur'an 3:64).

It should come as no surprise, therefore, that the Islamic world has preserved the oldest Jewish synagogues, Christian churches, and even pagan temples. They and their owners enjoyed the protection of a tolerant Islamic code of law, whereas the oldest mosques in Europe are hardly a century old. The Islamic world also ensured that the various Muslim sects could coexist. Genocidal wars or wars of ethnic cleansing were unknown, with some exceptional incidents. In fact, the Islamic world was a refuge for persecuted people of every confession. Among the human rights that Islam guarantees are the freedoms to think, proselytize, spread information, and hold religious debates, since these freedoms are practical applications of the principle that there should be no compulsion in religion.

The Pakistani Islamist thinker Sayyid Abu'l A'la Mawdudi, who is usually described as a hard-liner, says:

> In the Islamic state, non-Muslims will have the same freedom as Muslims to preach, write, express their opinions, think, and assemble. In this respect they will face the same restrictions and obligations as Muslims.

HUMAN RIGHTS IN ISLAM 141

They will be allowed to criticize the government and its personnel, even the head of the government, within the limits of the law. They will have the right to criticize the Islamic religion, in the same way as Muslims will have the right to criticize their religions and creeds.

Muslims will have to observe the limits of the law when they criticize these other religions, in the same way as non-Muslims. They will have complete freedom to sing the praises of their own religions, and if Muslims apostatize, the consequences will fall on their own heads and it will not be held against any non-Muslim. In the Islamic state, non-Muslims will not be forced to believe anything or do anything that goes against their consciences.

They will be allowed to do whatever suits their consciences, as long as it does not violate the state's laws.[3]

This right might be contested on the question of apostasy, although the Qur'an, while threatening apostates with the severest punishment on the Day of Judgment, does not specify a punishment in this world. But it is specified in the hadith, which has made it possible for Islamic thinkers to treat apostasy as a matter on which the Prophet Muhammad could make executive decisions. By extension he left it to state institutions in each historical period to assess the danger posed by apostasy and deal with it on that basis, distinguishing between individual acts of apostasy, which are not dangerous, and communal acts of apostasy that threaten the polity, as happened in early Islam when apostasy took the form of an armed political rebellion that threatened the political system, the political crime of sedition, and not just an idea that could be treated like other such ideas. This means that it is not in conflict with the principle of freedom of belief, which is guaranteed under Islamic law.

Islam also confirms the right of individuals to own property and to enjoy the fruits of their labor. It sees property as a social function exercised by individuals, guided by their religious consciences and by the authority of society, bearing in mind the interests of the community and the limits set by *shari'a* under the theory that human beings are God's deputies or vicegerents [caliphs] on Earth. We also must not lose sight of the fact that the objective of

[3] [See Syed Abul A'la Maudoodi, "Rights of Non-Muslims in an Islamic State," Appendix I in *Islamic Law and Constitution* (Karachi: Jamaat-e Islami Publications, 1955), 191–192, under the subsection "Freedom of Expression." Ghannouchi quotes from the Arabic translation, *Naẓariyyat al-Islām wa hadyih fi'l-siyāsa wa'l-qānūn wa'l-dustūr* (Damascus: Dār al-Fikr, 1964), 316. —Ed.]

142   ON MUSLIM DEMOCRACY

property ownership is to preserve the social balance, with all that implies in the way of banning the existence of classes based on inequality, especially if that inequality stems from illegal practices such as fraud, monopolies, theft, exploiting the needs of the poor (in usury, for example), or the use of political influence. Private property is thus guaranteed, but the Islamic concept is radically different from the capitalist concept—private property should be based on legitimate work and respectful of the public interest.

As far as social rights are concerned, work is a religious obligation, and the poor have a recognized claim on the wealth of the rich. Those in need can assert that claim if the state does not do so. Wealth is not sacrosanct as long as there are people in need in society. Social rights include the right to education, which is compulsory (a religious obligation); the right to health care, housing, clothing, and to start a family; freedom of movement; the inviolability of private residences; the right to go on strike to change unfair contracts that the strong impose on the weak and that have to be fulfilled. "And let him who owes the debt dictate" (Qur'an 2:282), meaning that the borrower should dictate the terms of the contract.

Other rights include the right to participate in public affairs. Starting out from the principle of equality, divine justice, and every Muslim's duty to promote virtue and prohibit vice, Islam was a revolt against tyrants with its call for participation in public life (". . . and who conduct their affairs by mutual consultation," Qur'an 42:38). It is no crime that Islam is happy with whatever humans are lucky enough to come up with when they develop specific consultation mechanisms, which in our times are expressed in the form of a democratic system. This makes it possible to put into practice the principle that the *umma* is sovereign and has authority over its rulers—appointing them, monitoring their activities, and removing them from office—on the basis of equality between citizens, political pluralism, freedom of expression, the transfer of political power through free, pluralistic, and regular elections, the independence of the judiciary, and the separation of powers.

There is nothing in the teachings or objectives of Islam that is incompatible with the fundamentals of democracy. In fact, they are the best that the human mind has yet produced in the way of good arrangements to clip the wings of tyrants. Islam seeks out the best in all matters. Islamic scholars are well aware that although the rules of politics are constants in Islam, the practical application of those rules is a worldly matter that can evolve and improve as reason and experience develop. The Prophet Muhammad said, "You know best about your worldly affairs," meaning the techniques and methods by which you organize your daily lives, in agriculture, industry, transport, and governance, since these are matters that achieve the aims of *shari'a* law and are not in conflict with its invariables.

Muslims have a right, in fact a duty, to act against wrongdoing, rebel against injustice, and advocate positive change by every possible means of protest—marches, sit-ins, media campaigns, and setting up associations and fronts—without resting till injustice is overthrown and justice established. If they do not do this, they are committing a sin. Islam guarantees the right to justice and protection from abuse. It established a social system based on the principle of justice. "Act justly," says the Qur'an (5:9): justice in governance, justice in the legal system and in all domains, and whatever is necessary to ensure the right to be protected from injustice and arbitrary abuse, including protection from torture. Remember that the Prophet told a story about a woman who went to Hell for starving a kitten.

Finally comes the right of safe haven or political asylum, which is a right that an Islamic state would guarantee to all regardless of race or religion. Anyone who appeals to Muslims and asks for their protection must be enabled to exercise this right and to be protected until they decide to go home or to go elsewhere. That is required by the Qur'an: "If a polytheist seeks your protection, grant him protection until he hears the word of God, then take him to where he feels safe" (9:6).

Ibn Kathir, an interpreter of the Qur'an, said, "If anyone comes from the Land of War to the Land of Islam to bring a message, to trade, seek reconciliation or a truce, or for any similar reason, and asks the Imam or his deputy for protection, he should be given protection for as long as he is visiting the Land of Islam and until he goes back to where he is safe and to his home country."

To sum up, the overall tendency in human rights declarations and international conventions is in harmony with Islamic law and its objectives—justice, freedom, and equality in divine respect for humans, which would be a commendable development if it were backed up by a reality that matches it, but human rights in Islam possess characteristics that make them superior.

The experience of history has shown that humans cannot live without adopting a god: "In the human soul there is a hunger that can be sated only by turning to God," as Ibn al-Qayyim said. The fundamental flaw in human rights declarations is that they are generally based on a secular philosophy that claims that humans can act independently of their Creator in how they organize their lives and achieve happiness. Despite partial progress, the result

144   ON MUSLIM DEMOCRACY

has been that the strong overwhelm the weak, destroy the environment, and dismantle networks of communication and empathy between humans.

To base human rights on man's Creator gives them a sacred aspect that discourages any attempts to tamper with them and gives all believers a stake in protecting them, since protecting them is a religious duty that people will be rewarded for performing or punished for neglecting. It also gives human rights human dimensions that ignore all gender, regional, and social differences, since God is the Lord of all beings and not the lord of one nation or community alone. All creatures are God's dependents.

When rights are derived from the Creator of mankind, they have a universality and positive aspect that save them from formalism or particularism, because God is the Creator of mankind and knows the real needs of His creatures better than anyone else. In this way the laws that protect these rights are reinforced by the authority of religious conscience, as is evident in the feeling among believers that God is always watching over them.

So why do contemporary Islamic countries rank at the bottom on human rights indicators among the countries of the world? It is nothing to do with Islam, since its principles and its experience as a civilization bear witness to its glory and the openness of Islamic societies. Nor with Muslims, because they are ruled by governments that do not represent them, but rather play them for fools. Their governments even abuse them, invoking against them an overwhelming international balance of power, until such time as "we give such days to people by turns" (Qur'an 3:140).

Philosophical-Theological Dialogues on Democracy, Pluralism, and Islam

Rached Ghannouchi and Andrew F. March

Biography and Formation

AFM: I am hoping that over the next week we can discuss a wide range of things, related to your thought from the earliest phases until today, as well as engage in some critical comparative dialogues between modern thought and its secular liberal counterpart, and so on.

I have many questions on your intellectual development from al-Hamah village to Gabes, Tunisia, Syria, London, Paris, and then your return to Tunisia. Of course, your political and intellectual experience encompasses more than just Islamic thought and politics. I am interested in your views on Islamic philosophy, your political trials, and how your views have developed from each of those two points of view, insofar as you now see a difference between them.

In addition, I have questions on the intellectual evolution and formulation of the broader Islamic trend.

So, the beginning, your childhood in al-Hamah. Can you tell me of your memories of the village, particularly about the concept of tradition and traditional Islam there?

RG: It is difficult for one to choose a starting point. Some scenes remain in memory from that phase and I will speak about them during our dialogue. There's imagery of my professional life, the village where I grew up, and my farming life when I tended to a palm-tree oasis. Doing so required climbing trees, and although I was quite young, I used

---

These conversations took place between December 2017 and January 2018 at Ghannouchi's home in Ariana, Tunisia. Translated and edited by Andrew F. March.

On Muslim Democracy. Rached Ghannouchi and Andrew F. March, Oxford University Press.
© Oxford University Press 2023. DOI: 10.1093/oso/9780197666876.003.0012

146 ON MUSLIM DEMOCRACY

to do it as the family needed it. When climbing treetops, I could see till the horizon. Palm trees invoke much love within me, as they are tall, straight, and have dangling fruit. It is such a beautiful sight, and this is why I was happy to find two such trees in this house when we moved in.

AFM: Was your father a shaykh in the village?

RG: Yes.

AFM: Was he a mufti?

RG: No. He memorized the Qur'an and would always recite it. This is another fixed image in my mind, as my father had always taken close care with our memorization of the Qur'an. He was very firm in raising us, as he was adamant about transferring to us his knowledge of the Qur'an. Whoever did not memorize what he had written that day on the board was punished with a beating.

My father never beat me, as I had always memorized everything. But my older brother had difficulty doing so, as his memory was not his best trait, and he would always receive a beating. But also, there was a session in which we would have to recite to our father what we had memorized, and it was a difficult session, one that we felt relief eluding when a guest would come to visit our father.

AFM: There was no regular school there at the time, just a school for Qur'an memorization, right?

RG: Yes.

AFM: There was no instruction on Maliki School thought or theology?

RG: No.

AFM: Was your father a teacher of jurisprudence in the village?

RG: No. He studied some scientific and jurisprudence books but did not give lessons, yet he used to lead prayers during Ramadan and pray *tarawih* [the additional night prayers during Ramadan]. Memorization of the Qur'an was a general trend in the family, as we were religious, and my father paid much attention to performing prayers and to leading the family during them. This was accompanied with fasting and ritual chanting of the name of God and His Messenger [*dhikr*]. On long winter nights, the family would stay up late working on making baskets, as this generated part of the family's income. The women in the family would weave wool clothing at night while at home and work in the field during the day. Women played a major role in our family, as most of the men had gone to the capital to pursue an education.

My late mother was keen on sending my two brothers to the capital to receive an education, as we were six brothers and four sisters. Although only two were my full brothers—the rest were my half siblings from my father's second wife. The males in the family studied at al-Zaytuna in the capital, and my sisters would work in the field instead of my two brothers who were pursuing an education. It was due to my mother's diligence and care that the males received a good education and that I got to be the man I am by having had the opportunity to study while she and my sisters worked in farming, weaving, cooking, and other jobs so that the money they made would allow us males to pursue an education. The state never provided us with financial assistance, and although education at al-Zaytuna was free, we still needed sustenance and spending money. I remember having had to work in the field from age ten to twelve and that I joined elementary school at the age of ten, but I had memorized the Qur'an by that time and already knew how to read and write.

I also remember that I was older than the other pupils attending the first elementary grade, as children usually entered their first year of education at the age of six, but I entered it at ten. Nonetheless, the school administration allowed me to skip grades so as to be alongside my peers.

AFM: Was the school in Gabes?

RG: It was in al-Hamah. We resided three kilometers from the city, and the journey back and forth required much effort, as I had to be home by midday for lunch. So I would sometimes have to remain at school without food till the evening, as we had no money, or I would go and take some money from my father to buy a dry piece of bread. Sometimes he had no money on him and I would go without lunch, a matter that my father said made his heart melt in sorrow.

During such times, I would play football at midday with my peers. But playing football with the other kids was unacceptable to my father, as football was considered a waste of time and foreign to our culture and so my father disapproved.

AFM: Was there some other more traditional game or sport your father preferred, or was he against all sports?

148 ON MUSLIM DEMOCRACY

RG: Other children played other games, but I liked football. My uncle would stand up for me and tell my father to allow me to play it. You see, my uncle was a merchant and more open-minded than farmers, and he was a political figure in the National Movement. I remember seeing my mother crying—a matter that saddened me dearly—when my uncle was jailed. People had the impression that only criminals were jailed, but from this event onward I began correlating between activism and jail. He was jailed for supporting the resistance movement, which had begun earlier in the mountains and reached al-Hamah in 1952, when I was eleven years old.

My mother would cry because her only brother was in jail for collecting money, food, and equipment to send to the revolutionaries in the mountains. He was a logistics officer and was jailed for six months. This influenced me to a great extent and introduced me to politics, resistance, occupation, and France. As a child, I also remember seeing the bludgeoned bodies of revolutionaries which the French army dumped in the village square.

AFM: What was the influence of French colonialism on the village of Hamah?

RG: There was none, as France to us was a barbaric occupier; the area had military administration and was dubbed a military zone, as no Frenchmen lived there.

AFM: Was there a French school there?

RG: There were schools of Qur'an and Arabic-French ones that taught both languages, and I studied in the latter.

But I studied for only two years there and was then directed by my father to discontinue elementary education, as he felt it had prevented me from memorizing the Qur'an after having realized I had forgotten what I had memorized of it earlier. At the same time, my father had grown older and needed a man to plow and reap the harvest outside the village, as my two brothers were studying in the capital. Part of the family income was from corn and wheat, which were not grown in the orchard. That area was thirty kilometers away and needed a man for the job. My uncles would go there, and I accompanied them afterward as there was none but me to represent our family. The task was difficult for a child of my age at the time, but it needed to be done nonetheless.

PHILOSOPHICAL-THEOLOGICAL DIALOGUES   149

That land was the property of our Bedouin friends, who had allowed us to use it. I had to leave school for a year at the age of twelve to do so, and it was difficult for me as it entailed sleeping in the wilderness and plowing the desert field. But a year later, when my two brothers graduated, I returned to school. One of my brothers became a teacher, and the second a judge and then a lawyer. The judiciary at the time was entirely Islamic [shar'i], and its affairs were carried out by Islamic law jurists [shar'iyyun] following the Maliki School. But a French court also existed alongside the shari'a courts. Shortly after, once my two brothers held jobs, we moved from the village to al-Hamah and then to Gabes.

AFM: This raises for me a somewhat precise philosophical question here. Some philosophers like Rousseau, Ibn Khaldun, and Sayyid Qutb regard people in the village as closer to human nature [fitra] than city dwellers. In other words, the simpler people in the village are closer to morality and natural human goodness, according to thinkers like this. Do you have any comments or observations on this?

RG: Life in the village has a kind of simplicity, humanity, solidarity, and empathy with fellow mankind. Its members act and react as one entity, with minimal focus on the personal and a stronger one on the communal. Villages are based on large and extended families who forge solidarity among each other. But humans tend to be envious and conflicting, and life stringent. Yet traditions and norms are important therein, not religion. The former is what constitutes social law that is affiliated with honor, revenge, vengeance, and non-sexual relationships among men and women.

AFM: Some academics say there is a difference between the Islam of the city and that of the village.

RG: Yes, true.

AFM: It is sometimes claimed that traditional Islam [largely embodied in texts and books] did not have solutions to modern problems nor any conception thereof. Is this correct in your view?

RG: Naturally, anyone who had studied at al-Zaytuna at the time had no connection to the era. We used to learn jurisprudence, but not that of modern times. Islamic sciences were also disconnected from modern times, and the ones we studied did not respond to the question regarding Islam's stance on modern issues.

150 ON MUSLIM DEMOCRACY

AFM: Even the works of Ibn 'Ashur?[1]

RG: Yes, even those. We used to study old books of hundreds of years earlier, which included no technical legal terms [mustalahat shar'iyya], no discourse on Islamic economy, politics, or modern issues like women and how one can be Muslim and abide by Islamic teaching today. There was a separation between Islam and modern times; whoever wanted Islam should refer to the old ages, and whoever wanted modern times should immerse himself in it. There were no books other than the old stagnant ones!

AFM: Before that, did you attend secondary school in Gabes?

RG: I studied at al-Zaytuna in al-Hamah, and this was among the reforms led by Ibn 'Ashur, as each Tunisian city established a branch of al-Zaytuna akin to the al-Azhar system in Egypt.

AFM: This was in Arabic?

RG: As of the morning of independence, the number of students studying at [Arabic-language] Zaytuna schools was twenty-seven thousand, whereas those studying in French schools were only forty-five hundred, as most of the teachers at the time had graduated from al-Zaytuna. But independence changed the equation, and the first decree issued by Habib Bourguiba was the closure of al-Zaytuna. When I studied there, it was on its last breath.

AFM: You read many French and Russian novels during this time, correct?

RG: I was in love with novels translated into Arabic, written by several Russian and French novelists like Victor Hugo, as well as by Egyptian writers like Ihsan Abdel Quddous[2] and others who I used to follow. I would escape my reality, in which I felt suffocated, into a world of imagination that gave me peace of mind.

AFM: You then moved to al-Zaytuna in the capital, correct?

RG: Yes. I moved there after finishing two years of education at al-Hamah and two more years in Gabes. Graduates of al-Zaytuna study for four years, then hold a degree called the "qualifier." I continued my education afterward at Ibn Khaldun School.

AFM: This was a high school, not university?

---

[1] Muhammad al-Tahir ibn 'Ashur (1879–1973), a prominent Tunisian scholar and legal theorist of the purposes of Islamic law (maqasid al-shari'a). He is referred to with some frequency in Ghannushi's writings.

[2] Ihsan Abdel Quddous (Ihsan 'Abd al-Quddus, 1919–1990) was an Egyptian writer, novelist, scriptwriter, journalist, and editor at the Egyptian Al-Akhbar and Al-Ahram newspapers. Many of his novels were adapted for film, TV, and radio.

PHILOSOPHICAL-THEOLOGICAL DIALOGUES   151

RG: Yes. Al-Zaytuna secondary education was seven years, four of which were for attaining the "qualifier" degree and two others for the first and second practicums. So three years in the capital and two at Ibn Khaldun. Part of our education was very traditional religious instruction that included jurisprudence and Arabic for three to four hours a week, and French, hadith, history, geography, physics, and mathematics. It was the same as was taught at French schools, but religious studies were traditional rather than modern, all taken from old books. Students would learn physics, mathematics, and modern sciences, but then when they studied religious sciences it was like they had gone back in time in terms of the terminology and subjects.

When we entered religious studies class, it was like we had gone back four centuries in time. It neither filled us with spiritual meaning nor gave us a sense of superiority or pride in Islam. Students were also not religious: of the three thousand attending the school, only five or six prayed.

There was no religious atmosphere, as all were inclined toward modernity, and Islam was in regression. Whenever some Muslims renewed their commitment to Islam, others would abandon it. It was an air of relinquishing Islam as the society ushered in the French era. The general atmosphere that Bourguiba brought was that Islam is from the past and constituted an obstacle to progress and development. People abandoned traditional dress; people who used to pray abandoned prayer; those who had abstained from wine began to drink it.

AFM: Was this difficult for someone coming from a village?

RG: Yes, it was. Those coming from villages found themselves marginalized and unable to cope.

AFM: At this time, your uncle Bashir had great influence on you, correct?

RG: My uncle was politicized and was following events occurring in Egypt. He was the first person to introduce the radio to al-Hamah, and we used to listen to Abdel Nasser's speeches through it. He took us to a space far beyond the confines of our small village.

AFM: You became an Arab nationalist, correct?

RG: I began to love Abdel Nasser and consider him among the sanctities!

AFM: At that time, you weren't aware of the ideological conflict between Arab nationalism and Islamism?

RG: No. At the onset of independence, there was a sense that Tunisia was heading West and al-Zaytuna remained part of the East and therefore began to be marginalized. Its graduates became disadvantaged

152 ON MUSLIM DEMOCRACY

vis-à-vis those graduating from French schools, producing success for modern education and its actors against the teachings of al-Zaytuna. Also, there was no Islamic movement, Islam, scholars, or traditions active at the end, but instead a movement of Westernization. Thus al-Zaytuna, its scholars, and all that related to Islam were dying.

AFM: How do you see the role of Zaytuna scholars in the independence movement?

RG: They took part in it but were not its leaders, despite the fact that the Constitutional Movement had emerged from al-Zaytuna at the hands of Shaykh ʿAbd al-ʿAziz al-Thaʿalibi.

AFM: No one like ʿAllal al-Fasi of Morocco?

RG: No. None of his like existed. Shaykh ʿAbd al-ʿAziz al-Thaʿalibi established the National Movement, but Bourguiba's movement defeated it when the Bourguibists joined Thaʿalibi's movement and caused a split in 1934. The Constitutional Movement was established in 1920. It was this splinter branch that brought forward independence as France found itself forced to exit Tunisia, particularly after Algeria's uprising in 1954. The front became comprised of Tunisia, Algeria, and Morocco, and France wanted to focus on Algeria, as it had no official government and was deemed French territory, unlike Tunisia and Morocco, which had their own distinct personalities.

France wanted a free hand in Algeria and therefore granted Tunisia and Morocco independence, although that of the former was mostly formal, as it did not include cultural or economic independence.

AFM: Had you developed any political ideology at that point?

RG: At this point my political ideology was primarily grounded in support for the Algerian cause and enthusiasm for the Algerian jihad. I met some Algerian students who had stayed at my place.

I also owned a radio and we would listen to a program entitled *The Voice of Algeria*, which was presented by a man with the nickname al-Masʿudi. It began with the Algerian national anthem, which was very powerful and nationalistic, and is so till this very day, and it filled us with enthusiasm.

AFM: Did the French react to this?

RG: France would conduct retaliatory bombings of some Tunisian villages along the border, like Sidi Yousef, as the Algerian resistance would conduct some of their action from Tunisian soil in areas like al-Qasrayn and others.

PHILOSOPHICAL-THEOLOGICAL DIALOGUES   153

I came to the capital in 1957 and remained till 1962, as the air was filled with resistance and the Algerian cause was omnipresent.

AFM: Did the ideology of pan-Arab nationalism influence the mood at the time?

RG: There existed a type of spiritual migration toward Egypt and a view that saw it as the future, savior, and ideal world. My two brothers followed the events occurring in Egypt, and one of them was in love with the singer Umm Kulthum and listened to all her songs. He looked at art from the Arab East with great admiration, not only Umm Kulthum but also Farid al-Attrash and Muhammad Abd al-Wahhab, in addition to Egyptian and Indian movies.

AFM: During this very time, many of the classical works of anti-colonial thought were written, like those of Frantz Fanon and Albert Memmi. Did you read any of these books?

RG: Not at that time, but later I read the former but not the latter.

AFM: So at that time, these anti-colonial works did not influence the development of your thought, correct?

RG: Correct. They did not.

AFM: You then went to university in Egypt?

RG: My university education was in Syria, but prior to that I had taught elementary education in Gafsa for sixteen months, yet I didn't find myself in it. I had wanted to pursue an education in the East, the land of dreams, and emigrated to Egypt in 1964, where I resided for months.

AFM: Then you traveled to Syria. Can you talk a little about the philosophy curriculum there at that time?

RG: Many renowned professors taught there, like ʿAdil al-ʿAwwa, Badiʿ al-Kasam, and ʿAbd al-Karim al-Yafi. The atmosphere at the university was filled with ideological struggle among Baathist and Nasserist nationalists, on the one hand, and the Islamist currents on the other, which included the Muslim Brotherhood, Hizb al-Tahrir, and the Salafist Movement. At the time, I joined the Nasserist Socialist Party, which struggled for the union of Egypt and Syria, and supported it during its existence between 1958 and 1961.

AFM: What was the ideological appeal for you of that nationalist party?

RG: I was a nationalist in my affections when I began learning about nationalism as it manifested itself within the party as well as in discussions between Islamists and nationalists in 1966, and I began to take notice of the difference between nationalism and Islam. In

154 ON MUSLIM DEMOCRACY

Tunisia and North Africa, there is no difference between Arabism and Islam, as all were Muslim in that region, but in the Syrian region there was conflict between Arabists and Turks. I began to discover new meanings of Arabism that were different from what we in Tunisia believed, and that Islam is not mere slogans but rather a way of life. This was the first time I had heard such discourse and that Islam is an entire culture and not merely acts of worship and rites. I also felt that I was not a true Muslim and that the Islam I had followed was a naive one and not deep. On June 15, 1966, I decided to make a transformation.

AFM: What happened on that day?

RG: It was the tipping point for me, and I developed a solid conviction that I was not a follower of true Islam.

AFM: You mean Islam and not political Islam as a way of life?

RG: Yes, Islam as a creed. Prior to that, I did not pray or adhere to Islam in my daily life.

AFM: Was this due to the influence of Nasir al-Din al-Albani or others?

RG: It was due to all the discussions at the university that I decided to transform myself and adopt Islam as the scale through which I measured my actions, life, and relationships, unlike the way it was for me before.

AFM: How did you understand true Islam at that time: as that present in the works of jurisprudence, the Qur'an, or theology?

RG: We find Islam in the Qur'an, the Sunna, and the writings of Islamic scholars, not in people's lives and customs, as the latter contain some things that are Islamic and much that is not Islamic.

AFM: What is the standard by which something is judged "non-Islamic" or "outside of Islam"?

RG: Texts, definitely.

AFM: Were there many of the various Islamic movements, like Scientific Salafism, Sufism, and the Muslim Brotherhood?

RG: Yes, there were Shaykh al-Buti and other movements. Islamism in Tunisia was setting, while in other countries it was rising.

I studied with al-Albani's small group for two years, in another small Sufi group with Ramadan al-Buti's father, and in a third of Sufi teacher Subhi Salih just to get an idea about their thought.

AFM: With regard to studying with Buti and studying jurisprudence, what did you read: classical or modern works?

PHILOSOPHICAL-THEOLOGICAL DIALOGUES 155

RG: He would refer to old commentaries [*tafasir*] but would discuss them using modern terminology.

I studied some jurisprudence but did not specialize in it, as I was seeking any form of Islam, because it came in different shapes according to the movements and traditional shaykhs teaching in houses, mosques, and Sufi lodges. I moved among them.

The Muslim Brotherhood was active and many of its scholars gave classes. There was a wide degree of freedom at the onset of the Baathist era, as it had not yet had a tight grip on people's lives. It was the era of Hafez al-Assad, but he was still the minister of defense at the time, and it was the era of frequent military coups.

AFM: During this period, did you adopt any specific trend, like Ikhwani, Salafi, or Sufi?

RG: I did not choose any specific trend; rather, I read many Brotherhood books, and others by al-Mawdudi, Malek Bennabi [Malik ibn Nabi], and Muhammed Iqbal.

I had conflicting feelings between the thought of Malek Bennabi and that of Sayyid Qutb. I would go back and forth between my inclination toward one or the other, but admired both.[3]

AFM: Which writings of Sayyid Qutb did you read?

RG: I read all of his and his brother's works.

AFM: Was this at the time of his death, or rather his execution?

RG: I was not affected by his execution, as I was unsure whether he was right or wrong, but later, after his execution, I became influenced by the writings of Qutb as well as Bennabi.

AFM: There is a view that Qutb is the one who influenced jihadist groups, including Bin Laden, particularly after the 1970s, when they adopted a part of his ideology. But during the 1960s [when you read him], how did people who accepted his ideology regard him: as an extremist or more like a renewer [*mujaddid*]?

RG: Qutb went through two phases: pre- and post-jail. In the first phase, he was a leftist social thinker and writer who rebelled against imperialism and the exploitation of workers. He was a writer and pupil of 'Abbas Mahmud al-'Aqqad[4] and supported the Nasserist revolution to the extent that he was offered the post of minister of education.

---

[3] See the essay in this volume: "Between Sayyid Qutb and Malek Bennabi."

[4] 'Abbas Mahmud al-'Aqqad (1889–1964) was an Egyptian journalist, poet, and literary critic who was an innovator of twentieth-century Arabic poetry and criticism.

156 ON MUSLIM DEMOCRACY

The second phase was when he traveled to the USA on an educational mission and changed when he saw American society. He was still there when Hasan al-Banna was killed and noticed a sort of gloating or glee in the media regarding that assassination. I do not know what he wrote in certain press venues, but you can research whatever articles he wrote even though they may be few.

One of his essays is entitled "The America I Have Seen," as he returned from there with a changed personality.[5] Despite that, and during the age of the revolution from 1952 till 1956, he was a proponent thereof, but when the Muslim Brotherhood members were imprisoned, he became a member of the movement's inner circle. Those leading the Brotherhood nowadays are the pupils of Sayyid Qutb, who were members of the secret organization of the Brotherhood from 1956 until 1962, when he was released, and then rearrested in 1964.

Qutb had unpublished writings such as "Scenes from Judgement Day in the Qur'an" and "The Glories of the Qur'an." I was a Nasserist during 1964 but would doubt the things that were attributed to Sayyid Qutb—for example, the claims of Nasserist propaganda that Qutb was involved in a conspiracy to assassinate Abdel Nasser. I used to think that if it were true, then he deserved it. But after the transformation, I became influenced by Qutb, as I believed the nationalist trend was entirely corrupt and un-Islamic.

AFM: What did you find in Qutb's works and thought?

RG: His writings stirred my emotions, as he presented a comprehensive picture of Islam as well as it being one of strength and pride. He held faith in high regard, and whoever read him would feel the same. He does not apologize for Islam's relationship to modern civilization but rather points out the former's superiority to the latter. This influences the young, as it gives them a sense of pride and self-confidence.

He spoke in a contemporary language and used modern terms. His thought was unapologetic and very critical of the West.

AFM: From the standpoint of identity or religious doctrine?

RG: Identity. When there is a wounded and beaten civilization and then a man comes along and questions why we have no self-confidence

---

[5] See Sayyid Qutb, "The America I Have Seen: In the Scale of Human Values (1951)," in Kamal Abdel-Malek, ed., *America in an Arab Mirror Images of America in Arabic Travel Literature: An Anthology 1895–1995* (New York: St. Martin's Press, 2000), pp. 9–27.

PHILOSOPHICAL-THEOLOGICAL DIALOGUES 157

when we possess a great civilization and religion, why we feel humiliated when our thought is not anti-science, he writes that Islam itself is civilization.

AFM: For Qutb, *only* Islam is deemed civilization, right?

RG: What Sayyid Qutb says is that Islam is a binding text and a divine mandate, whereas civilization is created by mankind. Humans may or may not produce civilization, according to how well they understand Islam. A Muslim may be civilized or uncivilized, just as a non-Muslim may be. It is this idea that woke me up and made me travel to Algeria to meet Malek Bennabi.

Malek Bennabi's works were translated from French into Arabic and published by an Arab printing press in Damascus.

AFM: What were the ideas that attracted you in Sayyid Qutb's thought?

RG: Comprehensiveness. That Islam is a comprehensive system of life, after which comes the idea of divine sovereignty [*hakimiyya*].

AFM: Was the relationship between human nature [*fitra*] and *shariʿa* seen as an important idea at the time?

RG: Very important, as he presented Islam as the basic principle of human nature and truth, and showed how Islam's provisions suit the inherent interests of mankind. Whoever departs from Islam is like a fish out of water, gasping and floundering.

AFM: Was this idea specific in any way to Sayyid Qutb?

RG: Modern Islamic thought, what is often called "political Islam," is based on the notion that Islam is both a religion and state and provides people with happiness in both this world and the next. Everyone says this.

Qutb is distinguished by his literary greatness, and he utilized this in describing Islam eloquently. Thus, the distinction between him and other Islamists is his literary ability, as he was a poet, novelist, story writer, and critic prior to becoming an Islamist. Hence, anyone reading Qutb would be attracted by his use of language. Many others share his same ideas, but they would express them with harshness and radicalism.

AFM: What about Mawdudi?

RG: He was Sayyid Qutb's teacher, and Qutb would speak of him with great reverence. The two shared the same ideas, but Qutb expressed them more eloquently.

AFM: But Mawdudi had some traditional training as a scholar?

158   ON MUSLIM DEMOCRACY

RG: He was not a classical scholar [*alim*] nor a graduate of traditional institutes. He studied on his own merit and established himself without assistance. He did not pursue traditional education,
and hence Islamists were not graduates of al-Zaytuna or al-Azhar.[6]
Jihadists, on the other hand, are men of struggle who also did not
graduate from formal religious education. It is quite rare to come
across an Azhari jihadist, as traditional religious education has a wide
space for relativity and does not produce such radicals.

AFM: The idea of universal vicegerency or caliphate, that the entire Muslim
nation is God's caliph or vicegerent—the foundational political idea
of modern Islamic thought—is first found in earnest in the books of
Mawdudi, in my reading. For example, you don't find it in Rashid Rida,
who was writing just before Mawdudi. Is this correct in your view?

RG: That is correct. This idea was stated to draw Islamic governance closer
to the modern state.

AFM: Can we go back now to your encounter with modern Islamism in
the late 1960s? How would you characterize the ideological conflict
among various Islamist thinkers at that time?

RG: There was intellectual discussion and conflict on usually narrow, de-
rivative matters concerning fatwas and hadiths that had to do with
the length of the beard, the hijab versus the niqab, and the like, which
are based on disagreed-upon hadith reports.

AFM: So the various Islamist groups at that time took a keen interest in
technical hadith scholarship?

RG: Yes, particularly the circles around [Muhammad Nasir al-Din] al-
Albani, whose gatherings they would attend, as they agreed upon his
sound knowledge, particularly of hadith.

AFM: But you were studying philosophy in the university. What was in the
curriculum of your philosophical studies?

RG: It was the philosophy of all eras, including Greek, medieval, and
modern, like that of Descartes to Kant, Spinoza, Hegel, and Sartre.
Some texts were translated, while others were abridged.

---

[6] In his study of Mawdudi and the Jama'at-i Islami of Pakistan, Seyyed Vali Nasr writes that
"Mawdudi received his early education in Urdu and Arabic, first at home and later in the traditional
schools of Hyderabad, Bhopal, and Delhi. As a young man in Delhi, he studied the *dars-i nizami*
curricula of the ulama with Deobandi tutors and received the certificate which would have permitted
him to join that sodality. He abandoned traditional education and the garb of the ulama, however, for
an education in modern subjects." Seyyed Vali Reza Nasr, *The Vanguard of the Islamic Revolution: The
Jama'at-i Islami of Pakistan* (Berkeley: University of California Press, 1994), 3.

AFM: Which branch of philosophy was regarded as most important? The philosophy of ethics?

RG: Modern philosophy dealt with current issues. We studied the *Discourse on Method* by Descartes, for example, and I was very enthusiastic about Kant's moral philosophy, as he was harmonizing reason and religion in his *Metaphysics of Morals* and *Critique of Practical Reason*. I believe Kant to be the peak of Western philosophy, as he harmonized reason and religion in his metaphysics and categorical imperative. He was a strict rationalist but religious at the same time, and his life had a discipline that I admired.

AFM: After that, when you went to Paris and the Sorbonne, what did you study?

RG: I only spent a year there, and it was a fairly miserable one materially, and it lacked an Islamic atmosphere, with only one mosque, under poor administration. The more unofficial or "popular" Islamic organizations on the ground were preaching and missionary groups [*da'wa wa tabligh*], mostly consisting of migrant Algerian workers who used to live in a modest house above the mosque. During this time, I would lead prayer and give sermons, and for the first time engaged in preaching and calling people to Islam. We would go to the cafes to call on people to pray and would then bring those who heeded our call back to the mosque.

AFM: Did you succeed in persuading many to attend prayer?

RG: We were able to convince several of them, and I spoke on the group's behalf. I tried to transform my Islamic language from a more abstract, refined level to a practical, accessible one. Most people we spoke with were from North Africa, and we would go to their neighborhoods. Their homes were very humble, and on the weekend we would go to the Latin Quarter near the Sorbonne. A student revolt was occurring at the time, and the Palestinian cause was among the issues being discussed.

AFM: Did you witness the student revolt of 1968?

RG: I used to attend the discussions occurring in the Latin Quarter at a time when a prominent student named Daniel Cohn-Bendit was there and who later became a member of the European Parliament. We had discussions on Arabism at a time when an Arab trend was becoming active. I had to work to sustain a living, and although working as a security guard was the most prevalent job for students, I was

160 ON MUSLIM DEMOCRACY

unable to get one and had to work in advertisement distribution. It would rain sometimes and it would be difficult for me to distribute three thousand papers. Sometimes my shoes would have holes in them. I also used to clean offices on Sundays and had to find a place to live, and when I couldn't, I would stay with friends. Food would also be unavailable at times, particularly halal meat. Afterward, I would go to a language center to improve my French and study for my PhD at the Sorbonne with a professor of education. It was a difficult year for me, and I could not continue with it, although I had just started.

AFM: How did your ethical, religious, and philosophical ideas develop during your time in Paris?

RG: I got to know some right-wing European movements that used to publish a magazine that was anti–Algerian independence and in support of the French right wing, and accordingly I was not drawn to their platform.

AFM: Were there Catholic students among you?

RG: I used to attend activities held by Catholic students at the Sorbonne to see what they and I had in common. I also attended their Mass sometimes to get to know their manner of thinking.

AFM: In my view, some of the conservative Catholic anti-modernist thought is popular among some Islamic thinkers in America. They see in it a critique of secularism and [modern] metaphysics. Did you encounter any such thought during this period?

RG: There was some literature by writers like Alexis Carrel, whose book *Man, the Unknown* Sayyid Qutb made extensive reference to in his works.

AFM: Did you study Marxism, and if so, what was interesting in it for you?

RG: I studied it while in Damascus and met Roger Garaudy in the 1970s, when he came to England after embracing Islam. I had some familiarity with it in the era that preceded my own turn to Islamism, as Nasserism was a form of Marxism. But after Islam, the Islamic theory that attracted me considered Marxism to be atheism to the extent that Mustafa al-Siba'i[7] wrote a book entitled *The Socialism of Islam*[8] in 1959 and dedicated it to Abdel Nasser as a gift. This was condemned

[7] Muṣṭafā al-Sibāʿī (1915–1964), a law professor and dean at the University of Damascus, trained at al-Azhar in Cairo and was the first general guide of the Muslim Brotherhood in Syria.

[8] Muṣṭafā al-Sibāʿī, *Ishtirākiyat al-Islām* (Damascus: Jāmiʿat Dimashq, 1959).

PHILOSOPHICAL-THEOLOGICAL DIALOGUES   161

by Islamists, as they considered Islam superior to any socialist or democratic ideologies, particularly since Sayyid Qutb ridiculed anyone who argued that Islam was socialist or democratic, since it is above all of these.

AFM: What about his own *Social Justice in Islam*?

RG: This was in a previous phase. Qutb's book *The Battle Between Islam and Capitalism*[9] and his literary books were also in a previous phase. This is in addition to his two articles on Farhat Hashid [Farhat Hached]—the Tunisian unionist who was assassinated by France.

AFM: If we can go back to your involvement in the Tablighi Jamaat at this time: were their activities in any way informed by these ideological debates, or only focused on bringing people to the practice of Islam?

RG: Practice only. We would talk about five topics: creed, prayer, Islamic fraternity, kindness toward Muslims, and not interfering in matters like politics.

AFM: But were your own ideas political at the time?

RG: At that time, young people needed to preserve their religion, and the Tabligh [Tablighi Jamaat] was a kind of incubator or shelter within which a young person could live in an atmosphere of spirituality that would protect him. As the plane flew over Paris, I wondered if I would be able to preserve my essence in this country that had already devoured tens of thousands of youth.

AFM: So you spent only one year in Paris?

RG: Yes. Afterward I returned to Tunisia with my brother, the judge, via Spain, where I visited Cordoba and its Grand Masjid. Then I went to visit Malek Bennabi in Algeria, who convinced me of the civilization issue—namely, that both Muslims and unbelievers [*kafir*] have the potential to be civilized or uncivilized.

AFM: He used the word "unbeliever" [*kafir*] or "non-Muslim"?

RG: *Kafir*.

Afterward, I began visiting Algeria on an annual basis to take part in a symposium held there every year on a topic dealt with by the Ministry of Religious Affairs. Muslims from all trends would attend it, including Shi'a.

AFM: Did you read the same books and theses?

---

[9] Sayyid Qutb, *Ma'rakat al-Islām wa'l-ra'smāliyya* (Cairo: Maṭba'at Dār al-Kitāb al-'Arabī, [1951]).

162   ON MUSLIM DEMOCRACY

RG: All topics and theses prevalent at the time were presented at the symposium, and this formed an opportunity for us to learn about the ideas being circulated throughout the Islamic world.

AFM: Did you discuss the same topics and problems as those discussed today?

RG: Some of them. Topics at the time were Islamic economy, non-Muslims in Islamic states, and the role of women—some of which are still being discussed till this day.

AFM: After you returned to Tunisia you taught philosophy and wrote a critique of the Western ideas you had been studying, correct?

RG: My article entitled "The Lost Generation" was published in the press in 1973 [in the journal *Al-Ma'rifa*] and then in a collection of articles.[10] In it, I criticized how Islam's abridged version of theology is marginal, useless, and dissociated from modern times, whereas other ideas present themselves as solutions for modern problems.

AFM: During this period, how did you discuss and treat the ideas of Darwin and Marx? Was it only a critical relationship, or were there any attractive ideas as well?

RG: The presentation was mainly critical, as the purpose was to highlight errors and weaknesses in comparison to the Islamic presentation, which was superior.

AFM: Did the Islamic presentation change due to discussing these ideas, such as the discovery of new problems?

RG: Naturally, viewing those ideas became more realistic, as they contained shortcomings in addition to goodness. Not all of them were invalidated, as this was human thought that contains correct ideas like those of Freud and Sartre, even if some of their ideas are exaggerated.

AFM: In the thought of Sartre: human freedom and the freedom to choose or determine the self?

RG: Self-determination and freedom. The notion of freedom's value as a pivotal one in life is a basic pillar. I believe that the most important addition to the Islamic movement in Tunisia is deeming freedom the key value through which human agency is to be interpreted.

---

[10] See Rāshid al-Ghannūshī, "Barāmij al-falsafa wa'l-jīl al-ḍayāʿ," in *Maqālāt: ḥarakat al-Islām bi-Tūnis* (Paris: Dār al-Karwān, 1984), 9–14.

PHILOSOPHICAL-THEOLOGICAL DIALOGUES   163

The way toward Islam is freedom. It is to pronounce freedom and to choose freely as a first step toward Islam, since the human is a free and responsible self.

AFM: For example, is this the lens through which you see your choice to transition from nationalism to Islamism in 1966—as a free choice for which you took personal responsibility, perhaps in the Sartrean sense?

RG: Yes, it was.

AFM: How long after your return to Tunis from Paris was it until the formation of the Jama'a Islamiyya [Islamic Group]?

RG: Not so long after. We embarked on this immediately. I had actually returned to Tunisia for personal reasons, as my elder brother had come to Paris to inform me that my mother was sick and that her illness was due to me being away. She had become diabetic during the 1967 war, while I was in Damascus. My mother was watching all the news and had many diseases during this time. I returned to Tunisia to visit my mother with the intention to return to my studies in Paris. My sense was that there was a kind of moral chaos in Tunisia at the time and thus I had not planned to settle there.

But I visited the capital and Zaytuna for the first time and saw a group of young men and women gathered around an imam giving them a lesson in religion, and I sat and listened in. I was happily surprised to see such piety in Tunisia and spoke with one of the young men there. He told me that a group of youth were active in a nearby mosque called al-Yousefi, or Sidi Yousef, and that they were meeting the next day, a Saturday, there. I went on time and saw five or six youths, and among them was the same young man with whom I had spoken. It turned out they were a group of youth led by an older imam who gave them lessons on Islam that they would then spread in other areas of the capital. I went out with them toward a working-class suburb called al-Kabbaria, and some we spoke with came to the mosque and prayed sunset prayers with us. I was then requested to give the lesson, marking the first time I had taught in Tunisia, and I noticed how well the people responded. They were religious lessons criticizing the social status quo and moral decay, and which called upon people to pray and adhere to Islam's teachings in raising their children. People's favorable reactions gave me a surge of hope, and we agreed on meeting the next day at al-Yousefi to go to another mosque in the city.

164   ON MUSLIM DEMOCRACY

The next day, I met Shaykh Abdelfattah Mourou,[11] who had not attended the group the day before. This is how our tours began. Mourou was a practicing Sufi at the time and was following a particular *tariqa* [order] in the city, although he later cut ties with me on the grounds that I was not a Sufi and was not drawn to this path. In any case, this marked the establishment of the first basic group, and we all became members of an association for the preservation of the Holy Qur'an, which was headed by a judge. We used to go on tours informing people of Islam and also speak with students on Islam's stance toward Marxism, existentialism, and other intellectual trends. I also taught philosophy in secondary school and would complement those discussions within the program. But the baccalaureate was limited, and we would go beyond it. Students would request that we continue discussions beyond classes, so we would invite them to the mosque, but they would laugh and say they would never enter one for a discussion when they had never entered one to pray.

This marked the launch of the Islamic Group's core in 1969, and I began teaching in October of the same year at the Ibn Sharaf institute in the capital. Later I was transferred to Qayrawan, where I stayed till 1973. A group from Sousse, one from Tunis led by Mourou. and a third from the coast agreed on meeting in Qayrawan. We numbered around a hundred and drew the attention of the security forces, who brought some of us to a police station asking who we were and who our leader was. It was the first time we had been arrested and they eventually ordered us to go home. This made us rethink our strategy, and we held a meeting in a city orchard owned by Shaykh 'Abd al-Qadir Salameh.[12] There were forty of us there, and we decided that outward public action did not suit a closed regime like Tunisia, so we decided to go underground—having been forced to do so by police actions after they had prevented us from working within mosques.

AFM: What were the public and internal activities, respectively, of the Islamic Group?

RG: The public action was calling to Islam and prayer at the mosque. Underground work revolved around formulating connections and

---

[11] Shaykh 'Abd al-Fattah Mourou (1948–) is cofounder, with Ghannouchi, of Ennahda, and long-serving vice president of the movement. He served as first deputy Speaker of the Assembly of the Representatives of the People 2014–2019.

[12] One of the founders of the Islamic Tendency Movement.

PHILOSOPHICAL-THEOLOGICAL DIALOGUES 165

instilling religious consciousness and principled action. The first conference of the group was held in 1979.

AFM: What can you say about the leading influences on the Islamic Group during the 1970s?

RG: The most prominent trend was that of the Muslim Brotherhood, as well as the books by Sayyid Qutb, Muhammed Qutb, Malek Bennabi, Mawdudi, Mustafa al-Siba'i, and Abu al-Hasan Nadwi.

AFM: Did you regard yourselves in Qutb's sense as a vanguard of the entire Muslim community?

RG: Yes, we did, and [chuckling] we thought we would change the whole world.

AFM: Were traditional Tunisian reformist ideas present in this milieu?

RG: No, not at this time. We were primarily influenced by the ideas of the Muslim Brotherhood, Mawdudi, and Malek Bennabi. The ideas of the Reformist Movement were not particularly represented at this time, as we were critical of Zaytuna imams because they did not defend Islam from secularism. We also did not admire them, as when Bourguiba had taken over their institution and public discourse they did not resist or struggle but rather surrendered.

AFM: Were you preparing for some kind of coup or a revolution?

RG: We used to say that if the people were put right, so then would the state be put right, as it is composed of the people. Therefore, we needed to reform the masses and deliver to them correct Islamic ideas and Islamic education, which would reform family, society, and then eventually the laws.

AFM: Were there discussions on the legitimacy of various means for political change such as violence or dialogue?

RG: We did not practice violence.

AFM: But were there debates around the legitimacy of using violence?

RG: I had written that during the 1970s the state was busy with the conflict with the Left and had had no prior experience with such opposition, as it was certain it had already managed Islam and achieved victory over it. It, therefore, did not pay much attention to such youth movements, which mildly criticized the state on social and ethical levels but did not confront it politically. We neither participated in nor led demonstrations, sit-ins, and the mobilization of university students, like the Left and trade unions did. We were addressing the people directly, not the state. Leftists claimed we were an opposition

166 ON MUSLIM DEMOCRACY

created by the state and a conspiracy to weaken the Left, but in reality we had no relationship with the state. They created relationships with Muhammed al-Sayyah[13] and other officials. But the state's might was directed against the Left during this period through trials, persecution, and jailing. Leftists would instigate strikes, and in 1978 a major general strike occurred that left hundreds of victims. This shocked us, and we had not expected it, as our main ideological enemy was Communism. The state made mistakes for sure, but making itself the enemy of Islam was not one of them. At the university, there was violent conflict between Islamist and Communist students [who were in control of the university]. When the Islamic current emerged, Communist students decided to suppress it by force, and there were fist and stick fights. Yet when the state intervened, it used lethal force.

The conflict was of ideological basis between Islamists and leftists. But when the general strike occurred, it was on a social level that was new to us, as we had believed the struggle was one between faith and atheism, insofar as the Communists wished to ban us and regard religion as the opiate of the masses.

AFM: So, the Bourguibist state did not represent atheism for you at this time?

RG: No. It represented a secular deviation, as states did not prevent the establishment of mosques, whereas Communists did. But the level of Communist animosity toward Islam was much greater than Bourguiba's deviations.

AFM: Was there any intellectual respect for Communists?

RG: No. We used to simply view Communism as atheism; they disavow faith and religion and claim it to be the opiate of the masses, and at the university they would attack those brothers and sisters who prayed, including sometimes with violence. But the events of 1978 made us realize that the matter is a social one, and that for the first time, conflict in society was not all about doctrine.

AFM: Had you not taken notice of Sayyid Qutb's *Social Justice in Islam* before that?

RG: We had not. That was when we began to study Islam's relationship with capitalism through Islamic writings. Then the Iranian revolt of the oppressed against the mighty gave us tools to express the

---

[13] A close ally of Tunisian president Bourguiba who held a number of ministerial portfolios from the 1960s to the 1980s.

PHILOSOPHICAL-THEOLOGICAL DIALOGUES 167

social conflict through Khomeini's ideology. For example, drawing on Chapter 28 of the Qur'an [Surat al-Qasas] and the conflict between Moses and Pharaoh, which was of a social nature. We are with Moses, of course, and the Iranian Revolution provided us with intellectual substance for our social struggle with an Islamic dimension.

AFM: So, you took on the problem of social justice more from the Iranian Revolution than from Sunni thinkers?

RG: We had begun to take notice of Sunni thought, like the book *The Socialism of Islam*, which we did not particularly respect at that time. We defended the Iranian Revolution, as it was one of the oppressed against the arrogant, the tyrants, and the agents of imperialism. Accordingly, we likened that revolt to our Tunisian reality, with Bourguiba as our own shah. Khomeini used to say that their war was against the shah and that all Muslims must struggle against their own shahs, that is, any oppressor. The shah as Pharaoh is not the name of a specific individual but rather a symbol of any tyrant and exploiter of his people. We adopted such discourse and defended the Iranian Revolution as being Islamic, whereas among Sunnis we witnessed reservations toward it.

We did so as we regarded the Iranian Revolution as an Islamic revolution and our movement was not based on sectarian affiliations. We did not speak of Sunnism, but rather of upholding all of Islam. The Muslim Brotherhood was also concerned with the same until before the emergence of sectarianism after the Iranian revolt. Then the discourse shifted to Salafism and Sunnism against Shi'ism. But the Brotherhood directed their words toward the Islamic *umma*, not just to Sunnis. This is why we find their discourse around things like "The State in Islam" and "Women in Islam," not of one sect or school. The Islamic movement developed as a non-sectarian one, yet it was the Iraq-Iran War that instigated the emergence of sectarianism, and Saudi Arabia did its utmost to shape this. It was then that discourse concerned itself with Sunnis and Shi'a, whereas the matter had not been so in either Sunni or Shi'a Islamic movements before.

AFM: Were you aware of Khomeini's ideas before the Iranian Revolution?

RG: I was not, nor was I aware of those of Ali Shariati. But with the Iranian Revolution we began taking notice of Iran, and not just of the shah and the Iranian singer Googoosh, whom Bourguiba would invite to

168   ON MUSLIM DEMOCRACY

sing like Umm Kulthum—who traveled throughout the Arab world. We had never even heard of Khomeini, and when I looked through our papers from Paris, I found some information about Khomeini, as we used to attend a Qur'anic association headed by an Iranian student. That association was a rare thing in the 1970s where Sunnis and Shi'a would meet up together as students.

That student would ask me to assist him in translating speeches into Arabic, which turned out to be by Khomeini, whom I had never heard of while in Paris.

On May 1, 1980, we celebrated Labor Day for the first time in a grand festival held at al-Tabi' Masjid and which was attended by five thousand people. We listened to a seminar on agricultural ownership in Islam as the state-owned land that it should distribute among the youth instead of having it monopolized by a small group.

On that Labor Day, the theme was workers' rights in Islam and justifying the right to strike, as when the contractual agreement is unjust and signed under duress or extreme need, and the pay is less than sufficient, employers may not demand that employees fulfill its terms. I therefore became involved with the labor union and began visiting al-Habeeb Ashour.

Before that, in the 1970s, when Communists would hold a strike on, say, education, we would aim to disrupt it, as we would never march with them. Later on, we decided that our mission was not to resist Communists but rather to support justice regardless of who calls for it. We perceived this as God's Will.

In 1979, we visited Hasan al-Turabi in Sudan and realized that there was openness in the relationship between women and men, that they participate together in a variety of activities, and that there was no separation between the worlds of each, even in schools. We had our own branch of female activism, but it was separate and influenced by the ideology of the Muslim Brotherhood.

AFM: So women participated in Turabi's movement in Sudan more than was the case with the movement in Tunisia?

RG: Yes. Actually, more than in all other Islamic movements, and it was joint action within the same movement. At the time, we did have women activists, yet contrary to the Sudanese case, they were not in the administration or leadership. In Sudan, women were on the Shura Council, in the executive office, and in labor sectors.

PHILOSOPHICAL-THEOLOGICAL DIALOGUES 169

We admired the thought of Turabi and his use of Islamic principles in his fatwas. I gave a lecture there entitled "Women's Participation in the Islamic Movement." Afterward, this was published as "Women in Islam." It was this kind of activism that made the Islamic movement inclusive.

AFM: Was there opposition to these ideas in Tunisia?

RG: Yes. For example, Salih Karkar[14] opposed the membership of women, but the movement became gradually more accepting of democratic and inclusivist ideologies nonetheless. The founder of the Movement of Socialist Democrats, Mr. Ahmed Mestiri, was a great leader and would encourage us to become even more open in our activities. Hence, our movement's work in mosques became politicized and addressed people's struggles, as well as international politics. Our discourse in mosques was also economic and political, not just religious.

AFM: What is the difference in your view between religious and political activism, since a premise of the Islamic movement is that Islam does not recognize a strict separation between religion and politics?

RG: The difference is that at first we used to discuss creed, rites, and jurisprudence, and then progressed toward matters of economy, state, educational policy, and foreign affairs. These matters became foundational for us, and we came to discuss the state's cultural policies as well. Our discourse attracted many people who had not been drawn in by our religious discourse, and our gatherings grew and we adopted the example of the Iranian Revolution. But the state adopted another stance, as it feared such a revolt, and therefore veered toward aiming its might against us after having had it focused on Communism and leftists. The attack was delayed for approximately a year, though, due to an event that occurred in Gafsa when an armed group trained by Gaddafi entered Tunis.[15] Yet the state's intention was clear, as it had embarked on releasing leftists and unionists from jails and replacing

[14] Salih Karkar (1948–2012) was an early leader of Ennahda, along with Ghannouchi, and served as the movement president for about eight months in 1987–1988 before receiving asylum in France. He was known as the leader of the more conservative wing of the movement.

[15] This is a reference to a January 1980 attack on the southern Tunisian city of Gafsa by a few hundred militants who entered from Libya and were thought to have been trained and sent by the Libyan government. See, for example, Ronald Koven, "Tunisia Puts Down Assault by 300 on Southern City," *Washington Post*, January 29, 1980, https://www.washingtonpost.com/archive/politics/1980/01/29/tunisia-puts-down-assault-by-300-on-southern-city/902b341e-9f48-4705-ae28-eb254f44716e/.

170 ON MUSLIM DEMOCRACY

them with Islamists, whom the state continued to confront up till the eruption of the revolution.

In 1979, we organized a national conference, but the state discovered it on December 5, 1980. They realized that we were more than merely an intellectual trend but rather an organization with a Shura Council and branches. Then we thought that since the state already knew who we were, why not just go ahead and tell the masses before the state speaks ill of us to them? The tradition in Islamic movements has been that once its symbolic leaders are discovered, they change them and go underground. But this way, we would announce ourselves out in the open and the state could not assassinate our characters.

We announced ourselves to the general public, and on April 9 Bourguiba said he did not mind openness nor the formation of political parties. We then held an exceptional conference on April 10, 1981, and decided to change our name from the Islamic Group to the Islamic Tendency Movement [MTI]. Then, on July 17, the state arrested many of our members when we applied for a license for our party. I remained in jail from 1981 till 1984.

AFM: In the public declaration of the formation of the Islamic Tendency [MTI], there was an acceptance of political pluralism. Was there debate on this acceptance?

RG: There was a leap in the group's way of thinking, and the declaration was very advanced and was coupled with a more general consciousness. The university played a role in developing the movement's views among Islamist and Communist students, which advanced the movement's humanitarian thought, as students were engaged in conflict but also in discussions with Communists who possessed a humanitarian and economic vision. During that time, I began taking notice of the anti-apartheid movement in South Africa. Prior to this, I had never heard of this issue or of other freedom movements, as all I cared about were Muslims. I then began to understand the human dimension and empathize with the marginalized in Vietnam, South Africa, and the USA. I also began realizing that the conflict was not merely about religious creed and commitment, but also about social oppressors and the oppressed. We must empathize with the oppressed regardless of their beliefs and stand against oppressors regardless of their beliefs, even if Muslim—and this in itself was a development for me.

PHILOSOPHICAL-THEOLOGICAL DIALOGUES   171

A facet of the conflict with leftists had humanitarian dimensions, but they were, and still are, radical bigots against religion, as there exist radical leftist parties that have remained stagnant, unlike their European peers, who have evolved on this.

In the early 1980s, we had relations with leftist parties like the Communist Party and the Popular Front. The state would accuse us of violence, and I published an article on renouncing violence, which refuted the state's claim. I did so to emphasize the principles of freedom and democracy that had spread across the movement. This represented a step forward in public awareness and aided in developing the movement, whose original foundation was the thought of the Muslim Brotherhood and Mawdudi. Social and economic ideologies were not as prominent at the time as the problem of religion, which divided people into believers and unbelievers, and which was contrary to the notion of citizenship.

We were the first Islamic movement that called for recognizing all parties. This was a development in Islamic political thought, as emphasizing the creedal facet alone does not give value to citizenship and renders non-Muslims second-class citizens. Hence, I paid particular attention to this matter while I was in jail, that is, the foundation of citizenship in the Islamic state.

AFM: "Non-Muslims" refers to Christians and Jews or also Communists, atheists, and other secularists?

RG: The dominant understanding is that only Jews and Christians are included in the term, while others are not. The Tunisian Islamic movement, however, decided that we would recognize the principle of equal citizenship and the sovereignty of the people as a foundation of the state; accordingly, such rights are gained via citizenship. This move became more prevalent in Islamist thought. Within our movement, the notion was embraced and gradually became accepted.

AFM: Was there a camp against these ideas?

RG: Resistance to this was at that time the dominant view in Islamic thought, and I myself had to retract and revise my own stance. The first documents on "public freedoms," which were prepared in the 1980s, recognized full citizenship for Muslims but only partial citizenship for others. I then retracted this view and called for full citizenship and for the right of non-Muslims to hold any office in an Islamic state, including that of the presidency. We also defended the

172 ON MUSLIM DEMOCRACY

right of Communists to have political parties. I remember that when Jordan allowed parties to participate in the political process there, but prevented Communists from obtaining licensing, we published a statement defending the right of the Jordanian Communist Party to receive accreditation.

AFM: At that time, did you consider Tunisian Communists to be simply non-Muslims or apostates and infidels, since they come ostensibly from Muslim families?

RG: Apostasy was a matter that I thought much about while in prison, and it worried me greatly, as I am a staunch believer in freedom as a basic value and as one of Islamic law's basic objectives [*maqasid*]. Islam came about to free humanity; hence, apostasy as treated historically contradicts this. All intellectuals and Islamic religious scholars claim to affirm freedom in matters of religious creed, and that of believing or not believing in Islam, but it is a one-way freedom that does not allow you to retract your stance once you accept Islam. This is what my mind could not accept—for how can there be the freedom to enter but not the same freedom to exit Islam? It became evident to me that apostasy was misunderstood, and that the Abu Bakr "apostasy wars" against certain Arab tribes corrupted the vision, combined political and creedal struggles, and inclined Islamic law toward seeing apostasy as a religious crime. But it is clear to me that apostasy was a political crime: treason and plotting against the legitimate state. This is akin to the state using violence for withholding taxes, as any state would carry out a defensive war to preserve itself. This is why Abu Bakr said, "By God, I shall fight those who differentiate between performing prayers and paying *zakat*." "Apostates" renounced the state, as it was a new notion to Arabs. They accepted Islam as a religion that included prayer, but they could not accept the notion of the state as an authority. Many Arab tribes at the time interpreted Islam tribally and viewed Islam as a means for the Quraysh to impose themselves on other tribes and take their money. Renouncing the state meant their return to tribalism and away from the state's grip.

In modern times, we notice how after the American invasion of Iraq, people reverted to their tribes and sects once the state had collapsed. Despite being a dictatorship, the Baathist Party had consisted of Shi'a, Sunnis, and Kurds, and was devoid of sectarianism and ethnic exclusion. Similarly, once the Prophet died, Arab tribes

PHILOSOPHICAL-THEOLOGICAL DIALOGUES   173

wished to revert to a lower civil status than that to which Islam elevated them. 'Umar himself was bewildered why he would fight them while they prayed and attested to the Oneness of God, but to Abu Bakr, Islam was both religion and state. Apostates rejected statehood and the legitimacy of the imam, while the Prophet had prohibited new Arabs who embraced Islam from returning to their Bedouin lifestyle, as Islam was a civilization, not a nomadic life of tribal ignorance. Islamic civilization established cities like Cairo, Qayrawan, and Kufa; hence the first capital of Islam was a city, not a desert.

AFM: Did you speak out about these views on apostasy while in prison between 1981 and 1984?

RG: I wrote an article, and the prison authority placed me with twenty members of the movement there so as not to influence other inmates. The area was large enough that we could hold Friday prayers. Each of us was imam for three months, and when my turn came, I focused on the rights of non-Muslims in an Islamic state and gave nineteen speeches. Later these were published as a short book on the rights of citizenship in Islam.[16]

AFM: During the 1981–1984 period when you were in prison, you read a lot and had access to many books, since there was a right for friends to bring books in without restriction.

RG: We used to read as groups, where each would read on a certain topic. We read on the Qur'anic economy through books like *Our Economy* by renowned non-sectarian Shi'a scholar Baqir al-Sadr. We also translated Malek Bennabi's booklet *Democracy in Islam*[17] from French. Other groups learned Italian and English, and I joined the latter. There were also classes on memorizing the Qur'an and its interpretation, and I joined that group as well even though I had memorized it as a young boy. It took me a year to re-memorize it, as I had forgotten some parts. We also had classes on Islamic tradition and jurisprudence.

AFM: I am curious about the ideas of Malik Bennabi, which are not as well known as those of Mawdudi, Qutb, and nineteenth-century reformers like 'Abduh. He was known to have argued that democracy is about

---

[16] See Rāshid al-Ghannūshī, *Ḥuqūq al-muwāṭana: waḍ'īyat ghayr al-Muslim fī'l-mujtama' al-Islāmī* (Tunis: Maṭba-at Tūnis Qarṭāj, 1989).

[17] See Malek Bennabi, *La démocratie en Islam* (Algiers: Alem El Afkar, 2016).

174 ON MUSLIM DEMOCRACY

an attitude toward the self, the other, and circumstances. What is the distinctly democratic method toward the self?

RG: Naturally, the human self requires direction, and there are barriers facing people and oneself, in addition to others beyond oneself. Bennabi catered to the self as well as to external barriers. Democracy was not just a struggle against others, but also against oneself. When one does not control himself, he may become a dictator even if elected democratically. One must control himself, as the enemy lies within as well, and a person must respect the selves of others. Therefore, one must render himself an icon to follow and to do only that which makes the world a better place.

AFM: Was Bennabi's theory of democracy in any way an Islamic one?

RG: Yes, as per the Prophetic hadith that one may not be a true believer until he likes for his brethren that which he likes for himself.

AFM: Does this conception of brotherhood include the relationship between Muslims and non-Muslims or is it primarily between believers, brothers in faith?

RG: Yes. My view is, and was, that there is human brotherhood, even with Communists, which was not the tendency in the seventies. At the time I argued that there exists complete citizenship and incomplete citizenship [on the basis of faith and commitment], but I renounced this last idea later and endorsed equal citizenship for all without regard to religion.

AFM: During your first prison stint, how much jurisprudence or legal theory were you able to read? For example, were the works of al-Shatibi, or summaries of them, available?

RG: We read the works of al-Shatibi and Ibn 'Ashur's modern treatise on the objectives of Islamic law and in this way discovered the Reformist School while in prison. So we began reading books by Khayr al-Din al-Tunisi, Ibn Diyaf, Ibn Khaldun's *Al-Muqaddima* [The Prolegomena], and Muhammad 'Abduh, which expanded our thought at the time.

AFM: The break from political activity also allowed you to write?

RG: I also prepared a small booklet called *The Right to Disagreement and the Duty to Unify* when I heard of discord occurring among our members on organizational matters. It was in a letter that I wrote and which we smuggled out. I also prepared a study entitled "The Civilized Nature of the Tunisian Society."

PHILOSOPHICAL-THEOLOGICAL DIALOGUES 175

AFM: You wrote all of these while in prison?

RG: Yes. The study on the composition of Tunisian society and Sufi orders was adopted by the movement in its 1984 conference. While in jail I also compiled the basic documents and first references for my book *Public Freedoms in the Islamic State*. Yet as they released us early, completing the writing of this book was delayed till 1986, when the state was readying itself to rearrest us. So I went underground for six months and wrote the book's first draft. The book was published in 1993, although it was composed in the summer of 1986, as the confrontation occurred in 1987 and I went into exile. Therefore, I could only publish it in 1993, although my plan was to have it as a doctoral dissertation at the Faculty of Shari'a at Zaytuna.

AFM: The book *Predestination in the Thought of Ibn Taymiyya* was a master's thesis?

RG: Yes. I studied for two years [1984–1986] in the Faculty of Shari'a and there was a measure of freedom at the time.

AFM: Why did Bourguiba give such wide freedom to read in prison at that time?

RG: He was a dictator but an educated man who read many books on history and literature and who also memorized Arabic and French poetry. Accordingly, culture was advanced during his rule and he was an intellectual, although he viewed Islam negatively. But Ben Ali was a non-intellectual and a crude dictator who denied us books, even the Qur'an, while we were in prison.

AFM: At this point, in the 1980s, what was lacking in your ideas about pluralism and disagreement?

RG: Ideas like that of citizenship were not accepted at the beginning, but gradually became so. In the prior theory, non-Muslims were part of the society but they were unable to hold certain government jobs or offices. Nonetheless, we have gone beyond this threshold and accepted the notion of non-discriminatory citizenship that only distinguishes between citizens on objective standards based on equality.

AFM: Who were the other intellectuals in the movement thinking deeply about Islamic ideology?

RG: Shaykh Mourou, 'Abd al-Majid al-Najjar, al-Dimni, and Karkar, who wrote books on economics.

AFM: Then there were two or three years of freedom and then the second imprisonment in 1987?

176   ON MUSLIM DEMOCRACY

RG: The period between 1986 and 1987 was actually the high point of
       the movement's flourishing in society. The student movement at the
       university became the largest of its kind and the general Tunisian
       federation of students (Union générale tunisienne des étudiants
       (UGTE)) was established. The federation was a large organization,
       had influence on the unions, and spread throughout Tunisia, with
       many branches in different provinces.

AFM: What were the political goals of the movement at that time? For ex-
       ample, a political opening in preparation for elections in order to
       pressure the regime?

RG: We called for an opening and struggled for recognition of our party,
       a request that was rejected in 1981. But we reapplied and the regime
       recognized the student arm of the movement and allowed us to pub-
       lish a newspaper as a compromise.

AFM: Was there also a secret newspaper?

RG: We had secret papers and internal correspondence, as it had become
       evident to the regime that the Islamic Movement represented a danger
       to it due to many embracing our principles. At the time, Bourguiba
       was also nearing the end of his rule, and many sought to succeed him;
       this included much conflict among his friends and with the unions.
       Ben Ali seemed the most favored for succession, as it appeared that the
       Islamic Movement would be the alternative to a weary ruling party.
       Hence, the party relied on strengthening its apparatuses so that Ben
       Ali might succeed in ruling the country, as he had been Bourguiba's
       staunchest arm. Yet although the latter ruled out the military control-
       ling state facets, he considered Ben Ali as the most capable of striking
       Islamists where it hurt, as Bourguiba was adamant on executing us.

AFM: They executed two from the leadership?

RG: They executed two, but they were not in leadership positions. Some
       youth were accused of carrying out bombings in hotels, and two
       others were blamed during Ben Ali's rule. But Bourguiba was fixated
       on executing thirty of our leadership.

AFM: And then Ben Ali's coup occurred, but at the same time there were
       some in the movement also preparing a coup against the regime?

RG: When Bourguiba seemed adamant on executing us, a group started
       thinking how they might sideline him, and it consisted of a number
       of junior officers who planned on removing and exiling him on
       November 8, 1987. But Ben Ali was also conspiring for such an act

PHILOSOPHICAL-THEOLOGICAL DIALOGUES 177

and held his coup a day earlier, thus circumventing the other group's action.

AFM: So Ben Ali saved your life in a way.

RG: He said this as well. He released me from prison in May 1987, and I met him at the palace two or three months later. He said that he intervened to save us and that he was expecting gratitude from us.

AFM: This was during the time of the proposed National Pact?

RG: Yes. There were steps toward recognizing the movement, and he promised me when we met that he would do so, but requested that we calm things down and be a little patient, as he would recognize the movement afterward as Ennahda. I took his words seriously, but I do not know why he changed his mind or whether he was just maneuvering to gain time. I assume it was the latter.

AFM: And then came the elections of 1989 and the movement won, whether as Ennahda or as independents.

RG: Yes, the movement won and emerged strong, technically as independent candidates. This shook the regime, as Ennahda proved itself to be the main power in the country instead of the ruling party. That was when Ben Ali was confused about how to act and whether to acknowledge the results or not. In the end, he decided to annul the ballots and grant all seats to his party. He promised to eradicate the movement and drew closer to the Communists and other parties, to whom he promised that he would establish democratic rule in Tunisia if they assisted him in eliminating Islamists. But, of course, he reneged on his promises the moment after they assisted him.

AFM: This was the year you fled to Algeria.

RG: Yes, in 1989. Shortly after the elections, I was disappointed and left for Germany to give a lecture to a Palestinian student association. It had been ten years since I had last traveled abroad, as I had been banned from doing so. This was in addition to the trials against me, which left me facing the death penalty. This gave me a reputation abroad, and whenever I left Tunisia, I would receive invitations to give lectures in many countries. I traveled to the USA, and to much of the Arab world, including Algeria and Morocco and Libya, among others. As matters developed adversely in Tunisia, my colleagues requested I not hasten my return and continue to monitor the situation there from abroad. It was escalating toward a confrontation, and it was not the right time for me to return.

178 ON MUSLIM DEMOCRACY

I went back to Algeria and decided to stay there and called on my family to join me. They did so by coming through the mountains to evade detection. Eventually we settled in London.

AFM: From 1993 to 2010, while you were in London, how would you describe the changes in your theoretical ideas about the legitimacy of an Islamic state and the role of the *shari'a* in politics? Were these core, foundational changes or only in the details?

RG: In the details. That is, the ideas of democracy and freedom deepened and expanded, and my trust in the interpretative method grew. The interpretation of Islam beginning with the value of freedom and the method of explaining scriptural texts widened my understanding of the meaning of freedom.

This was new ground, as this type of thinking was not part of the intellectual matrix in the 1980s. The explanatory method and the framework of human rights existed, but it came to occupy a greater sphere, probably due to the need for struggle in Tunisia, and there was a greater need for thinking in terms of civil society and human rights.

AFM: How do you interpret these transformations?

RG: They were positive transformations that assisted in removing Ben Ali and contributed to drawing the various Tunisian opposition forces together. It also paved the way for meetings between us and other opposition groups to coordinate the struggle against the regime, and a common intellectual ground between us and them. This led to intellectual discussions that produced some important documents in 2005 on the relationship of religion to the state, democracy, and women's rights. This was dubbed the "Collectif du 18 Octobre," or the "18 October Coalition for Rights and Freedoms in Tunisia," in 2005. Such cooperation between Islamists and secularists was extremely important for deposing Ben Ali, and after the 2011 revolution this provided the groundwork for establishing shared democratic governance between Islamists and secularists in the form of a coalition between one Islamic political party and two secular ones.

AFM: Who participated in these dialogues?

RG: Participants included those who were released from prison, like Ali Larayedh and Samir Dilou from Ennahda, Hamma al-Hamami from the Communist Party, the group around Ahmad Najib al-Shabi, and Moncef Marzouki's Congress for the Republic. Consultations occurred inside the headquarters of the legally accredited Progressive Democratic Party.

PHILOSOPHICAL-THEOLOGICAL DIALOGUES   179

AFM: This contributed to the forming of the alliance after the revolution.

RG: Yes, it assisted in creating the Troika coalition.

AFM: If we can come back then to the development of your thought during this period, and what you meant by the expansion and deepening of your understanding of the concept of freedom?

RG: There are varied meanings of freedom. I am free when I act without being coerced, so the more I can act, the wider the freedom of action I have. This means that there is freedom vis-à-vis others, when they do not coerce me to adhere to a certain behavior. Furthermore, there is freedom visa-à-vis all types of coercion, which include political, economic, and social. I am free with regard to my whims and desires, and thus free with regard to myself, if I am able to master my own desires. This is the reason I say that God placed reason in a position of highest authority and rendered all desires beneath it, so that that which is higher must be sovereign over that which is lower and baser.

This is also the reason I considered worshipping God as a step toward emancipation. Freedom is the ability to control and possess yourself. For example, during the month of Ramadan, one is extremely hungry within the first four or five hours and the food is right there in front of you. In one sense, freedom could simply be not being coerced from acting in a certain way. This kind of freedom is our freedom as an animal, in the sense of acting on immediate desires. But mankind's behavior contains a further element—namely, our will. Acts of worship discipline and educate our human will. Consider what the people chanted during the Tunisian revolution: "The people 'want,'" which can also suggest "The people *will*." Accordingly, between the "desire" and its fulfillment is a fundamental element—namely, the *will*. Mankind is free to say no and to control the self. Thus, there is freedom vis-à-vis internal coercion or impediments, like our desires, and vis-à-vis external economic, social, and political ones.

What distinguished the Islamic trend in Tunisia is that when we announced ourselves to the public back in 1981, we did not demand *shari'a* but rather freedom, because we considered it the main entry toward reform, progress, and eventually the application of Islam. We interpreted this ranging from political freedom to all other intellectual freedoms, and we focused on human rights as the path toward reforming society and people's affairs. From here came my explanation of the subject of legitimacy, the relationship with non-Muslims,

180 ON MUSLIM DEMOCRACY

and the rights of minorities and women, all of which sprang from the basic principle of freedom.

Equality is also among the meanings of freedom because one of the basic implications of freedom is justice and one of the main implications of justice is equality between persons. Accordingly, Muslims are considered brethren in the sense that they have equal human value and no one can claim to be better than another, as we are made of the same clay.

AFM: You have said, in this vein, that your exile in London gave you the chance to see the operation of a democratic system with certain political liberties directly.

RG: Yes, I attended some seminars at universities to learn about the situation in Tunisia, and also learned a lot from Professor John Keane, working on the application of democracy and the importance of civil society. I also deepened my understanding of rights and how they are not merely political but also social, and how one must achieve balance between the social and the political.

I also kept abreast of how the electoral process, in parliament and on the streets, operated. During the Iraq War, for example, millions would march against it, to the extent that I once gave a speech in one of London's squares and led the march with Jeremy Corbyn in 2003. It was the first time that the English Left allied with Islamists and the broader European Left opened itself up to Islamists, because democracy does not only possess a political face but also is about international relationships. English democracy was transcended to the extent that the democratic scene contained cultural, intellectual, and humanitarian dimensions beyond just that which affected the English themselves.

AFM: Given overwhelming public opposition to the war in Iraq and the fact that this judgment was redeemed as accurate, I wanted to ask whether you think that the idea expressed in the famous hadith "The *umma* will not agree on error" bears comparison to Rousseau's general will, "which can never be wrong," and what is sometimes called today "epistemic democracy."

RG: The stance against the war on Iraq became a general humanitarian will, not only a national one, against Tony Blair, who always insisted that Iraq possessed weapons of mass destruction. This emphasizes how democracy can fall into error and can justify injustice by deceiving public opinion.

PHILOSOPHICAL-THEOLOGICAL DIALOGUES 181

AFM: To what extent was exile in London a break from day-to-day political activity and an opportunity for prioritizing intellectual work?

RG: Yes, the pace was slow and there was opportunity for intellectual action. But this space has narrowed since returning to Tunisia and the daily practice of politics.

AFM: Can we talk a little more about this topic?

RG: I mean that the opportunities for intellectual activities were greater in the UK, and I gave lectures and took part in seminars throughout the country after having been prevented from doing so in many countries like the US, Germany, and France. It became evident that the values of human rights in some European countries were deeper than in others. Scandinavian countries, for example, were unconvinced by Ben Ali's claims that I was a terrorist, as they did not have any great state interests in Tunisia. But Ben Ali was able to convince many others that I was a terrorist, including all Arab countries except Qatar, and I was unable to travel to those other countries.

Scandinavian countries are more faithful in their practice of human rights. They have great respect for others, and foreigners there have rights.

AFM: So there was no dialogue at all with Ben Ali during this period.

RG: No, there was no dialogue, as he completely rejected it and refused to deal with us as a movement, but only as individuals. This period I spent in England was important for reading and for observing firsthand how a democracy operates in political and social spheres.

Democracy, Sovereignty, and Morality

AFM: Having covered the outlines of your intellectual trajectory before the 2011 revolution, I would like to turn to a discussion of your writings in more depth. I would like to read a bit from *Public Freedoms in the Islamic State*. I have a set of concepts and topics that I want us to discuss, the first being the concept of democracy and the critique of Western democracy in the book. And so, to begin, on page 34 in the 1993 edition:

Yet even when the Westerner attributes rights to the human person and defends them, when he convenes assemblies, establishes

182 ON MUSLIM DEMOCRACY

judicial, administrative, media, and economic institutions to make sure they are applied, and even protests their violation, he is in fact lying. For what he calls "human being" is actually only the "citizen" in the best of instances.

In these texts, the term "human being" is inserted in a misleading way, the healthy mixed in with the mangy, though French, English, and other Western languages generally add to it the noun "citizen," a misleading repetition in which the second word is of lesser value. Even this human being/citizen has no honor in himself, simply because he is human, and in fact that honor comes from his belonging to a particular historical, social, and cultural context—nation, class, or European race....

Thus there remains no moral foundation upon which to base the covenants of rights and liberties in the West, unless it is a bundle of connections and historical, social, and cultural convergences and interests, perhaps on the basis of class, race, or nation. No matter how the civilization expands and its humanity develops, it will not be able to grow out of its Western orbit, wherein there is no god but matter, no authority but brute force, and wherein the Machiavellian ruler is allowed to subject everything to his will and do all that he can to protect, extend, and consolidate his own power, while seeking the support of God and religion.[18]

And elsewhere [from page 83 of the 1993 edition of *Public Freedoms*]:

Fundamentally, the principle of legitimacy, that is, the state's submission to the law and popular sovereignty, is seen in the state's legislative authority. No authority supersedes it, and it will not submit to any exterior authority. Then, too, its authority is derived from the people by means of general elections. These two principles, therefore, form the essence of the Western state. And because their establishment represents an important step in affirming the authority of the law and the people's authority above that of the ruler, and

---

[18] Rāshid al-Ghannūshī, *Al-ḥurriyyāt al-ʿāmma fi'l-dawla al-Islāmiyya* (Beirut: Markaz Dirāsat al-Wiḥda al-ʿArabiyya, 1993), 34–35. See the English-language translation by David Johnston, *Public Freedoms in the Islamic State* (New Haven, CT: Yale University Press (2022)).

PHILOSOPHICAL-THEOLOGICAL DIALOGUES   183

because of the conferring of fixed rights to the citizens, and thereby giving them the means to resist autocracy, the political conundrum remains in all its gravity. How can you restrain the human desire to dominate others while exploiting their need to live in society? There is no satisfactory solution to this problem within the framework of the Western state's two essential principles—legitimacy and the sovereignty of the people.[19]

AFM: So the first question is, do you have any comment on these ideas today? Has your critique changed between 1993 and 2018?

RG: No. The problem remains in the state, its law being upheld as the highest authority, as that which its institutions decide. There exists no ethical value beyond or higher than the will of the parliament. It is true that there are human rights values, but they remain ideals. If states decide to colonize Vietnam, it becomes legal; if Algeria is colonized and 1.5 million are killed, it also becomes a moral cause. This means that the parliament and the constitutional court have concurred, and it becomes a matter of state sovereignty. What states decide upon through their democratic mechanisms is a right above all else. In America, what the Congress decides is also supreme, although the president may object through the veto. Yet when it overrides that with a two-thirds majority, its decision becomes the supreme law and highest authority. There will always remain a problem of sovereignty in the state—for example, when Congress decides to reject the climate pact regardless of that decision's adverse impact on all humanity. What matters is that the interest of the American economy is upheld. But this is to the benefit of CEOs and capitalists, and not in the best interest of the American people, never mind humanity as such. American public opinion may also be bought via influencing the media within constitutional institutions under the banner of the "national interest," but it is actually in the interest of a certain class or group. Even if it is in the national interest for all Americans, should the climate agreement be annulled given how this will affect the rest of the world?

AFM: But I think there is a distinction here between saying that sovereignty means that what is enacted by the state is *law* and saying that it is therefore *right*.

---

[19] Ghannūshī, *Al-ḥurriyyāt al-ʿāmma*, 83.

184 ON MUSLIM DEMOCRACY

RG: It is the right, it is the law; it is the supreme authority. This will always remain the problem of sovereignty in the modern state.

AFM: But Western states usually possess some kind of human rights documents, or like with the European Convention on Human Rights, there is an effort to codify the protection of human rights above the state level. These are precisely meant to serve as a higher moral constraint on the exercise of state sovereignty. Is there a difference between the principle of absolute popular sovereignty, often expressed as the sovereignty of parliament or the nation-state, and these efforts to guarantee humans rights through these constitutions or conventions?

RG: There are attempts to come up with a moral authority like the International Criminal Court and to oppose the authority of the nation-state, but the state itself may also oppose these efforts in turn. In Britain, for example, citizens may object to the ruling of a local court at the European Court, but this does not necessarily mean that the British state must adhere to it. The state may pay citizens money and not be subject to its ruling. The persistent problem is that state sovereignty supersedes everything else, including the church and human rights, on the pretext that it represents the public will. As the state is the entity that represents this will and discharges it as it wishes, it could colonize another country or repress another people, as the public will represents the interests of a particular people and not ethical principles.

AFM: Is the problem in Western, secular democracy a problem of institutional design, that is, that the institutions ostensibly created to guarantee human rights on the basis of conventions or constitutions simply do not have sovereign power over the state and what is perceived as the public interest, or is the problem a more ontological-metaphysical one of the foundation and origins of morality? That is, is the problem not just that these institutions are not powerful enough vis-à-vis the state, but that they do not rest on a true underlying foundation of morality and justice?

RG: There is an important formal development, as there are institutions that have developed from the form of personalism when it was in the hands of the ruler to another phase where there are elected parliaments and the rule of law in the form of courts. All of these minimize despotism in that there exist authorities that limit the absolute rule of the state or even the people in the form of the executive,

PHILOSOPHICAL-THEOLOGICAL DIALOGUES 185

legislative, and judicial authorities. There is also public opinion adopted by elite intellectuals, the media, and the United Nations, which reduces a state's authority. But even the UN itself is limited in its authority through the Security Council, which is headed by five countries that can veto any motion regarding any country.

AFM: We can acknowledge the problem of authoritarianism and a lack of balance of powers, that is, the fact that human rights are often not upheld or honored. This is a problem of how things operate in practice. But are you also still talking about a philosophical or ethical problem in the very notion of human rights as understood by these instruments? Are the very values or ideals represented by human rights or the UN Charter also deficient from a philosophical, ontological, metaphysical, or moral standpoint? Is the problem also a deficiency in the very ideas and values themselves that are meant to order the world or the state?

RG: The ethical dilemma is that people and members of the UN are both unequal in their own right. But formally, all are equal. When viewing the UN, we realize it is an organization whose members are states on the premise of equality, yet there is an order rendering differences between larger states and smaller ones. The standard here is not ethics, but rather strength! Since the big five possess nuclear weapons, they are deemed as such, and if you do not possess them, then you are considered small. Although the United Nations is established on the basis that all mankind is free, the strong do what they please, and hence the ethical dilemma. This is an ontological problem, as it means that mankind is not equal, because while it ought to be the case that strength is subordinate to justice, in reality it is the opposite. Eventually, all that which is done by the strong is deemed righteous.

AFM: As the ancient Greek historian Thucydides said, "The strong do what they will and the weak suffer what they must."

RG: This blows up both the UN system and ethics, leading to an ontological problem of people being unequal and might making right. Power is not forced to answer and submit to justice, but justice submits to power, and the strong do whatever they wish and regard whatever they do as moral.

AFM: But couldn't your foundational criticism of the nation-state and Western constitutions also be applied to the post-revolutionary [2014] constitution of Tunisia, which Ennahda of course helped draft

186 ON MUSLIM DEMOCRACY

and adopt, insofar as Tunisia has a juridical and state structure identical to that of Western states?

RG: The Tunisian constitution, as is the case with all other constitutions, is likely to contain errors and allow for exploitation and corruption. But it contains human values, like those of human rights and dignity, and Islamic values. The two constant principles, in the form of two unamendable articles, are that Tunisia is a civil and Muslim state. The Constitutional Court can annul any law that contravenes these two principles, as parliament does not possess absolute power and is monitored by the Constitutional Court. The Constitutional Court can also strike down any law that violates the constitution and the principles of justice, equality, Islam, and human rights. The Constitutional Court may nonetheless err, but the sovereignty of parliament is not absolute and is subject to the constitution, with the latter being monitored by both the Constitutional Court and public opinion in civil society.

AFM: But how is this different from what we earlier established about other constitutions in European and other Western states, all of which also have constitutional courts and some codified commitment to human or civil rights?

RG: All constitutions are monitored by constitutional courts, yet they do not prevent the emergence of authoritarianism, just as all of colonialism occurred within the framework of existing courts and public opinion. All of this is indicative of the fallibility and imperfection of humankind. Prophetic hadith states that all of Adam's children err in this world, just as Aristotle describes this world as one of change, corruption, and degeneration rather than perfection. Thus, we speak of another world, the afterlife, that is the abode of perfection. Mankind is not perfect but aspires to perfection; one is not free but seeks to free oneself. Sartre said we are without metaphysical guarantees and so "man is condemned to be free." Well, we Muslims say that only God is perfect and that mankind is imperfect but our condition is one of striving toward God. For this reason, God has His blessed names, or His attributes of perfection, but mankind is fundamentally deficient and imperfect.

AFM: So perhaps what we can say about your conception of politics, progress, and justice is that there is no single moment of founding a justice, ideal state, or utopia, but a constant progression and movement

PHILOSOPHICAL-THEOLOGICAL DIALOGUES   187

toward that. And so in any given moment we can accept imperfection and error, and perhaps compare this to Jacques Derrida's notion of a "democracy-to-come."

RG: This agrees with the Islamic concept that man is a fallible being but may rectify his mistakes and resist himself via resisting his desires due to the incompleteness of his nature and his ability to ascend toward higher ideals. Yet despite his deficient nature, mankind possesses dispositions and capabilities for seeking perfection and progress.

AFM: In your opinion, is the Islamic conception of mankind, or its theological anthropology, fundamentally more positive about humanity than the Christian, Marxist, or secular ones in general? Is it more optimistic than these other conceptions, or has there been a shift in Islamic views on the human in modernity from the premodern, classical one?

RG: It remains within the path toward integration, development, and elevating oneself. This path remains open, and Islam grants mankind the possibilities and opportunities for greater individual and collective progress, since Islam addresses mankind as an individual, a group, and as humanity at large by saying, "O people, We have created you males and females and made you peoples and tribes so that you may get to know one another" [Qur'an 49:13].

AFM: What specifically are the opportunities that Islam extends for the sake of progress and perfection?

RG: There are individual and collective remedies. God requires humans to remedy themselves via worship and virtues as well as through cooperating with others as a society. One is to cooperate with Muslim and non-Muslim friends on the basis of goodness, justice, and piety toward whatever benefits all. This is required of Muslims since all human beings are a single family, all God's children, and the best among us in God's eyes is the one who benefits other people.

AFM: Given its grounding in Islamic truth-claims, what is the outer limit of moral perfection, progress, good, and virtue that non-Muslims can attain in this world?

RG: As God is just, he does not do injustice to non-Muslims in either this life or the afterlife. Therefore, if one does an ounce of goodness or of evil, he or she will see the same in the hereafter. For example, if an unbeliever is put in charge of agriculture, if he does this well, then God will not withhold the reward for this. If non-Muslims are proficient

188   ON MUSLIM DEMOCRACY

at politics and established a state on the basis of justice, God will not withhold good results from them. It is also like one who endows a university and a good educational system, where God will not deny him a good outcome, as He is Just. So there is a legal system based on justice which, if one follows it, one's outcomes will be good, one will receive riches from God. Whoever does well will receive good consequences, and whoever does ill will receive bad consequences, whether they are a believer or unbeliever. Similarly, whether Muslims or unbelievers commit bad deeds, God will give them ill results.

The basic law of this world, that is, natural law, is based on reason and equality among people. Of course, there is the question of people's intentions and aims behind their deeds. In this world, consequences and rewards are based on what is apparent. Only rewards in the hereafter are based on the intention behind them, that is, whether they are intended as obedience to God, in which case one will receive good rewards now and in the afterlife. But if it was an action intended to benefit others in this life, not as an act of obedience toward God, He will grant you its rewards in life, but not in the afterlife. So if one quits alcohol because God orders such, he receives rewards in this life and the next, but if he quits it as being adverse to one's health, he would receive health benefits and save money in this life but will get no reward in the next. The same can be said for fasting and other acts that may have worldly motivations and benefits but also be attached to the promise of reward in the afterlife as worship and obedience to God.

AFM: Political philosophies that seek to explore the outer possibilities for justice and order in society often go back to "theological anthropology" and "philosophical anthropology," that is, the attempt to explain what is human and the essence of humanity. These theories also try to explain or interpret the cause of evil and imperfection in the world. Some Christian theories, like that of Augustine, speak of evil as the result of original sin, but this concept does not exist in Islam. Or Rousseau talks about evil as an abject form of human self-love with its origins not in original sin but in private property and "the first person who, having enclosed a plot of land, took it into his head to say this is mine." Then we might speak of the Platonic and Neoplatonic traditions, like Plotinus and those who followed him in the third, fourth, and fifth centuries, which identified the source of evil as matter itself. Whereas God Himself is only spirit and reason,

PHILOSOPHICAL-THEOLOGICAL DIALOGUES   189

we are made partly of matter and all matter is subject to imperfection and degeneration. Now, in the Islamic conception, and your own view, what is the corresponding theory that explains the existence of evil in the world? What is the original source of error and the tendency of some humans to incline toward evil and error and not toward good and justice?

RG: Mankind is innately innocent. Just like the presumption of innocence in the law, Islam states that mankind is not born in original sin but in a state of original innocence and goodness. God created mankind with the dispositions and capacities for both good and evil, but he was not born evil, and the freedom of choice comes into play here, as one is always in a position to do one or the other. This is how I understand Islam, that it orders and encourages us to do good deeds that would lead to happiness and rewards in this life and the next. I also understand that God has warned us from the other path of Satan, wrongdoing, and following our lusts and temptations. God has also provided us with the means of repenting so that if we lose our way momentarily, we would be welcomed back into the bosom of Islam. Thus mankind is in a constant battle, as each of us has been born with a conflict with evil inside of our souls and evil outside of ourselves. But God has given us the means of resistance for victory in this battle. Therefore, Muslims are optimistic, since even when they lose a battle to evil, they have hope to renew their strength for the sake of victory. God loves good and there is always another opportunity. So we are not left in despair, which is a crime and unbelief in Islam. For example, the prophet Ya'qub [Jacob] told his sons not to despair of God's guidance and to continue looking for their brother Yusuf [Joseph]. Despair is considered disbelief, since faith holds the meaning of optimism, and one of the meanings of faith is to hold your head above the water. You always have hope that God will not leave you to your own devices but will extend His hand to you. You should never feel alone but always feel that God is with you, and He was with Moses at sea when He said to him, "Do not be sad for God is with you."

This is the secret behind the strength of Muslims, and the essence of their faith is this feeling that God is with you and you are not alone. Without this feeling is despair, terror, suicide, nihilism, and frustration. Faith gives you the sense of never being alone in the world or without hope in victory, even in front of the gallows or before the

190 ON MUSLIM DEMOCRACY

enemy, illness, or poverty. The true problem before you is nihilism and the sense of meaninglessness or absurdity, like we read in Camus or Sartre.

AFM: Nietzsche, on the contrary, said that perhaps the meaning of life is that man looks at the reality of this absurdity or void and finds within himself the power to advance in life, to create his own values and purposes.

RG: Without this sense of accompaniment by God there are only feelings of isolation, selfishness, triviality, meaninglessness, and eventually suicide.

AFM: So to bring this back to politics and the problem of resisting tyranny: You put a lot of emphasis on the importance of a moral foundation not only in constitutions and laws but in the general culture and beliefs of a society. Where should we see the manifestation of virtue and the power to check tyranny? In an Islamic society, are the citizens believing Muslims who believe in the fusion of ethics in political life, thus providing a check against tyranny? Or in an Islamic state, should we see institutions like the Shura Council [parliament] or others as the ones that apply morality and act as the check on despotism?

RG: Is there only one means for preventing tyranny? In my book *Public Freedoms in the Islamic State* I spoke about the various mechanisms that prevent tyranny. Islam is accused of being a cause for tyranny and that belief in predestination is one of the reasons for this. I wrote on how we can resist tyranny through a variety of means, as there is more than one cause of it. We must work together and utilize new tools like democracy, pluralism, the rule of law, constitutions, courts, public opinion, and popular participation in the political process. This is a legal matrix that needs to work together, as the Prophet Muhammad stated that the *umma* will not agree on evil.

AFM: Aristotle also held that democracy was superior because the majority of the people will not err, something we call today the theory of "epistemic democracy," that is, that democracy is a means to truth and to superior decisions because a majority is wiser and smarter than a minority or individual.

RG: We must not rely on one cause, but rather utilize all mechanisms for reducing this deficiency so as to overcome its ontological counterpart in mankind. But we need to minimize it, not destroy it completely, as we are no angels and the world is based on imperfection and degeneration, in the Aristotelian sense. The universe is established upon imperfection, but humans are honored in that we are called upon to perfect it. Marx says that the difference between a clever bee and a stupid engineer is that the former builds its hive the same way throughout its history, whereas the latter always renews his design, as he relies on intellect, not repetition, to redesign a house that crumbled in the past, regardless of how stupid he may be compared to other engineers.[20]

Hence, we are required to evolve continuously, learn from our mistakes, and not rely on one specific method in curing our shortcomings. So, in the political realm, we must utilize different means for resisting tyranny, and humanity has definitely evolved in this regard. The UN system is a good tool for acknowledging human rights and that mankind has inalienable rights without discrimination. But many shortcomings still exist, as the Security Council has five nations with the exclusive right of controlling the entire world. For example, although almost 95 percent of the international body agrees that Jerusalem is not the capital of Israel, the US disregards all and says it is. So humans are not in effect equal, the world order is not a good one, and, for example, an American president might exert disproportionate domination on his own.

AFM: And is this still your view on Islam, that there is no solution for this lack and deficiency except through the religion of Islam?

RG: The problem is not in the mechanisms of democracy, as they are the best that mankind has created to this point. It is in the spirit active in the transformation of this system into a philosophy that recognizes humanity in all its facets, not as a physical entity alone. The major defect in modern philosophy is believing that a political system that pleases mankind is one that is independent of God. This is man's vanity in believing he can establish an independent life by ignoring God. French democracy, for example, is built upon the notion

---

[20] In Chapter 7 of *Das Kapital* ("The Labor Process and the Valorization Process"), Marx writes, "A spider conducts operations that resemble those of a weaver, and a bee would put many a human architect to shame by the construction of its honeycomb cells. But what distinguishes the worst architect from the best of bees is that the architect builds the cell in his mind before he constructs it in wax. At the end of every labor process, a result emerges which had already been conceived by the worker at the beginning, hence already existed ideally." See Karl Marx, *Selected Writings*, edited by Lawrence H. Simon (Indianapolis, IN: Hackett, 1994), 274.

192 ON MUSLIM DEMOCRACY

of combatting God; English and American democracies say that whether He exists or not, our minds can establish a political system that brings about human happiness. So the belief in arranging a universe that is void of God cannot bring happiness to mankind, as it does not acknowledge his complexity of soul and ethics because man is body, mind, and soul all in one.

AFM: But let us dwell on this philosophy that there might be a system, or a theory of justice, that says that people can create or institute a political system purely on human values alone, while remaining silent about the [metaphysical] questions of whether there is a Divine Creator. Such a theory neither denies nor asserts, but is rather simply silent on this, since we have knowledge of certain purely human values.

RG: The question of humanity and human nature is not a small matter, such that we can be silent about it. Similarly, believing or not believing in God is no minor issue for us to marginalize and consider nonexistent. When we read the Qur'an and see how many times God's name is mentioned in it, we realize that it is no small, insignificant matter. Similarly, God's place in this universe is no minor issue, as you cannot explain anything in the human body or in nature without referring to God. So the effort to construct a conception of the human or to adopt a system for mankind without God is ignorant.

AFM: But Islamic jurists famously said that it is possible to imagine a just but unbelieving order, or ruler, as well as an unjust but believing one.

RG: It is possible, yet only in theory. When we view all of mankind's facets, we notice his short life and his eternal afterlife. Man is destined to live a maximum of eighty or so years, in general, and then return to the earth, but we must also believe that these eighty or so years are not the end. We need to realize that man's mission is not so insignificant as to be encompassed within these few years, but rather that he was created for a more sustained reason encompassing a life and an afterlife where he can achieve happiness in both. It is the afterlife that is longer and which should obviously matter more.

AFM: Is it the role of worldly political life and governance to prepare people for the journey to the next world, and how does it do this—through laws, and the creation of a certain environment, circumstances, and means?

RG: In my book *Public Freedoms*, I said that the mission of the state is not to force Islam upon people but rather to provide them with services that make the path toward Islam easy and desirable. The path toward non-Islam should be possible but not easy. For example, sexual relations make marriage desirable. Extramarital sex is possible but entails punishments, although it does remain possible. Marriage is made easy, in that the state's mission is to make virtue easy and vice difficult but possible. Unfortunately, today it is the opposite, as virtue is hard and vice is made easy.

AFM: I have one final question here. We began this discussion around *Public Freedoms* on the problem of the lack of an ethical foundation for Western democracy and the problem of the absolute sovereignty of the modern nation-state, even if those states have constitutions or human rights commitments. We called this the crisis of Western democracy, and you have claimed there is no solution to this crisis except for that provided by an Islamic state. So how can we synthesize the necessary Islamic solution for the protection and guarantee of human rights and morality in an Islamic democratic state, as opposed to secular democracies? How does this Islamic foundation succeed at guaranteeing morality, the limitation of sovereign power, the supremacy of law, and human rights where Western democracy fails?

RG: There is no perfect system and the world we live in is not an abode for establishing an ideal society. There are only attempts to get closer to the ideal, but we do not reach it. This requires intellectual and cultural reform so as to strengthen the moral and spiritual aspect of mankind, as mankind possesses many evils. Hence, that which is needed is to alleviate such evils and strengthen mankind's good side.

AFM: So this depends on institutions and constitutional procedures, but also on virtue within the citizens in society.

RG: Virtue, mankind's virtue, goodness, and inclination toward social cooperation must all be strengthened. We do not only regard democracy as a set of tools alone, but also rather as values that facilitate the strengthening of virtue, cooperation, charity, equality, and belief in human dignity among people regardless of their nationalities. We need to strengthen mankind's values and intellectual facets and decide upon the means that will assist us in doing so, and then after that come the procedures. The national state is a reality now, but we need to mitigate its sovereignty via both human morals and international law.

194 ON MUSLIM DEMOCRACY

Both virtue and law are useful for achieving our goal because international law is based on the premise of human brotherhood and God-given dignity, and thus human equality. Human rights law invokes this and represents these values. We are called upon to strengthen these values so that the supreme standard of values is not the national interest but human interests and human rights. This requires action, the right culture, and also mechanisms and institutions.

The Universal Caliphate, Democracy, and the Meaning of the *Shari'a*

AFM: Can we speak a little about the theory of universal human vicegerency of God [*istikhlaf*]? This is among the most important ideas in modern Islamic thought; indeed you call it the pillar of modern Islamic political thought. Is this political interpretation of the idea strictly modern and contemporary? Did the scholars and philosophers of Islam from the beginning understand it in the same way, or is it a kind of revolution in Islamic political thought?

RG: These meanings are found in abundance in Islamic thought and texts, but their wording is modern. The idea is old and instilled in Muslim minds and in Islamic culture and civilization that there is cohesion between the transfer of text and the mind. This idea was emphasized by Ibn Rushd in a treatise entitled *Fasl al-maqal fi ma bayn al-hikma wa al-shari'a min al-ittisal* [often translated as "The Decisive Treatise on the Harmony of Philosophy and the Law"].[21] In modern reformist thought it was phrased as the correlation between authenticity and modernism and seeking commonalities on how to bring together the *shari'a*, reason, and freedom. This resulted in the predominant emphasis on *shura* [public consultation] and democracy. Accordingly, such analysis leads to the conclusion that the entire Islamic system is based on the correspondence between revelation and reason. And thus mankind's vicegerency of God on earth is embodied in the

---

[21] In English, see the translations of George F. Hourani, *Averroes on the Harmony of Religion and Philosophy: A Translation, with Introduction and Notes, of Ibn Rushd's* Kitab Faşl Al-maqal, *with Its Appendix (Ḍamima) and an Extract from* Kitab Al-kashf 'an Manahij al-adilla (London: Luzac, 1961) and Charles Butterworth, *The Book of the Decisive Treatise Determining the Connection Between the Law and Wisdom; &, Epistle Dedicatory*, Islamic Translation Series (Provo, UT: Brigham Young University Press, 2001).

PHILOSOPHICAL-THEOLOGICAL DIALOGUES   195

public seeking of truth [*ijtihad*], and thus the role and status of humanity collectively on earth are as God's deputy and trustee, whether we are aware of it or not. God delegated and transferred much of His authority to humanity and provided it with a road map and an axis to guide itself with. All other creations, like plants, animals, rivers, and the like, are controlled directly by God without awareness or will of their own. But mankind is in control of his life and is deputized and entrusted by God in the sense that mankind is given a mandate and freedom, but also given revelation as a road map and guide that also requires active human interpretation and judgment in application. This is the space of human responsibility, and thus I believe that speaking of the collective vicegerency of God is a new form of speaking about ancient meanings, and the new form of an Islamic political entity is nonetheless based on a synthesis of revelation and *shari'a*, on the one hand, and human freedom on the other. For on my view one cannot say "Only *shari'a*!" or "Only freedom!" because the *shari'a* is more a matter of principles than specific provisions, and every person is called on to interpret these and thus to be a *mujtahid*.

AFM: Are these general principles of the *shari'a* found only in texts [of revelation], or also in the human conscience or reason? That is, do we as humans need text to acquire knowledge of these principles, or are reason or conscience sufficient?

RG: Mankind must utilize all capabilities given to him by God in doing so, and he will be judged by God accordingly. Therefore, the judgment of the educated will be harsher than that of the ignorant, as will be that of one who has learned of Islam and another who hasn't.

AFM: When I read classical Islamic political theories, say up until the nineteenth century and the emergence of reformers like Khayr al-Din or Bin Diyaf or Muhammad 'Abduh, those classical theories do not rely on the concept of the universal human vicegerency to the same extent. That is, I don't really find this concept that all of mankind is God's deputy on Earth as the pillar or foundation of Islamic political philosophy. In my view, this concept is distinctly modern, and so I am curious what change this turn or development brought about. Did it deepen the power or authority of the people in politics or have some other primary impact?

RG: Sufi schools have written on mankind as being a vicegerent, and this is found in the writings of al-Isfahani. [Senior Ennahda activist]

196 ON MUSLIM DEMOCRACY

'Abd al-Majid al-Najjar wrote about al-Isfahani's book on mankind and affirmed it as an important text. Al-Najjar is among the Tunisian Islamist movement's leaders and a member of the Shura Council, and wrote a book entitled *The Vicegerency of Man, Between Revelation and Reason*, which is considered a major doctrinal foundation of the movement.[22]

AFM: You connected this to the problem of divine wisdom and the meaning of wisdom of the Islamic *shari'a*. Has there been some development in your thought since the writing of *Public Freedoms* until today?

RG: There has been more clarity. The meaning of mankind's vicegerency of God and adhering to God's law is related to elevating the status of the rule of law that is drawn from Islam and the Islamic order. It is about political values more than those of jurisprudence, where political philosophy and values are more important, since in this conception there is no divine ruler, or absolute or supreme authority. What is at stake is constitutional authority governed by a constitution, that is, by Islamic values, which regulate society and which are drawn from Islam. Accordingly, Islam has waged campaigns against oppressors and pharaohs—incidentally, which does not refer to the name of an individual but to a title for the ruler that denotes "supreme lord" or "deity." Islam waged a campaign against political paganism, as the pharaoh was a kind of political icon, and among the traits most loathed by the Prophet, peace be upon him, of Persian rulers was that of *shahanshah*, that is, king of kings, which Islam regards as a despicable title for a mortal ruler to claim. So, Islam came as a revolution against both theological and political paganism, which is autocratic rule that places supreme authority not in the law but in the will and whim of an individual man. Islam introduced the authority of the *shari'a*, the meaning of which is that the rule of law is higher than that of the ruler, which is merely executive.

AFM: The ruler does not have supreme legislative authority, but then neither do the people, since this supreme legislative authority is found in divinely revealed texts.

---

[22] 'Abd al-Majid al-Najjar, *Khilafat al-insan bayna al-wahy wa-al-'aql: bahth fi jadaliyyat al-nass wa'l-'aql wa'l-waqi'* (Beirut: Dar al-Gharb al-Islami, 1987). See the English translation: 'Abd al-Majid al-Najjar, *The Vicegerency of Man, Between Revelation and Reason: A Critique of the Dialectic of the Text, Reason, and Reality*, translated by Aref T. Atari (Herndon, VA: International Institute of Islamic Thought, 2000).

PHILOSOPHICAL-THEOLOGICAL DIALOGUES 197

RG: This legislative authority belongs to the people who believe in the *shariʿa* and who will create a jurisprudence in accord with it. This is not the jurisprudence made by the people and scholars as it is set in light of *shariʿa*, because mankind is not an original ruler but rather a deputy of God. Hence, mankind acquires fixed rights that are derived from God, who granted them to mankind, and these fixed rights are what prohibit dictatorship.

AFM: But in my view this is not the only question. You just said a short while ago that the legitimate law is the law that issues from a people that believe in Islamic legitimacy.

RG: This is when we speak about an Islamic government as one whose laws are legislated by Muslim jurists and who formulate them in accordance with the *shariʿa*, that is, supreme Islamic and political values.

AFM: But in the case of a people or nation in which not all of the members believe in *shariʿa* and in which not all citizens aim at legislation in accordance with the spirit of the *shariʿa*, is this law legitimate?

RG: It is not called a legitimate law when legislating does not occur within the framework of *shariʿa*,[23] but rather a rational judgment [*hukm al-ʿaql*]. I took this notion from Ibn Khaldun, who divides governance into that of nature, reason, or the Islamic caliphate. Rational governance is the rule of a group of rational people that adheres to justice but is not derived from the Islamic *shariʿa*. In Ibn Khaldun's writings, he said that the main difference between rational governance and governance by the divine law or the caliphate is that both provide for justice and welfare in this world, but only the latter provides for human welfare and happiness in the next world.

AFM: But what about a society that is pluralist in its values and trends, like Tunisia today?

RG: Tunisia is a Muslim country and may not legislate that which contradicts Islam, particularly as it rules over a people the vast majority of whom are Muslim. So the foundational principle is that of not adopting any legislation repugnant to Islam.

---

[23] In Arabic, the common word for "legitimate" in the politico-legal sense is *sharʿi*, and the word for "legitimacy" is *sharʿiyya*. These are obviously derived from same root as *shariʿa* in the sense of the divinely revealed law (as opposed to other words for law, like *qanun*). Thus in this passage, Ghannouchi is referring to "legitimate" (*sharʿi*) and "legislation" (*tashriʿ*) as defined by the revealed law, the *shariʿa*, even though in modern Arabic the term *sharʿiyya* as "legitimacy" is used more broadly in the context of legal, political, and constitutional legitimacy.

198   ON MUSLIM DEMOCRACY

AFM: It *cannot*, or it *may* not?

RG: The principle is that it cannot.

AFM: That is, the law can be struck down?

RG: And the Constitutional Court may annul it as being contradictory to the constitution.

AFM: So whatever the Tunisian Constitutional Court declares is in accord with *shari'a* or Islam?

RG: The premise is that the Constitutional Court adheres to Islam and does not allow the passage of a law if it is not in accord with the *shari'a*.

AFM: And the members of this court also understand their role in this way?

RG: Supposedly.

AFM: So how are these two ideas compatible? First, the idea that the nation can either accept its status as God's vicegerent on Earth and its adherence to Islam and *shari'a*, or the path of unbelief and injustice. How is that compatible with the ideas of pluralism and toleration? That is, how are the ideas of pluralism and toleration of those who do not choose Islam compatible with the obligation to judge according to *shari'a* collectively?

RG: No law is of any value if forcibly imposed on people. If the public culture of a society is not an Islamic one, laws have no value when they are imposed from the top down and do not fall on receptive groups. Laws must fall on the appropriate, receptive ground while originating from the bottom up. Accordingly, we speak of a Muslim society that is eager to have its laws and regulations in tune with its faith and conscience and does not expect the issuance of contradictory laws. A democratic country does not anticipate the issuance of laws that shock public opinion.

      For example, when Essebsi considered changing the inheritance laws, he gave a directive, formed a committee, and directed its members to develop this law in light of equality between the sexes and in a way that does not create a conflict with public opinion, that is, Islam. Hence, any development of a law must take into consideration that it is a law for a Muslim people.

AFM: Well, for example, today Tunisian women have the right to marry non-Muslim men?

RG: It should be if Islam's intentions and scripture allow it, but if they do not, then it is anti-Islamic, and in such a case, there needs to be

PHILOSOPHICAL-THEOLOGICAL DIALOGUES 199

consensus among Islamic jurists on whether or not it is permissible, as there are differing opinions on the matter. I, for example, am a member of the European Fatwa Council, and I remember that a woman who had embraced Islam came to ask for our opinion on continuing to be with her husband, who had not also converted to Islam. The matter confused us, since in Islam a Muslim woman cannot initiate a marriage with a non-Muslim, but as her marriage had already occurred prior to her embracing of Islam, then what should the fatwa be? So in order for this marriage, which had produced children, not to be dissolved and torn apart, we issued a fatwa that she remain in the marriage as long as she had hope that one day, through her encouragement and example, her husband might embrace Islam as well if he was not hostile to Islam. So in essence, she was giving him an indefinite grace period to do so. But there were jurists like Shaykh Hasan al-Turabi and others who have the response that Islam's provisions are not clear and straightforward [*sariha*] enough in this area. For example, the original texts differentiated between religions of the Book and pagan marriages, and this had great bearing on the matter but leaves uncertainty about it. So it was not clear whether or not we were in consensus, and hence the Constitutional Court can look into the matter and decide accordingly, as it is one concerning Islamic values and principles, not pure jurisprudence.

AFM: But we are talking about texts and not just values.

RG: We are talking about texts, but they have been concerned with instilling values and did not delve into particulars. This is why we need jurisprudence, as it interreacts with the society and the political system throughout changes in time and place. Thus, Islamic jurisprudence is pluralistic and not unitary.

AFM: The right of *ijtihad* in jurisprudence is not only for jurists but belongs to the whole system, so what is binding and obligatory in the *shari'a*?

RG: He who issues a fatwa must be a jurist and knowledgeable in the realm of jurisprudence, competent to provide an opinion that is based on the interpretation of scripture. This is a specialized science. Yet one may give a fatwa for himself, as at a certain point a person may need to do so for himself. But when issuing a fatwa for a society and a state, you must be specialized in this, and this is why members of the Constitutional Court must be specialists.

200 ON MUSLIM DEMOCRACY

AFM: But today in Tunisia the members of the Constitutional Court are experts in the positive law, not Islamic law.

RG: Yes, there exists a statutory law, and there are experts in positive law, the *shari'a*, and the interpretation of scripture. This is a specialized expertise, and not all people are capable of such interpretation.

AFM Where are the *mujtahid*s and experts in jurisprudence in Tunisia today?

RG: We have a university and women and men of law and *shari'a*.

AFM: From al-Zaytuna?

RG: Yes, Zaytuna. We nominated a jurist for the Constitutional Court, which consists of twelve judges, four of which are chosen by the parliament. So we recommended some experts in the positive law and in the *shari'a* who are from and who are still at al-Zaytuna.

AFM: So Ennahda nominated judges who are experts in positive law or the Islamic *shari'a*?

RG: The matter is still under deliberation.

AFM: But they are not from Ennahda?

RG: They must be independents and cannot be members of any party.

AFM: I have a question on the relationship of *shari'a* to the restriction of the freedom of a Muslim people, the ruler, and the political system to engage in political or legislative activity. Should the sovereignty of the *shari'a* and its restriction of legislation and politics be seen as pre-political, that is, as something known and existing before the creation of political institutions, or is the authority of *shari'a* something that is discovered within political activity? In other words, does *shari'a* constrain politics, or does politics create *shari'a*?

For example, by comparison, there are systems within which constitutions and human rights declarations attempt to set a specific and limited space for politics and legislation. For example, they might say that congress or parliament never has the freedom or right to permit torture, that the separation of church and state means that congress may not adopt an official religion. We might say that these are pre-political constraints on the sphere of politics and legislation rather than principles that are discovered and created through political activity.

RG: Political action is of course based on the law and the constitution, and political parties are formed accordingly. Otherwise, they may not be licensed. Similarly, parliamentary legislation is subject to conditions

PHILOSOPHICAL-THEOLOGICAL DIALOGUES   201

established by the constitution unless the constitution itself is changed. There are also unamendable constitutional provisions, like Tunisia being a country whose language is Arabic and whose religion is Islam. As Tunisia is a civil state, the parliament has bounded itself, thrown away the key, and vowed that this would never change unless a revolution occurred and did away with all that which has been established. Accordingly, legislating is bound by prior principles and values, or precommitment devices, most notably the provisions on Tunisia's language, religion, and civil status.

AFM: But even these kinds of apparently clear provisions may require some elucidation, and so is it fair to say that political action then produces this meaning and is not something that is known prior to this political action?

RG: In these cases, the constitution explains the meaning of "Islamic," "civil," and that the national language is Arabic in that it cannot be Amazigh, and subsequent statutory law comes later to give details.

AFM: For example, American law might prohibit torture ["cruel and unusual punishment"], but what counts as torture? It is the Supreme Court that decides this. Today in America there are many people who regard the use of solitary confinement in prison as horrific torture, including almost all experts in psychology. But so far, the Supreme Court has not accepted this view and has not declared solitary confinement to be unconstitutional and thus impermissible in the US. And so the principle might be written down in the Constitution, but the interpretation of it is something that [is not pre-political but rather] emerges from political decisions. Now, is the situation the same with regard to *shari'a* [and political life]?

RG: For you in the US, the Declaration of Independence states that mankind has God-given rights that may not be touched, denied, or stripped from him.

AFM: But the Declaration of Independence was not law or a constitution, and we know that the American Constitution, as the highest law, preserved slavery. However, as an aside, it is true that Abraham Lincoln, as he was attempting to create a principle for forbidding slavery, did say in many of his speeches and writings that the supreme law in America was not the Constitution but rather the Declaration of Independence. Indeed, he claimed that the foundation of the Constitution was not just the will of the people but also the principles

202 ON MUSLIM DEMOCRACY

found in the Declaration of Independence, which were a kind of law or will, higher than the Constitution. The American Constitution as a temporal, statutory law contained within it all kinds of concessions to reality, whereas the Declaration of Independence reflected better the natural law.

RG: "Natural" is, in fact, "religious," as these are divine rights.

AFM: But we know that those who wrote the Declaration of Independence, like Thomas Jefferson and Benjamin Franklin, were not orthodox Christians. Their theology, you might say, was more like that of Ibn Sina or Aristotle.

RG: They were not speaking of only nature, but of a divine law with both divine and natural rights.

AFM: But what are the attributes of this Creator according to them? In the view of most historians, Thomas Jefferson, for example, did not share the theology of Protestants like Luther or the Anglican Church, but had a more philosophical [Deist] theology, perhaps similar to that of Ibn Sina or Aristotle, for example, with the view that God does not know particulars.

RG: For us, the *shari'a* gives the *umma* its identity, as we are not merely Tunisians or people who happen to live in this area, but Muslims. So if we change, it would be similar to a revolution in identity and essence, and the transfer from one system to another.

We were part of an Islamic system and became part of a non-Islamic one. The *shari'a* set certain standards and values, but these are not in themselves law in the modern sense, as they are rites of worship, ethics, and ultimate goals. There has been confusion between the idea of *shari'a* and positive law [*qanun*], on one hand, and between the *shari'a* and Islamic jurisprudence [*fiqh*], on the other. The idea of *shari'a* itself is higher than the human practice of jurisprudence [*fiqh*]; the latter is derived from the former. Furthermore, the *shari'a* contains objectives and values, and some similar texts are interpreted according to this more general perspective agreed upon by Muslims, because while some texts are clear and perspicuous in meaning, others are unclear or ambiguous, and therefore some revealed texts might seem on the surface to contradict each other.

AFM: But there are, of course, some clear texts with a firm, decisive meaning.

RG: Yes, these are a part of the *shari'a*, although they are relatively few. These texts are fixed in their source and clear in their meaning. They

PHILOSOPHICAL-THEOLOGICAL DIALOGUES   203

represent the general framework of the *shari'a*, and the practice of jurisprudence [*fiqh*] operates within this framework.

AFM: And what is this framework?

RG: Consensus around what Muslims have all agreed upon.

AFM: But can there be disagreement even about the framework itself?

RG: There can be partial disagreement, but Islam states that that which is permissible is clear and that which is impermissible is clear. So there are matters of clarity, like Islamic creed, most obviously that God is one, not two or three. Similarly, we cannot say that alcohol or lying is permissible.

AFM: So there is a consensus in Islam that wine is forbidden, but in Tunisian law it is legal.

RG: This is a different matter and has to do with the existing conditions being suitable for prohibiting wine and other alcohol or not. In America, alcohol was prohibited in 1920 but was allowed ten years later. Such was the government's assessment of whether society was ready for it or not. Even those who drink alcohol in Tunisia know that Islam prohibits it. Drinking is one thing, but asserting that it is permitted in Islam means that a person has gone beyond the realm of Islam. Yet people say they know it is prohibited but that they are addicted to it, while others say it pacifies them like a medicine, or they give other excuses. But all of these so-called reasons are nothing but chatter, as what matters is to acknowledge the Islamic standard of value, which determines what is permissible and what is forbidden, and then act upon each in accordance with your individual capability and circumstances.

AFM: In my opinion, among the most important contributions of the theories in *Public Freedoms* is the legislative authority accorded the people. The people do not just have the right of consultation, like in older theories, and not just the right to choose and supervise the ruler. Moreover, the nation's legislative authority is not just over worldly matters, like what classical Islamic political theory referred to as *qanun* [legal edicts issued by the ruler] or *siyasa* [discretionary policy judgments], but also over matters of Islamic jurisprudence in religious matters.

In your view, what are the circumstances or necessary conditions for us to speak about the authority of the nation or the people such that the rulings or laws it produces can be referred to as Islamic rulings, or part of the *shari'a*?

204 ON MUSLIM DEMOCRACY

RG: There are matters that are of human awareness to the extent that the knowledgeable and the ignorant, the educated and the uneducated, the expert and the common person agree upon. Things that all are knowledgeable of or ignorant of. So, a revolution occurring against a tyrannical and oppressive ruler is a matter all agree upon. Similarly, all Muslims agree on the Palestinian cause and that Trump is unqualified to grant that which he does not own to others who do not have a right to it. So, there are issues that are so clear that all agree upon them regardless of their levels of education, while there are other technical ones that require specialization and expertise. Therefore, the *umma* participates in *ijtihad* and legislation within the political realm, and the highest level of consensus [*ijma'*] is in the parliamentary elections and referendums on war and peace that affect all. Exceptional events like revolutions and the establishment of sovereignty are matters that must not only rely on the consensus of the elite, but require the general public for legitimacy. Questions of national security possibly belong here as well, as these are great matters that the public is invested in. Politics is inescapable here because consensus about them must be discovered, unlike, say, issues like the basic pillars of Islam, about which there is no disagreement or change. But in politics, consensus is mutable and what people may agree upon in a certain era may change. In Tunisia, for example, jurists at one point agreed on the religious prohibition against taking up French citizenship, as this was an assault on Tunisia's Islamic character. It was a matter that jurists, politicians, and the general public agreed upon to the extent that one who possessed both nationalities could not be buried in an Islamic cemetery, as he had left Islam by taking French citizenship. But, obviously, this consensus no longer holds.

AFM: In the traditional political theory of Islam, that is, the theory of *al-siyasa al-shar'iyya*, there is an important distinction between two kinds of law: *fiqh* law, which belongs to the jurists and represents the *shari'a* and that which does not change much, or as rapidly, in Islam, and *siyasa* law, or the law of the sultan or ruler, which can change often and does not represent the continuity of Islam and the Islamic identity of the society. So *fiqh* covers personal status, contracts, marriage and divorce, inheritance, property, transactions, and so on, and the authority of the ruler covers more worldly, transient affairs like public policy, foreign relations, and decisions over public order and

PHILOSOPHICAL-THEOLOGICAL DIALOGUES   205

security. There is theoretically a distinction between the authority of the jurists and the authority of rulers [in this classical theory]. But in the modern state there is a unity of legal authority, a kind of legal monism, without a distinction between, say, the legitimacy of the laws of marriage and personal status [and all the laws based on *fiqh*] and the legitimacy of laws on finance or others that are not based on *fiqh*. Again, there is a unity of laws and codification based on the authority of the state. Now, in modern Islamic thought, is there a difference between legislation and codification in areas on which religious texts speak and about which there were classical *fiqh* rules, and legislation in more neutral matters for religion, like whether we drive on the left or right side of the road? In my view, there is a very important question about the Islamic state—namely, whether it is imagined that every law must somehow be in accordance with Islam, or only specific laws that are important from a religious perspective and which the texts of revelation speak to in some way.

RG: All laws must conform to, or at the very least not blatantly contradict, the *shari'a*. As jurisprudence itself is divided into that of worship and that of social relations, the former is supported by detailed texts, while the latter is treated in general terms. Hence, change and *ijtihad* are present in the jurisprudence of social relations, but not in worship. How we pray, fast, perform *hajj*, and marry are matters that scripture has described in detail. Whereas matters like sales, international relations, and wars were not. Issues of how to worship God are treated in detail because reason cannot arrive at knowledge of how God wants to be worshipped. But the jurisprudence of transactions deals with the general sphere, not the private and personal, like with marriage, for example.

AFM: But doesn't marriage concern both the private and the public? For example, the prohibition on polygyny in Tunisia is both a private and public matter and was justified on both private and public grounds.

RG: This is all due to being influenced by the intrusive atheist French culture, and we accepted it pragmatically, as we do not view it as a core issue. Polygyny is not obligatory in Islam, but rather merely permitted. That which is permissible in Islamic legal theory allows the ruler to regulate on the premise of restricting that which is permissible.

AFM: Like the prohibition on slavery, for example, when the Tunisian ruler Ahmad Bey outlawed it.

206 ON MUSLIM DEMOCRACY

RG: The percentage of men practicing polygyny in Tunisia before it was banned was less than one in a thousand. So it wasn't really a burning social issue. The real issue has to do with the question of the place of genuine *ijtihad* within the jurisprudence of social relations in which a small number of texts were revealed of a general nature. So the question at stake is political jurisprudence [*al-fiqh al-siyasi*], the jurisprudence of the state and the realization of justice in the courts. Would a unitary judiciary with a single code of justice or a plural system of courts and adjudication realize justice better? These are important questions of argument and judgment [*masa'il ijtihadiyya*], but the important thing by which various positions are evaluated is the realization of justice and consultation. How they are realized is not a fixed principle of religion but is left to reason, discernment [*ijtihad*], the benefits of all human experience in achieving justice, consultation, intellectual progress, and peace. Consider by comparison the question of the best way to defend Islam. Is it through jihad, or the defense of its principles, or the creation of educational and university research centers? Expansionary, or aggressive, jihad belonged to a closed world, but today the world is open and so whoever talks about "opening" [*fath*, the word used for military conquest] France or Europe is talking about opening doors that are already open.

AFM: I would like us to talk a little about the question of jurists, *mujtahids* and experts in jurisprudence in an Islamic state. A role for this kind of expertise is a pillar of all modern Islamic constitutional thought, including your own writings. But when we turn to something like the post-2014 constitutional order in Tunisia, how can we consider, for example, the supreme Constitutional Court in Tunisia to be akin to a committee of senior scholars in the theory of Islamic governance?

RG: We sought the assistance of the supreme or Constitutional Court to interpret scripture in accordance with the verse "If you disagree on a matter, refer it to God and the Messenger, if you believe in God and the Last Day" [Qur'an 4:59]. Yet neither God nor the Messenger is available to us to consult directly, so "refer to God and the Messenger" refers to consulting the Qur'an and the Sunna if there are people who disagree on some issue. But this is not a simple matter, and so it requires turning to jurists who understand its interpretation. In essence, it is transferring an individual matter to an institutional one. Muslims have had shortcomings in translating Islamic values to the institutional level, although this is necessary for understanding an absolute text, particularly as the scholars themselves often disagree on matters of interpretation. This is an area where Western thought has been more developed, in establishing institutions that translate authoritatively its political thought. For example, consider the very general and abstract value of the authority of the people. What does this mean in practice? If there were no elections or parliament, how would the people govern? The authority to interpret texts must also exist. Otherwise, how will they transform into public opinion and legitimate authority? Thus, these values require the existence of institutions.

AFM: In the ideal Islamic regime we can speak about two institutions: a legislative assembly with deputies elected by the people, and a committee of scholars—*mujtahids*, experts in the *shari'a*. So there are two sources of legislation: that which comes from the will of the people and that which comes from the knowledge of the scholars. So there can be a conflict between these two forms of law, and in this ideal Islamic regime, one of the two must ultimately have supremacy over the other.

RG: The referral to experts, jurists, and judges may be before or after the formation of legislation. The draft law must be sent to parliament and presented to experts who would state whether or not this law, which was drafted by the government, is consistent with the constitution and applicable laws. The council would then decide upon the matter and the government would need to modify the law prior to referring it to parliament. This process can also occur after the issuance of the law having been discussed in the council and the Constitutional Court, to see whether it does or does not concur with the constitution, and in the case of the latter, it will be returned to the council.

As we possess a temporary transitional Constitutional Court, its opinion is binding, and if it decides that a law is in opposition to the constitution, the council must reconsider it. The Constitutional Court's work is not political but rather technical, as it views laws according to technical standards, not political or value-based ones.

AFM: So you imagine in the ideal Islamic regime that there isn't competition between the representatives of the people and the representatives of the texts of jurisprudence, but rather cooperation and unity between them?

208   ON MUSLIM DEMOCRACY

RG: The premise is that there exists cohesion and interoperability among the state's apparatuses, yet state institutions have levels and hierarchies.

AFM: There is a chapter in *Public Freedoms* about the foundation of the state and the constitutional principles informing how a Muslim community can constitute the state and what the limits of its constituent freedoms are. If there is an ideal Islamic order and there is a committee of religious scholars with some authority, should they be regarded as representatives of the people, and thus the people as sovereign in this state, or are the scholars representatives of God and the texts of revelation?

RG: The Islamic system is closer to a parliamentary one and is not an executive authority. So, the government is a tool for implementing that which the parliament legislates. The entire process occurs in parliament, and the Constitutional Court itself is considered part of the legislative authority that assists parliament. Members of parliament are elected officials who derive their authority from the people rather than from their knowledge. So, they are not experts. For example, they may be elected because they are close to the people or tribal leaders and thus are representative of the people. But when transforming that into law, they seek the assistance of experts. I regard these elected members of parliament as the elite or "the holders of authority," as referred to in the Qur'an [4:59] and Islamic tradition; if they decide on anything regarding the nation, their decisions must be accepted, as each member represents part of the population. If elections are valid and not manipulated, then these MPs are in fact the rulers and supreme authority, and when they agree on a matter, it must be accepted by the people. This is because the consensus of "the holders of authority" in Islam is in fact the consensus of the people. If they decide on war or on peace, their decision must be carried out.

       We are the bloc [Ennahda] that strongly defended the parliamentary system in opposition to the dominant tradition in Tunisia, which is very strongly presidential. Bourguiba's norms were strongly presidential, as was much of the history of governance in Tunisia. So we wanted a definitive break with this history. I once discussed a matter with Yusuf al-Qaradawi, who said that the parliamentary system is similar to the Islamic one. The important point is that the Islamic experience is closer to a federal system, as a caliph's authority was for the

PHILOSOPHICAL-THEOLOGICAL DIALOGUES   209

most part symbolic but each province or administrative region had its own conditions and the head of government there enjoyed executive authority.

AFM: This discussion of the limits of legal authority and legitimacy brings us back to the central theme of your thought, modern Islamic political thought in general, and our discussion: the idea of mankind as God's deputy or caliph on earth. On my reading, this concept does not apply only to the *umma* at large but also to individual believers, and it thus raises fascinating and complex questions about the obligation to obey the law and the right to civil disobedience. For example, let us take a passage from your book *Democracy and Human Rights in Islam*:

> Considering that God is the Absolute Sovereign—that supreme, indivisible, and exclusive authority belongs to God; that God's sovereignty is expressed through revealed texts, the Qur'an and Sunna; that the community, which has vicegerency on earth, is collectively responsible for upholding God's Law and that the ruler is nothing more than a mechanism, among others, to fulfill this duty, there are certain limits to state authority with regards to legislation and policymaking, particularly in matters pertaining to the economy, culture, and education. Here lies a major point of distinction with the modern-day secular state and its institutions, which know no bounds to their authority and stand as the supreme arbiter over right and wrong, and good and evil. Justice is, then, its law and whatever it decides. Thus, if it chooses to destroy a people and loot its riches—even by spreading drugs among them or through wars of extermination—or decides to pollute the sources of livelihood on the entire planet, its decisions are legitimate as long as they have emanated from its institutions, and no citizen has the right to refuse to abide by them. However, in an Islamically based political system, it is not just a right of every citizen, but a duty, to weigh all state policies against higher norms, and to refuse to obey any policies that contradict the supreme power in the state, namely, divine texts.[24]

---

[24] Ghannushi, *al-Dimuqratiyya wa ḥuquq al-insan fi'l-Islam*, 20–21.

210 ON MUSLIM DEMOCRACY

This strikes me as an extremely important and attractive idea. If the covenant of vicegerency is the theological foundation of popular sovereignty in modern Islamic thought, can we therefore say that this sovereignty does not only belong to the people, or the *umma*, collectively, but to each individual, as so we might speak about a "sovereign believer"?

RG: True. This is based on the notion that mankind as an individual is the vicegerent, not just the *umma*. The meaning of vicegerency is that man is directly responsible before God as an individual and will be questioned by Him. It is not the people collectively that come before God, but every individual. It is not the people collectively that God will ask about their deeds, and it is not the right of an individual to say he did something because the *umma* or the collective did it. It is the duty of the individual to speak the truth, to bear witness to God and to the truth, and to guide to it, as well as to denounce the forbidden to the extent of his capacities, even if it is only in his heart, like when he says to himself, "O Lord, this is wrong." This is a basic issue in Islam, that each individual is God's vicegerent on earth and is responsible before God.

AFM: After Trump entered the White House, he tried to ban the citizens of some Muslim countries from entering the United States. There were widespread demonstrations, indeed from the beginning of his assumption of the office, and this was based on a similar idea of collective and individual responsibility. What is the difference between legitimate civil disobedience in the defense of the rights of others and unjust civil disobedience?

RG: This is where the need for God arises, as we may not forsake Him in times of knowledge because when times of darkness reign, we will need His guidance to show us the path of righteousness.

AFM: Okay, but in America there are also those who say that following the word of God requires them not only to oppose same-sex marriage or migration of Latin Americans to America but also to resist and defy such laws.

RG: We consider it following one's whims, as if they had set their personal wishes aside and were true in seeking the immortal truth, they would find it.

AFM: And is this search always superior to the civil law?

PHILOSOPHICAL-THEOLOGICAL DIALOGUES 211

RG: Yes. Mankind cannot forsake the Almighty, as his mind cannot answer all of our questions.

AFM: In American Christianity and the history of Christian theology on the relationship to morality and natural law, there is the view that God does not will for anything other than universal human love, without regard to citizenship or other characteristics. But of course there is this other particularistic tendency to see America as having a special, exceptional status in the world and in the eyes of God.

RG: Islam states that the entire nation cannot agree on wrongdoing, and similarly neither can humanity. If we respect the Declaration of Human Rights, then the freedom of movement would be guaranteed for mankind, and I would not need permission to travel anywhere I wanted. The law on human rights is but one of many other rights; yet due to mankind's tyrannical behavior and aggression, we have such barriers as exist nowadays. It is not the United Nations system that grants non-criminal Mexicans the right to enter American soil. But America does not respect the right to free movement nor the right to a clean environment. Accordingly, the problem is with mankind's selfishness, not with principles and values.

AFM: But is contemporary international human rights law independent of God?

RG: It is drawn from God, as those who worded the Universal Declaration of Human Rights included a number of religious members who drew on the wording from all religions. On the other hand, the human experience is drawn from religions, with religion as the foundation of the law. Without religion, there would have never been either law or the state.

AFM: Even, let's say, radically atheist states like the former Soviet Union?

RG: Yes, despite its claims. But its avowed atheism is also why it was shorter-lived than other empires, as it combatted religion. It did not try to restrain itself through neutrality toward religion, but waged war against it. After all, a law that opposes morality is no law at all.

AFM: But as you know, today there are serious disagreements between people about the status of religion in the law.

RG: Yes, there are differences among human beings. This is why if coexistence among mankind is required, a law is decreed, and it remains the right of the individual to decide whether it is a just or an unjust one.

212   ON MUSLIM DEMOCRACY

AFM: In Islam supposedly all state policies are meant to be weighed by the scales of the *shari'a*. So the judgment of the justness or not of a law is not merely subjective. But today in Tunis there are many laws that do not even claim to be based on considerations of the *shari'a*. Are citizens meant to judge their justness based on their conscience or sense of justice, or the *shari'a*?

RG: They must abide by the law which is applied to a group of people, but I believe that I have the right to say it is unjust. But there is always a law that is applied to all, so I respect it, yet work toward changing, not breaking, it, from the standpoint of respecting the principle of group coexistence. There is a collective interest in not disobeying every unjust law when other possibilities exist for changing it that I respect.

AFM: Can we compare this to Kant's political philosophy in "What is Enlightenment?", in which he says that it is the duty of persons acting outside of official posts to never forswear their freedom of conscience both in matters of justice and in religious doctrine?

RG: There is the right to conscience and the right to abstain from doing something that contradicts with one's conscience.

AFM: In America there were many who defied the draft to fight in Vietnam on grounds of conscience who were imprisoned.

RG: The right to abstain. But when there exists a social force seeking to corrupt or undermine society, there may be constraints, as Islam is anti-sedition [*fitna*]. Hence, one must choose the lesser evil by following the position of the collective even against one's own conscience on the premise that "necessities make the forbidden permissible."

AFM: In my opinion the question of how far morality can be said to govern the political is crucial. You see this as a recurring theme in Western political philosophy, with debates between moralists like Kant and realists like Machiavelli. On my reading it is also one of the great values of Islamic political thought, which puts an emphasis on the realities of power that are a condition for the realization of rules, as well as how to think about exceptional situations and the need for judgment and prudence [rather than just rules] in balancing between various harms.

RG: This is where disciplined judgment [*ijtihad*] comes in, that is, how to apply the general principles of justice, brotherhood, and *shura* to particular and partial realities.

AFM: This kind of judgment is prone to error and does not admit of perfection or infallibility.

PHILOSOPHICAL-THEOLOGICAL DIALOGUES 213

RG: Yes, errors will occur. But Islam encourages all efforts of truth-seeking [*ijtihad*] if the intention is pure. Islam states that if one does his best to apply general principles to specific realities and acts in a correct value-based manner, whether committing mistakes or not, then he or she is rewarded. Of course, such *ijtihad* may be prone to error, as it is not based on clear-cut rules. The Prophet, peace be upon him, says that Adam's descendants do not just err but err frequently, and yet must still take a stance on matters and must judge on their own.

AFM: There are many areas on which there is disagreement on whether they violate or agree with the law. Does *ijtihad* continue in these circumstances?

RG: Here one compares between benefit and detriment, or among detriments, and chooses the least harmful.

AFM: And where are the limits of "commanding the right and forbidding the wrong" for ordinary citizens?

RG: This is a topic on which Muslim jurists of this time have disagreed. Both Sunnis and Shi'a have disagreed among themselves on the limitations of commanding the right and forbidding the wrong. Yet it is available for every Muslim to condemn the wrong through speech at least, in a reasonable way, as it is Muslims' duty to do so. As for condemning it physically, "with the hand," for example, suppose there is a wine house that the state has not shut down, and a citizen takes it upon himself to shut it down instead. Most Sunni jurists say that denouncing and opposing wrongdoing by the hand, through physical force, is the duty of the state, not the citizens. The latter may do so through words or even in their own hearts. For example, with the boycott of Israeli goods, the individual is not forcibly shutting down shops but is simply declining to shop in them. The same applies to strikes. It is not the right of citizens to take the law into their own hands, as this may cause more harm than the wrong action itself. In a democracy, there can be changes of government and not just one single permanent government, and so I believe forbidding wrongdoing "by the hand" is the responsibility of the state and that our role is to criticize the state, not to take its place outside of the law.

If a law is unjust, we do not forcibly prevent its implementation, but rather work toward changing it, as the government's mission is to implement laws and we do not try to take the place of the state. Apart from the justness of any individual law, the continuity of the

214   ON MUSLIM DEMOCRACY

government is a religious, humanitarian, and national interest that must be preserved.

In Egypt, when Faraj Foda[25]—may God have mercy on his soul—was killed and the group that killed him was brought to justice, they said they applied the *shari'a*, as the state had failed in preventing this man from attacking Islam and denouncing it. In Tunisia, when Ben Ali was persecuting us in 1992, the government would have him speak to the masses during Ramadan and badmouth the members of Ennahda as a justification for oppressing us. Instead of listening to an imam during Ramadan who would educate people about their religion, they would bring Faraj Foda to insult Ennahda when it was not his right to do so, as the regime he supported was a tyrannical one.

But the important point is that the Gama'a Islamiyya in Egypt said they carried out an Islamic ruling and so Shaykh Muhammed al-Ghazali was brought forward to testify and he said it was not Foda's right to attack Islam like that, but that it was the state's duty to prevent him from doing so, as the Egyptian constitution states that the *shari'a* is the main source of legislation. But when asked if his killers should be punished for carrying out a duty that the state had failed to do, he said he did not know. He said that Foda and the state were both at fault, and left the matter open.

Freedom, Pluralism, and Toleration

AFM: I would like to shift our focus slightly in order to go into more detail on the problem of public authority and pluralism. A common view in modern Islamic thought is the idea of freedom and emancipation. The common Islamist view is that Islam came to liberate mankind from authoritarianism, but also from itself, from its own passions, errors, wrongdoing, mistaken ideas, et cetera. This is one idea. But a second idea is that of freedom of belief and conscience. And there are some very strong statements to this effect in *Public Freedoms*, for example on page 44:

[25] Farag Foda was an Egyptian professor, writer, and human rights activist who was assassinated on June 8, 1992, by members of the al-Gama'a al-Islamiyya after being accused of apostasy by a committee of scholars at al-Azhar.

PHILOSOPHICAL-THEOLOGICAL DIALOGUES 215

Freedom of Conviction and Its Roots: The aim here is for the individual to freely choose his own belief system without any outside pressure. The *shari'a* guarantees this freedom of conviction and forbids all methods of compulsion. At the same time, it spares no effort to highlight the necessity of presenting the truth, of establishing the proofs of the creed with certainty, and holding individuals and the community responsible for maintaining and defending it. Moreover, it forbids those who have embraced it from stoking discord [*fitna*], and it urges them to make every effort to subvert the evil ploys of their opponents.

So, again, we have two ideas here. The first idea is that there is a single true conception of human freedom and happiness. This idea holds that Islam implies worship of God, and that the Islamic way of life is the only rational one for humans to choose. Islam's system of action, worship, and creed is the sole path to human liberation and perfection. This conception is thus the foundation for political life. The second idea is that each individual is responsible for herself and is free in matters of conscience and way of life, and that there is absolutely no room for violence or coercion.

So the question is this. Let us go back to your above statement about the role of the state in making virtue easy and vice difficult. Is it necessary in a well-ordered society for the majority of the people in such a society to understand and to accept this theoretical foundation of political life? And is it necessary for people who live within this system to agree that it is the proper role for politics and governance to perfect life and to assist people in becoming virtuous, in living a religious life—a Muslim life? Or, rather, is it not necessary for the masses of citizens to comprehend and agree with this concept [of the purpose and role of political life]?

RG: There needs to be a general order that is based upon public opinion, as if none of the sort existed, the regime would be authoritarian. A regime cannot be based on tyranny and coercion, and if we exclude the latter, it means that an Islamic system can only be applied to Muslims. The *shari'a* does not chase down people so as to rule them, but it is the people who seek its justice.

AFM: So first we need a Muslim society, a Muslim community, and then after that a state and system of rule. But you said that a system or

216 ON MUSLIM DEMOCRACY

government or state is what is required in the first place to attain such a Muslim society or community.

RG: The relationship is one of reciprocity, as an Islamic regime can only be established over a Muslim society. But the Islamic system serves a Muslim society, instills its convictions, provides services, and sustains the Muslim society. But when one lives beyond this system, one will be in a state of anguish and worry like a fish out of water, as the regime is at one end and one is at another.

AFM: Did your experience in London represent for you a certain freedom after anxiety and worry?

RG: Definitely, or at least to a certain extent. People are prone to flee tyranny to freedom regardless of the latter's Islamic or non-Islamic framework. Had the Tunisian society then been a Muslim society, I would have preferred to stay there. But when a Muslim lives in a non-Muslim society yet has some rights, it becomes a civilized society, like that of the UK, but not like that of Burma, where the Muslim minority is ruled over by a dictatorship. It is also similar to non-Muslim minorities who lived throughout history in Islamic countries with no trouble but were still considered a minority.

AFM: But there is something lacking in such a life and the place of a community or individual who does not choose this conception of happiness, perfection, or virtue in a Muslim society. You concede that this can be a free decision to choose another path, another conception [of the good], or another ultimate end for happiness in life. And so what is their place in a perfectionist Muslim society?

RG: There is public life and there is private life. Islam respects people's private lives in how they think, what they believe, and what they do in their homes. There are public affairs related to the law and private ones related to preaching to people with "good-willed exhortation" [Qur'an 16:125]. The state has no business regulating how people think or what they believe in, as it should only monitor public matters and provide security and cohesion for its people.

AFM: But in any event, the methods of governance and politics are violent ones by nature. Even education is coercive insofar as an educational system might be mandatory and must identify the limits of freedom of conscience. For example, in an ideal well-ordered Islamic society, is there space for teaching Darwin's theory of evolution on the origins of man, or the theories of Einstein on the origins of the cosmos? That

PHILOSOPHICAL-THEOLOGICAL DIALOGUES 217

is, what is the role of politics and governance in educating, indeed creating, virtuous Muslim citizens?

RG: Western countries as per the French model do not consider themselves as reflecting public will, but rather as protectors and creators of it and of national identity. It is a dogmatic state [*dawla 'aqa'idiyya*], based on advancing the truth of a particular doctrine, not neutral. The Islamic model is far from the French one in that it is also a dogmatic state but at the same time an open one. So there may exist a multitude of legal systems within the Islamic state, as the historical ones contained courts for Jews. In Islam, there are courts that follow different legal schools, like the Hanafi and Maliki Schools that traditionally coexisted in Ottoman North Africa. But this is completely alien to modern states that have created a unitary legal code for all. During the Ottoman caliphate there was the so-called *millet* system, which allowed confessional communities self-governance, as well as many different courts and legal systems within the state itself. The USA has a similar system, although on a smaller scale than that of the Islamic civilization, as each of the states has its own legislative body. I wrote on education in *Public Freedoms in the Islamic State* that there may exist different educational systems within the Islamic state and not just one. So why do you wish to impose upon me a specific way of how to raise my child? In Denmark, trade unions have schools following their own educational system, where one follows a liberal method and another does not. So why are you insisting that I follow a specific one? There is no necessary perfect correspondence between law [*qanun*] and sovereignty in Islam, and many different legal systems may exist within one state, and it is not necessary that only one court exists.

AFM: So the conflict among them is only in the public sphere?

RG: The public sphere should not be controlled entirely by the state. There may exist a multitude of legal systems and educational schools where Christians, Jews, and Muslims each have their own but who are united in their protection of the nation under the banner of civil education.

AFM: What is the difference between this conception and the neutralist state?

RG: It is closer to the neutralist state than that of the Danish, French, Kemalist, Bourguibist, Iranian, or Saudi, which are all adamant about the state having a tight grasp on society, the economy, education, and law—which is a type of tyranny.

218   ON MUSLIM DEMOCRACY

AFM: The modern conception of the Islamic society and Islamic public order is about expanding possibilities for a variety of ways of life, not only religious ones but also materialist, secular ones?

RG: When taking a look at the historical Iraqi society of the ninth century, you find it as one open to all religions, sects, and philosophies. All sects used to hold debates at kings' courts on the existence of God and on matters at the core of religion without ending up in bloodshed.

AFM: Was this idea of radical pluralism present in the first printing of *Public Freedoms*? Was this conception there from the beginning rather than being a later development?

RG: It was from the beginning, along with the ideas of freedom of conscience and discussing apostasy.

AFM: At that time did you imagine that the kind of pluralism present in Tunisian society, that is, socialists, secularists, Muslims, et cetera, was a kind of permanent or temporary pluralism? In other words, was the acceptance of pluralism seen as a kind of concession from an ideal regime or the Islamic ideal, or was this a permanent acceptance?

RG: This is a main concept in our intellectual matrix. Pluralism is an ontological matter in that God willed it even in religion and even in denying the existence of God Himself. God says, "And had We willed, We would have created you all as one nation" [Qur'an 5:48]. That is, if God had willed, we could have all been of a single heart, a single path, a single religion. But instead God willed that we be free, which implies that we will differ, and God gave us reason and freedom, which also imply that we will disagree. The genius of this is how we may unite, and through our difference create unity and civilization. It is the role of our intelligence and reason to reach consensus and a common opinion, and the role of democracy to prepare for unity in the context of disagreement through the tools that democracy provides.

AFM: What kind of unity specifically do you have in mind?

RG: Unity of decision and the general will is like going into labor, which eventually gives birth to a general will among differences. We neither sacrifice difference nor fall into chaos and mayhem. So we achieve unity through our differences.

AFM: But at the time, Islam came to liberate all mankind from false ideas, correct?

PHILOSOPHICAL-THEOLOGICAL DIALOGUES 219

RG: The Qur'an is clear in showing that difference is a divine will. I also have an article on this entitled "The Dialectic of Unity and Difference."[26]

AFM: But every system or theory requires boundaries or limits of difference or disagreement—for example, the way in which we would draw a line at racist ideas. That is, every system of freedom and justice has a notion of both reasonable and unreasonable disagreement.

RG: Freedom does not mean that rights must negate themselves, as the right to freedom must not negate other freedoms and thus annul the notion of freedom itself. A freedom that does not eliminate freedom itself. And one who transgresses on the freedom of others is not free herself.

AFM: Does the right to individual freedom extend to the right to harm oneself?

RG: No, there is no such right.

AFM: But isn't rejecting Islam considered a type of harming oneself?

RG: It is a type of self-harm, but God gave mankind the right to do themselves injustice if they so choose. This denotes a difference between the ontological facet and that of rights. So, you have the right to choose between going to the mosque and to the pub, but it is your responsibility. Having been given the right does not mean that you are encouraged to do so, or that God is pleased with it, as God does not accept wrongdoing, but He does not prevent people from doing evil. God says, "God commands justice and charity and does not command immorality or evil." God has given mankind the ability to do what they will, whether steal, kill, oppress others, or harm the self, but He did state we must not do so and that He will punish us if we do.

AFM: Have your ideas about pluralism and respect for disagreement and for the other changed between that period and now, that is, since the 2011 revolution?

RG: In the realm of accepting inclusion and generalizing and expanding the notion of pluralism, human rights, and the rights of women, there is more acceptance of such ideals, and the application thereof has sustained these through the newly formulated constitution. We found no problem in accepting the freedoms demanded by secularists, like that of conscience, as we had established a basis for this years before.

[26] This volume, Chapter 2.

220 ON MUSLIM DEMOCRACY

We had no problem whatsoever in accepting and acknowledging the freedoms of belief, pluralism, difference, personal responsibility, and that of conscience.

AFM: Some Western moral philosophers who write on justice and pluralism claim that the problem of pluralism is not only an existential or ontological problem but is more specifically a historical problem. For example, John Rawls argues that religious and metaphysical pluralism in the West is a legacy of the Wars of Religion between Catholics and Protestants. From this time there is no universal unity or agreement around a single political, ethical doctrine, and so in this particular historical period pluralism must be accepted and regarded as reasonable. But, again, this is a historical phenomenon, which has a beginning and possibly an end. And so, there are people who say that pluralism is also a historical fact in Islam, that is, something new. And that prior to colonialism and modernization there was a kind of moral unity in the Islamic nation. That is, there may have been political and even sectarian disagreements in Islam, but there was a universal agreement about adherence to Islam and that the lack of this kind of agreement and moral unity is a sort of disaster or catastrophe, which has been caused only by colonialism, [forced] modernization, dictatorship, and [coercive] secularism [like in Turkey, Tunisia, and Egypt]. And thus the important thing is a return to moral and intellectual unity and agreement around belonging to Islam. Now, you yourself reject this idea about a difference between the ideal and the reality [in a Muslim society], correct?

RG: We are convinced that Islam is viable for all times, places, and peoples, as it is the religion of human nature [*din al-fitra*] that suits mankind, whether in the twentieth century or the seventieth, that is, it suits the white, the black, the rich, the poor, women, and men. It is the religion of the natural human disposition [*fitra*] and does not change as such, but rather adapts to the human condition. It is a religion that assists in solving mankind's problems and that provides them with direction on what to do when in jail, when a free man, or in times of prosperity or need, both as an individual and as a group. Such flexibility mandates embracing pluralism and acknowledging that realities have changed. As a religion of the natural human disposition, Islam must be able to accompany and guide humans in all their trials, not mandate that others be of a certain status in order to interact with

PHILOSOPHICAL-THEOLOGICAL DIALOGUES 221

Muslims. Humans are diverse, and so are their conditions; so is Islam, with its high flexibility that one must study well in order to gain its riches.

AFM: This is like the Protestant notion within Christianity, that every believer can read Scripture directly.

RG: Every believer can read directly but must exert strenuous effort [*ijtihad*] to understand the scripture and practice his or her right in doing so. It is not a matter that only Muslim jurists are entitled to do, as God demands that all Muslims toil as individuals and as members of groups because they bear direct responsibility for their actions in front of God, not just in front of mankind. Believers' actions should be guided by Islam's light, and they may be correct at times or may err, but in both cases they have gained goodness and reward from the Almighty, as He encourages the freedom of thought and toiling to find answers.

Pluralism and difference are ontological matters on the basis of people's differences, not merely passing or conditional ones. Throughout Islam, Muslim societies have been varied and multiple. I am personally very fond of the history of Iraq, in particular, as it was the most pluralistic during the grand 'Abbasid civilization. Grand scholars and legislators like Abu Hanifa, al-Shafi'i, and Ja'far al-Sadiq lived during that time, and not one of them issued a fatwa limiting the existing pluralism of that society. Iraqi society included all Muslim sects, excommunicated Christian groups, Nestorians, Assyrians, Yazidis, Sabeans, and devil worshippers, rendering it a natural history museum of religions. But what value and intellectual foundation was it that protected these minorities? It was Islam, as a civilizational concept that established the 'Abbasid state, which was also home to renowned poet Abu Nuwas, who sang for and praised alcohol consumption. Such a society produced many of this man's kind, as it possessed literary, intellectual, and artistic pluralism under the banner of a state that governed according to Islamic law. Not a single one of its grand jurists issued a fatwa to rid the masses of these artists. For evidence, it also suffices to look at the example of Andalusia and the manifold cultures that thrived and flourished during Islamic rule there.

AFM: Is it not necessary that this pluralism be somehow under the sovereignty of Islam, or some leadership or Islamic public authority?

RG: Islam should be applied according to people's abilities and needs. Pluralism is not a new, exceptional, or contingent idea, but as it is

222   ON MUSLIM DEMOCRACY

ontological and a component of Islam, Islamic civilizations have always had pluralism.

AFM: Is radical pluralism not just the plurality of Islamic schools?

RG: No. Even natural religions, the worship of trees and devils, have all existed, signifying the emergence of a philosophical perspective that establishes pluralism as a fact.

AFM: Is not the idea of [mere] toleration of the People of the Book the dominant idea in Islam?

RG: Throughout Islam's history, there have been no religious wars but only wars over political power. Muslims did not succeed in regulating political pluralism, but their wars were not on a religious or sectarian basis, as was the case in Europe.

AFM: But Islam is valid for all times and places, and is the religion of truth, and if humans all have the same natural disposition [*fitra*] in all times and places, and if it is what directs us to Islam, to the acceptance of God and the Prophet Muhammad, then why do some people accept Islam and others do not? That is, if we all have the same natural disposition and rationality?

RG: God created all as free people. I was once attending a seminar in the USA that John Esposito was at and he explained the notion of Islam quite well. So, the students asked him why he did not embrace Islam, and he said that God was yet to guide him toward it. Hence, there are psychological reasons and the human self is stubborn. Also, social experience is to blame sometimes, as someone may have had a bad experience with a Muslim, was too self-centered, or feared for his interests within society in terms of how people will look upon him if he changed his religion. Thus, psychological, social, and practical considerations enter into the matter.

AFM: But also considerations of reason and rational persuasion?

RG: I remember once telling a friend who I sensed was convinced of Islam not to announce it publicly if he was considering embracing it, as I feared for his life.

AFM: I mean what about the following scenario. Someone looks at the universe, that is, at the origins of the cosmos, and holds that the world does not have a Creator, but instead is just matter, chance, and natural, physical laws. Is this a potentially rational theory of being or just error plain and simple?

RG: God is Compassionate and Merciful and is not tyrannical but rather Just. He loves humans. Hence, if He sees His subjects honest in seeking

PHILOSOPHICAL-THEOLOGICAL DIALOGUES   223

truth, He will definitely guide and aid them. But if He sees them as arrogant and self-centered, He will not, as God does not guide the arrogant. God says, "I shall turn away from My signs those who are arrogant without any right" [Qur'an 7:146].

AFM: So denying the Creator is simply a human, psychological error?

RG: If one is sincere and faithful toward knowing God, He will guide him; but if arrogant, He will not. God created mankind with inclinations and capacities toward goodness and evil and provided them with reason that would guide them toward the good, and also sent messengers to assist mankind, as reason alone is insufficient. Most of those who use their reason sincerely arrive at belief in God. The greatest philosophers also believed in God, but this also often required the arrival of prophets for a more civilized life that included ethical values and tranquility among people. Hence, prophets were sent to assist mankind in this, as we possess capacities for both good and evil and possess reason that can guide us if we use it properly. There are proofs for contrary views, but we are still possessed of a nature that allows us to arrive at the truth.

So, difference is represented in the varied levels of preparedness for goodness and evil, but always there is reason capable of guidance and prophecy available for assistance.

AFM: So our innate nature [fitra] is distinct from the assistance given by prophecy?

RG: Differences exist so that we may be guided toward the truth, so that we may walk the path of truth, and we have prophecy to assist us in doing so.

AFM: Some, like Immanuel Kant, hold that the disagreement between these various proofs is internal to human reason, that there must be an equipollence of these proofs or arguments, what he called the antinomies of reason.

RG: But Kant did not stop at that and said that pure intellect leads us to neither faith nor disbelief. So equal proofs allow us to identify faith and secularism. But he connected faith to ethics and said that life cannot be ethical except through intellectual faith.

AFM: But there is no [definitive] rational proof for the existence of God.

RG: No, but there is ethical proof.

AFM: We agree on the philosophical theory, that there is no rational, demonstrative proof for the createdness or eternity of the world, but rather the proof is only moral.

224   ON MUSLIM DEMOCRACY

RG: There is no rational, demonstrative proof but the Qur'an in its entirety from beginning to end focuses on faith and belief. As one of the poets said, "And in every thing there is a verse testifying that He is the One." Meaning that the entire Qur'an, in all of its verses, are rational proofs. Kant was mistaken regarding the equipollence of arguments or the antinomies, for how may one imagine a universe without a Creator? The mind itself does not imagine itself if by mind we mean just the brain, since when you consider the brain where do you suppose it comes from?

AFM: So Darwin was also wrong?

RG: Yes, of course. Can life evolve on its own? Of course not. It is just like the Library of Congress, which did not establish itself on its own, but rather it was effort and civilization that made it what it is. But we cannot in any way claim that movements or disruptions in nature or in the Atlantic Ocean created the Library of Congress!

AFM: Okay, so the position of a Muslim toward the one who rejects or denies this truth is only a position of toleration, and not one of recognition or respect.

RG: Tolerance in itself is respect; the two are the same. It is an acknowledgment of the truth that people are allowed to think differently and that it is not my right to hate them or coerce them otherwise. This prohibition is clearly stated in the Qur'an, and the Prophet, peace be upon him, said that we are only required to inform people of righteousness. Hence, our duty is to deliver this message just like the Prophet did not impose his dogma on the people of Medina—which was already a pluralistic society. In Medina there existed pagans and Christians brought together with Muslims via a constitutional document, dubbed al-Sahifa, that regulated this pluralism and which all parties signed. So a Muslim believes himself to be right, but also acknowledges the right of others to believe differently.

AFM: But the relation is one of persuasion, discussion, debate . . .

RG: It is one of respect and of debate with goodwill, as per the commands of God and the Prophet. If an informed debate, it should be with proofs, and if a common one, then with kind persuasion.

AFM: Is this a debate that only goes in one direction, or both?

RG: Muslims must seek wisdom even if found in China.

AFM: Earlier you mentioned freedom of conscience, but at the same time the idea of Islamic legislation and subjecting the state to law

PHILOSOPHICAL-THEOLOGICAL DIALOGUES 225

and in fact to Islamic *shari'a*. Is there compatibility between these two ideas?

RG: The Islamic *shari'a* is a civil law in that legislation is entrusted to the parliament, which legislates based on its assessment of society's will. Such legislation develops in accordance with the development in public opinion, since there is both sovereignty and active legal reasoning [*ijtihad*]. Those who seek and reason about the *shari'a* [*al-mujtahidun*] are the members of parliament in what we may dub as collective *ijtihad*.

AFM: So, for example, Beji Caid Essebsi[27] participates in this form of public *ijtihad*?

RG: Caid Essebsi expresses the present state of public opinion, but when the latter develops and the quality of Islam rises to the point of being prevalent in society, the head of state and the parliament would follow this development. But we do not wish to impose anything on the masses and therefore possess no supreme authority, as legitimacy rises from the bottom up.

AFM: Right, so it becomes possible to see public deliberation and reason as constituting public *ijtihad* when the people below are Muslims and believers. The discussions and debates in the British parliament around human rights and justice, for example, are not considered "Islamic *ijtihad*." Rather, Islamic *ijtihad* is present when there is a nation or community that aims at this as an expression of the public interest in accordance with revelation—a kind of "deliberative *shari'a*."

RG: That which is right and that which is the truth cannot be concealed, whether spoken by a Muslim or a non-Muslim. If legislation agrees with Islam, then it is of it whether legislated by a Muslim or a non-Muslim. This is why the Prophet said that wisdom, wherever one may find it, is the property of believers.

AFM: Even when such a regime is silent on these goals, that is, it doesn't publicly proclaim them as the intention behind the legislation?

RG: Even if it is not called Islamic, it is still of Islam's principles, as Islam seeks content, not form.

AFM: I am curious how you understand the differences between the moral pluralism that shaped the modern West and post-colonial Muslim

---

[27] Beji Caid Essebsi (1926–2019) was president of Tunisia from December 31, 2014, until his death on July 25, 2019. He represented the old secularist guard elected as a bulwark against Ennahda.

226 ON MUSLIM DEMOCRACY

societies like Tunisia. On my understanding, in the Western republican conception of Madison and Montesquieu the presence of differences and disagreements [around religion and the good] is permanent in society, and so we cannot presume any moral unity around faith or religion. Whereas the theory presented in *Public Freedoms* imagines and expects a kind of moral unity around ultimate ends, goals, and objectives, defined by religion. You write in *Public Freedoms* that this theory of Montesquieu and Madison was restricted to Western secular circumstances. But in reality, isn't the description of conditions in the West [as characterized by moral pluralism] the same situation as in Tunisia today? For isn't there a kind of moral pluralism, according to which some people adhere to a materialist philosophy of life, and isn't there the same kind of moral conflict between different ways of life, religions, and theories of morality and value?

RG: The concept that mankind is evil is that of Hobbes, where a dictator was thus needed to govern an unruly people. Madison does not see mankind as evil; rather, mankind overcomes evil through a balancing of interests and managing the conflict between the interests of various groups. Through this struggle, each limits the other, and thus neither is capable of dominating society. Therefore, the fear is if people become of one dominant creed or racial group they would establish tyranny over the others. In other words, conflict or competition is not necessarily to be feared or prevented but encouraged because in the right circumstances this is what prevents any single group from monopolizing power. This is also the theory of the separation of powers whereby the political process regulates differences so that no one branch or party may overpower another.

AFM: But Madison says that the sources of this conflict are in the "hearts of men" and not only in the conditions of society, because people differ in their desires, ideas, goals, philosophies, religious conceptions, and moral doctrines. Thus, this kind of fundamental disagreement is not an exception but rather the norm.

RG: In this text, my aim was to criticize the principle of a harsh and rigid separation of powers. Some separation of powers is, of course, necessary, but not a radical or rigid form, as cooperation between powers and institutions is ultimately more important. One of the Islamic system's values is cooperation, as per the verse of the Qur'an: "cooperate toward goodness and piety" [Qur'an 5:2], not

PHILOSOPHICAL-THEOLOGICAL DIALOGUES   227

earthly interests. Thus in a genuine Islamic system, the powers and institutions of government should cooperate and complement each other rather than be strictly separated.

AFM: Like the British model in which the members of the government are members of parliament.

RG: And only the queen is representative of all authorities, including the church, of which she is the head. In this vision there is a limit to the separation between the religious and the earthly and of various state authorities. There needs to be a unity of state, nation, religion, and worldly life, unlike the total separation between religious and worldly matters, as in the French system.

AFM: The traditional British system is thus attractive to you from an Islamic standpoint?

RG: Yes, it is close to the ideal of cooperation rather than competition between various institutions and powers, including the earthly and the religious.

AFM: Who represents this unity in Tunisia today?

RG: The head of state.

AFM: He represents this ethical, religious, and Islamic unity in Tunisia today?

RG: Supposedly.

AFM: Would this come as a surprise to Mr. Essebsi himself?

RG: Constitutionally speaking, he is. The state's unity and Islamicity are the responsibility of the head of state, as the seat of power adapts to whoever sits on it. The seat itself can be large or small depending on who sits on it. When a person like De Gaulle sits on it, its authorities expand, and when someone like Hollande does the same, it contracts.

AFM: There is an important philosophical question here. We have discussed pluralism, and if I understand you correctly, your view is that difference up to and including rejection of Islam itself is a matter of divine decree. That is, not all people will agree on accepting Islam, and even some people who hear Islam presented to them and then reject it are not doing so out of their own hearts or minds, but because it is a permanent decree of God that not all will accept Islam. But in the liberal, republican philosophy, disagreement about religion, ethics, ideal conceptions of the good is natural, because in our nature, our minds and reason, we are shaped or created to disagree on these matters. It then follows that if this disagreement is natural, and the source of it is

228   ON MUSLIM DEMOCRACY

necessary, then we are obliged to accept this disagreement as reasonable. And so there is fundamental conflict between the Islamic conception of pluralism and the Islamic explanation for pluralism, and the liberal, secular explanation thereof.

Again, Madison says that these disagreements are internal to us, the way that two people watch the same film and disagree on its merits. Or like in Kant's critique of pure reason: two people look at the same proofs for certain metaphysical arguments about the origination of the cosmos and arrive at different conclusions. Unlike in mathematics or physics, in the realm of ethics, religion, politics, and metaphysics, there are no decisive [apodeictic] proofs such that any rational, sane person must accept them. For them, these disagreements are reasonable. But in the Islamic conception not all disagreements are reasonable, and in particular the decision to reject Islam after knowledge of it has been presented to one is not a rational, reasonable decision, but rather reflects a lack of some sort. Do I understand the difference between the two philosophies clearly?

RG: According to the belief in mankind's responsibility, if one has been presented with the call to Islam and yet does not embrace it, then it is the responsibility of Islam to explain this. If it is presented to him in a good manner and he is sincere in seeking the truth, that is, rational and earnest, such a person would accept the truth of Islam in all cases.

AFM: So some professor of physics at Stanford or Harvard, an expert on theories of the origins of the universe, says she doesn't know the origins of the atom or matter involved in the Big Bang and is not sure if there is a Divine Creator behind it. So we can call this person an unbeliever, since she does not believe in a God with all of the traditional divine attributes like knowledge, will, power, and perhaps justice. Now, is it your view that if this person was presented with the proofs of Islam then she, a sincere seeker of truth about existence, would accept the theory of a just, knowledgeable, and powerful creator?

RG: [Pause] What does this have to do with politics?

AFM: In my opinion it has a great and important relationship to politics— namely, the foundation of the state. For if there is reasonable disagreement between believers and unbelievers, then it is unjust for the state to privilege belief over unbelief, as well as unbelief over belief, but rather might strive to be neutral between them, as impossible as it is to be neutral in the effect of state laws and policies on different

PHILOSOPHICAL-THEOLOGICAL DIALOGUES 229

ways of life. But consider the situation of faith in a country like France or other more militantly secular theories like Marxist ones, where faith might be regarded as irrational and backward. That is, perhaps some Communists and some republicans in France regard religion as something belonging to the past, something unreasonable, and something that is necessary to emancipate humanity from. On the other hand, some liberal philosophers say that faith and religion can be regarded as epistemically and morally reasonable, that not every believer is stupid, and that it is not necessary to emancipate everyone from religion. So this question is very important for politics, because the liberal philosopher who regards religion as a potentially rational and reasonable, and thus acceptable, phenomenon will say that it is not just for the state to violate the rights of the religious. This recognition is, on this view, the foundation of religious freedom—namely, that the religious live a respect-worthy life, and that the foundations of this life are rational and reasonable. Even if one does not agree with those foundations with regard to a specific religion, liberal citizenship suggests that we should nonetheless respect the soundness of their minds and reason. There is a big difference between this kind of aspiring neutralist liberalism and anti-religious militant liberalism that wants to emancipate people from religion completely.

RG: One might say that a kind of Islamic liberalism shares in this, as it holds that Islam must not be imposed on the non-religious and the state has no right to do so, as its duty is to spread knowledge of Islam but not to compel acceptance of it. The state's duty is to open up the possibilities and then to "let whoever wills believe and whoever wills disbelieve" [Qur'an 18:29]. So, whoever wishes to go to the mosque or the church, or to drink alcohol, may do just that.

AFM: Is there a difference between this "liberal Islam" and the theories in *Public Freedoms*?

RG: There is no difference in giving this freedom to everyone, as the state is not a church that monopolizes the interpretation of scripture. It does not impose Islam but rather leaves people with the freedom of choice.

AFM: But the state is based on the *shari'a* . . .

RG: It is based on the *shari'a* with relation to its consultative and democratic mechanisms. In other words, if the *society* demands something, then the state will respond to its requests if they are of an

230 ON MUSLIM DEMOCRACY

Islamic nature in that they are based on the freedom of choice, on the authority of the people, and on the respect of private and public freedoms. If the people demand a certain law, it is the state's responsibility to respond accordingly through its parliamentary and representative institutions. As for those who do not believe in the Islamic creed, there is no law that forces belief or faith on them. Spreading the Islamic call [*tabligh*] is the duty of those popular, civil institutions within civil society and there is no time limit on this mission. Calling to Islam is not something that is completed within a day, or two, or three, but is an open-ended horizon. So no one is told, "You have this set time period to hear and choose to respond to the Islamic call." The scholars of Islam are responsible for presenting Islam in public and responding to questions or objections, and then to leave it before the people. They have no other task than presenting Islam, and they must not exceed the boundary of clarifying Islam by responding to questions and doubts, without ever saying that there is a limited time period for people to respond to this call.

The problem is that states interfere in private freedoms in every place, despite the fact that states have no legitimate authority over individual conscience and private freedoms.

AFM: Yet, on a view that derives the state from popular sovereignty, like your own theory in *Public Freedoms* and elsewhere, isn't the authority of the state none other than the authority of the society and the individuals in it?

RG: When a state deprives women of their natural rights, like driving a car or receiving an education, then this is a problem. This is how the state interferes in people's personal rights, and it is a matter connected to the dominant culture in a society.

The state should not interfere in people's lives except within very narrowly defined limits. For example, why should the state care whether the driver is man or woman?

AFM: Unlike Madison, Montesquieu, Rawls, Habermas, and so on, as we have discussed, if there is a kind of unity in the ideal Islamic system with regard to morality, ends, and cooperation around them between all state institutions, where does this unity come from? And if in an ideal Tunisia, for example, all people would converge around the goals and moral principles of Islam, is this unity and agreement original, or must it be produced through the mechanisms of politics and education? That is, is it the right of the state to produce virtuous citizens, virtuous Muslims, to teach Islam exclusively in the schools, and to assist people on the path to Islamic moral progress?

RG: The state is required to provide health, security, judicial, economic, cultural, and educational services that benefit and unite its people, but it must still respect differences. For example, a secular or religious state that is fighting a longtime adversary will see this struggle influence its educational system, as is the case in France and the Soviet Union. These states consider the school as a generator of national citizens and are accordingly adamant about controlling it because it is the key to producing the right kind of national subject or personality to struggle against whatever the national enemy is perceived as—for example, religion in the French example. This is not the historical experience of Islam, because then the schools followed sects, like those of the Shi'a and Sunnis or, under Ottoman society, that were based in the religious communities [the *milal*]. In addition to education, these communities also, of course, administered law through their own courts, and the unity of the state did not also mean one education system, one law, one judiciary, or even one language.

AFM: Yes, but this is not the modern state. The same was true about premodern European societies.

RG: I speak of the Islamic state as I see it, not as merely one form of modernization, as there are many: British, French, Marxist, Turkish, and American. There is a wide range of possibilities. There could be a subject on national education, history, or the political or social system, for example, but with other subjects taught to specific communities. In Belgium, the same school has Catholic teachers teaching Catholic students and Muslim teachers giving religious education to Muslim students. So, the students share the topic but on different foundations, each according to their own.

Even the idea that the provisions or laws of the *shari'a* and Islamic jurisprudence must be assigned to a single code or judiciary is an idea adopted in modernity, based on the principle of a single state will; it is based on modernization and the idea that state's sovereign will requires a unitary legal code. But why is that? This is a French notion that the belief in the general will requires a single legal code. But why should we accept this?

232 ON MUSLIM DEMOCRACY

AFM: Right, in Islam there was never a single unitary codification of law.

RG: In Britain nowadays, there are Islamic courts, so-called Muslim arbitration tribunals, catering to matters of marriage, divorce, and inheritance. Even with regard to financial cases, we find Islamic economics
applied there, with the possibility for transactions thereof to also be
according to Islamic law. This all reflects a new kind of openness.

AFM: An expansion of choice of law?

RG: All of it correlates with the notion of freedom for mankind so that the
state does not become a prison and one does not lose his or her personal freedom. This is what happens in the modern or militant secularism that fights to suppress religion entirely.

A Muslim who is conscious of his or her religion only subscribes
to Islamic ruling, although in cases of necessity may choose a secular
system. But a Muslim who is genuinely conscious of Islam and has the
opportunity to choose between secular laws and Islamic laws may not
freely choose the secular laws. If one does, it means that he or she does
not have a complete awareness of Islam or has somehow received a
negative image of it.

AFM: There are other forms of legal pluralism. In the United States, every
state has its own personal status law; for example, some states have
community property between spouses [and others don't].

RG: Even in Tunisia, when the marriage contract is being prepared, the
one writing it asks the bride and groom if they want joint or separate
ownership.

AFM: But also in the West there are people who engage in Islamic same-
sex marriages, claiming that in Islam marriage is just a contract, not a
matter of worship or a sacrament, like in the Catholic Church.[28]

RG: Yes, marriage is not sacred or a form of worship per se, yet contracts
must be based on the terms of the *shari'a*.

AFM: So if same-sex marriage departs from the terms of the *shari'a*, then
some might enter a civil marriage and leave Islam out of it, which is
legal in America. We might then say that two men live together and
share property like a company, and what happens outside of this is
private, we are silent about it, but there still exists a private law contract that doesn't need to say anything about sexual relations.

---

[28] See Adrian Goldberg, "British Gay Muslims Seek Islamic Weddings," BBC News, February 20,
2011, https://www.bbc.com/news/uk-12486003.

PHILOSOPHICAL-THEOLOGICAL DIALOGUES 233

RG: Not all contracts are permissible.

AFM: Shifting focus, I would like to talk a bit about how the state manages both a unitary identity and pluralism. In both *Public Freedoms* and *Democracy and Human Rights in Islam* you argue that the state is based on the *shari'a* and the texts of Islam, but also that the duties of the state are "civil" [*madani*]. But the state itself is founded on religion and turning to revelation for judgment and authority. Can we tell others, non-Muslims in this state, that it is "civil"?

RG: We must first specify what we mean by "civil" [*madani*]. The Prophet Muhammad, peace be upon him, established the state and called it *al-madina* [the city], as civilization is only established in cities. Hence, Islam's mission was twofold: religious and "civilizing-urbanizing" [*hadariyya madaniyya*], with the former focusing on transforming people from being unbelievers to ones who concur in God's unicity—as had been the mission of all prophets throughout time. The second mission was transforming Arabs from nomadic life to an urban, civilized one. This is why when some of the Prophet's Companions who had inhabited the desert wished to return to their Bedouin life, the Prophet ordered them not to and said that whoever did so has forsaken Islam. The city [*al-madina*] was governed by a law and a pact, while the desert was not, and Islam established cities wherever it reigned—like Cairo, Kufa, Qayrawan—and did not demolish any cities it conquered. Islam also established institutions of knowledge and other forms of civilization and considered "corruption in the land"—that is, rebellion or banditry that threatened civilized life—to be a crime. Islam did not come to destroy but to build and to "civilize the earth" [*'imarat al-ard*] rather than spoil it.

Rulers did not need to possess a religious rank or status, as there is no clergy or priesthood in Islam. Hence, we are not speaking of a state ruled by "men of religion," that is, a clerical hierarchy, nor of a state that is infallible on the premise that it receives its orders from God. Rather, these are rulers chosen by the people, and they can be criticized by them, as their actions are merely human and subject to error. So, what would you call such a state other than "civil" in that it excludes clerics and banishes tyranny? A state in which the rule does not ascend from below but descends from heaven does not exist in Islam.

234 ON MUSLIM DEMOCRACY

AFM: Some Islamic reformist political thinkers, yourself included, speak about the formation of a state in relation to the Prophet's state in Medina and the centrality of a constitution like the so-called Sahifa of Medina. This view holds that Islam is a religion of civilization and desires all the goods of civilization, like science, education, and economic development. Should one not regard this view of politics as quasi-secular?

RG: We do not seek a state based on the rule of clerics. We wish for civil governance to oppose military rule. Civilization and the civil nature of politics here do not mean outright confrontation against religious government, unless it is against the kinds of theocracies we associate with the Middle Ages. Our state is a state of a Muslim people, or as Essebsi says, "A civil state for a Muslim people."

*

AFM: So to bring our conversation to a close, let us return once more to the central theme of your thought: how both Western and Islamic democracy endeavor to solve the problem of constitutionalism and the grounding of morality in politics. If I understood correctly, even in those modern constitutions that attempt to protect rights and freedoms through institutional means there is a lack and imperfection, both in the moral foundation of these rights and in the institutional mechanisms for preventing tyranny. As I understand it, Islamic societies have a possible solution to this problem in that such societies are comprised of citizens who are believers and virtuous, and they actively believe in and are committed to the necessity of virtue in politics. That is, in addition to a set of institutions that correspond to the institutional vision of republican theorists like Madison—in the Islamic state these would be institutions like a *shura* council, a council of jurists or experts, or a supreme court to apply the *shari'a* and standards of justice and morality—Islamic theories of democracy also presume that there is a somewhat virtuous citizenry of believers and elites without which no good institutions could hope to succeed on their own. Unlike Madisonian theories, this view presumes that without widespread virtue among the many and the few no just regime can hope to be stable and avoid despotism. Do you see your theory in *Public Freedoms* as stressing more the role of unique

PHILOSOPHICAL-THEOLOGICAL DIALOGUES 235

institutions that prevent an unjust, tyrannical will from overpowering the state, or the presence of a virtuous public?

RG: There is no single solution for preventing tyranny. I have spoken in the plural of checks against authoritarianism. The Islamic civilization is accused of being one of despotism and that Islam and its theology of predestination are the cause of this. In *Public Freedoms*, I spoke of the reasons for resisting authoritarianism and that we must benefit from the modern experience of adopting important democratic mechanisms like elections, pluralism, the rule of law, constitutional oversight, constitutional courts, monitoring by public opinion, and popular participation in the political process, all of which create a legal-institutional apparatus. But this apparatus is insufficient and must be accompanied by spiritual and moral education, as the Prophet said that the entire people cannot agree on error.

We must not rely on only one source of stability and justice, but rather utilize all possible tools to mitigate shortcomings and overcome mankind's ontological imperfection, which can only be limited, not eradicated completely.

Index

For the benefit of digital users, indexed terms that span two pages (e.g., 52–53) may, on occasion, appear on only one of those pages

Abbasid Dynasty, 44–45, 73, 124–26, 221
Abdel Nasser, Gamal (Jamal 'Abd al-
    Nasir), 81, 151, 153, 155, 156, 160
'Abduh, Muhammad, 46–47, 57–58, 173,
    174, 195
Abu Bakr, first caliph of Islam, 43, 54,
    69–71, 111–12, 172
Agonism, 1–2, 29–30
Albani, Nasir al-Din al-, 154, 158
Algeria, 79, 80, 93, 98, 109, 112, 152–53,
    157, 161, 177–78, 183
'Ali ibn Abi Talib, fourth caliph of Islam,
    45–46, 72, 139
Alms (*see Zakat*)
Andalusia, 52, 53, 140, 221
Apostasy, 54, 55, 57, 73–74, 128, 141, 172,
    173, 218
Arab nationalism, 109, 151, 153
Authoritarianism (*see* Despotism)
Autocracy (*see* Despotism)

Banna, Hasan al-, 57–58, 85, 156
Ben Ali, Zine El Abidine, 2–3, 5, 25–26,
    175, 176–77, 178, 181, 214
Bennabi, Malek, 91–99, 155, 157, 161, 165,
    173–74
Blasphemy, 6–7, 21, 134–35
Bourguiba, Habib, 2–3, 5, 81, 150, 151, 152,
    165, 166, 167, 170, 175, 176, 208–9

Caliph, mankind as God's (*see* Mankind as
    God's deputy on earth)
Caliphate, as political office, 44, 60–61,
    71–72, 112, 197, 217
Citizenship, equal rights to, 17–18, 19–21,
    27–28, 51, 57–59, 68–69, 73–74, 87,
    88–89, 100–7, 129, 139–40, 171, 173,
    174, 175, 228

Civil society, 1–2, 5, 19, 44–45, 50–56, 106,
    173, 180, 186, 229
Civil state (*dawla madaniyya*), concept
    of, 6–7, 22–23, 27–28, 133, 200, 225,
    233–34
Collectif du 18 Octobre (18 October
    Coalition for Rights and Freedoms in
    Tunisia), 178
Colonialism, 95, 148, 186, 220
Communism, 15–16, 75–76, 165–66, 168,
    169, 170, 171–72, 174, 177, 228
Conflict, as condition of politics, 13, 19,
    30–31, 51, 53, 66–67, 96, 116, 120,
    121, 128, 149, 166, 170–71, 225–26,
    227
Constituent power, popular, 12–13, 16–17,
    21, 208
Constitution, in general, 10, 27, 75, 196
    Egyptian, 214
    Sahifa of Medina as (*see* Medina, Sahifa
        (Constitution) of)
    Tunisia (2014), 5–9, 16–18, 21–22–, 26–
        28, 29, 130–36, 185–86, 198, 200–1,
        207, 219
    Tunisia (2022), 3–4
    United States, 201
Consultation (*Shura*), 13, 19–20, 42–43,
    44–45, 46–47, 57–58, 59, 63–64, 65–
    77, 84–85, 112, 113, 123, 126, 131–32,
    142, 194, 203, 206, 212, 234
Contract, politics as, 11, 12, 18, 20–21, 43–
    44, 53, 57–58, 59
Coup, 25, 57, 85–86, 155, 165
    Algeria (1992), 112
    Egypt (July 2013), 8–9, 91n.2
    Tunisia (1987), 176–77
    Tunisia (July 2021), 1, 2–4, 5–6, 29
    Umayyad victory as, 112

238 INDEX

Democracy, in general, 4, 5, 10–11, 13–14, 19–20, 22–23, 43, 45–47, 73–74, 75–77, 79, 83–84, 87–88, 100–1, 105–6, 115, 131–33, 142–43, 148–80, 181, 184, 190–91, 193, 194, 213, 218, 234
Tunisia 2011-2021, 2–3
Democratic transition, 2, 5–10, 25–26, 30
Despotism, 1–2, 4, 10, 18–19, 22–23, 42–43, 45–46, 51, 53–54, 55–56, 57, 59, 67–68, 75, 76–77, 83, 84, 86–87, 89, 93, 96, 111, 115, 131, 133, 182–83, 184, 186, 190, 197, 214, 216, 220, 234–35
Dhimma (*see* non-Muslims)
Dictatorship (*see* Despotism)
Disagreement, ideological, moral and political, 2–3, 18, 22, 23, 26, 28, 30–31, 55, 60–61, 63–64, 67–68, 124–25, 132, 134, 135, 174, 175, 203, 213, 218, 219, 223, 226, 227, 228

Education, 44–45, 49, 50–51, 66–67, 69, 96–97, 98–99, 109, 110, 113–14, 117, 126–27, 128, 142, 147, 151, 158, 165, 179, 204, 205, 209, 216–17, 230–31, 235
Egypt, 2, 5, 8–9, 25, 52, 53, 79, 84–85, 95, 97, 109, 150, 151, 153, 214
Ennahda Party, 1–2, 4, 5, 6–8, 10, 15–17, 21, 24–26, 30–31, 75–76, 132n.5, 134–35nn.13–14, 177, 178, 185, 200, 214
2016 Party Congress of, 7–8, 16–17
Essebsi, Beji Caid, 2–4, 198, 225, 225n.27, 227, 234

Fanon, Frantz, 95, 153
Fitra (*see* Human nature)
Freedom, 11–12, 18–21, 23, 27–29, 31, 35–42, 43, 44–45, 46–49, 51–52, 53–54, 55–56, 57–58, 60, 73–75, 78, 79, 83–90, 96, 105, 106–7, 108, 111, 115–16, 122, 126, 127, 129, 133–34, 138–39, 140, 143, 155, 162–63, 171, 172, 178, 179–80, 189, 194, 200, 214–15, 218, 219, 229–30, 232, 234
"Negative" conception of, 18–19, 23–24, 138, 215, 219, 230
of association, 27–28

of expression, information, press, speech, 45, 79, 86, 142
of movement, 41–42, 142, 150
of property, 47–48, 141–42
of religion, belief, and conscience, 11–12, 18, 23–24, 28, 37, 41–42, 44–45, 76–77, 106, 125, 128–29, 130–31, 131n.4, 133–34, 134n.13, 139, 140, 141, 172, 212, 214–16, 218, 221, 224, 228
"Positive" conception of, 18, 55, 214, 215, 218
Public, 9, 10, 18, 43, 138, 171, 229

Gender and women's rights, 21, 23, 48–50, 84, 86, 88, 89–90, 100, 106–7, 134, 144, 169, 178, 179–80, 198, 219, 230
right to hold political power, 74–75, 84, 89–90, 168–69

Hanbal, Ahmad b., 125–26
Hizb al-Tahrir, 115, 153
Human nature, 19–20, 60–61, 66–67, 149, 157, 187, 188–90, 192, 220, 222, 223
Human rights, 6–7, 11–12, 21, 22–24, 25–26, 27–29, 41–42, 49, 59–60, 105, 132–33, 134, 137–44, 178, 179–80, 181, 183, 184–85, 186, 191, 193, 200, 211, 219, 225
Human values (as harmonious with Islamic values), 22–23, 80–81, 132–33, 186, 192
Hypocrites (*Munafiqun*), 51, 53, 127, 128, 129

Ibn ʿAshur, Muhammad Al-Tahir, 39, 40, 62, 64, 105, 115, 123, 124, 139, 150, 174
Ibn Diyaf, Ahmad, 132n.6, 174, 195
Ibn Khaldun, 91–92, 149, 174, 197
Ibn Rushd, 36, 53, 194
Ijtihad, 67, 123, 194, 199, 204, 205, 206, 212, 213, 221, 225
Iqbal, Muhammad, 39, 156
Iraq War (2003), 106, 108, 112, 172–73, 180
Islamic democracy, theory of, 8–9, 10–15, 26–28, 234

INDEX 239

Islamic law (*see Shari'a*)
Islamic Tendency Movement (MTI), 5, 10, 15–16, 75–76, 170

Jama'a al-Islamiyya, al- (precursor to the Islamic Tendency Movement), 163–67, 170
Jihad, 52, 106, 112, 206
  as non-violent action, 65–67, 106
  Jihadist movements, 2–3, 152, 155, 158
Justice, 20–21, 22–23, 26, 28–29, 36, 40, 41–43, 51, 53–54, 55–56, 57, 71–73, 80–81, 84, 86–87, 92, 95, 96, 104–5, 106–7, 108, 110, 111, 113, 118, 119, 124, 131–32, 133, 143, 167, 168, 180, 184, 185, 186, 187, 188, 192, 197, 206, 209, 212, 215, 219, 220, 225, 228, 234, 235

Kant, Immanuel, 59–60, 158, 159, 212, 223, 224, 228
Karkar, Salih, 169, 175
Kharijites, 45–46, 72–73, 110
Khayr al-Din al-Tunisi, 57–58, 174, 195
Khomeini, Ayatollah Ruhollah, 72–73, 166, 167–68

Legitimacy, 7–8, 9, 12–13, 21–23, 43, 45, 46, 57, 72, 84, 88–89, 100, 103–4, 133, 135–36, 173, 178, 179–80, 182–83, 196n.22, 197, 204, 209, 223

Madison, James, 1–2, 12–13, 225, 230
Malik b. Anas, 124–25
Mankind, as God's deputy (vicegerent, caliph) on earth, 11, 13–15, 17–18, 23–24, 27–28, 35, 47, 61–62, 65–67, 138, 141–42, 158, 194, 195, 197, 209, 210
Marxism, 127, 160, 162, 164, 187, 190, 228, 231
Marzouki, Moncef, 178
Maslaha (*see* Public interest)
Mawdudi, Abu'l-A'la, 18, 40, 84, 114–15, 140, 155, 157–58, 165, 171, 173
Medina, Sahifa (Constitution) of, 20, 40n.6, 51, 58–59, 68–69, 88–89, 101–2, 122–23, 139, 234
Mixed presidential-parliamentary system of democracy, 6–7, 21, 135

Moderate Islamism (*See Wasat, Wasatiyya*)
Montesquieu, Charles Louis de Secondat, 1–2, 12–13, 225, 230
Mourou, Shaykh Abdelfattah, 164, 175
Muhammad, Prophet of Islam, 36, 38, 40, 41, 42, 44, 51, 52–53, 63–64, 67, 69–70, 82, 86, 104–5, 111–12, 114, 115, 128, 130–31, 133, 138–39, 141, 142–43, 190, 222, 233
Muslim Brotherhood, 2, 25, 75–76, 84–85, 89–90, 96, 153, 154, 155, 156, 158, 165, 167, 168, 171, 194–97, 198, 209–10
Muslim democracy, theory of, 9–10, 11, 15–31

Najjar, 'Abd al-Majid al-, 175, 195
National Constituent Assembly (of Tunisia, 2011-2014), 6–7, 6n.9, 24–25, 123, 130–36
Neutrality, of the state toward religion, 121, 122, 124–25, 127, 211
Non-Muslims, 10, 19–20, 51, 84–85, 87, 94, 99, 102, 103–4, 106–7, 139–40, 141, 162, 171–72, 173, 174, 175, 179–80, 187, 233

Ottoman Empire, 44–45, 53, 73, 112, 217, 231
Ownership (*see* Property)

Palestine, 78–79, 81, 102, 106, 108
Parliamentary system of democracy, 1, 6–7, 10, 21, 135–36, 208–9, 229
Perfectionism (in political theory), 11–12, 13–14, 17–19, 23–24, 186, 187, 215, 216
Pharaoh, 42–43, 96, 111, 166–67, 196
Political Islam, 7–9, 15–17, 78, 79–80, 154, 157
Pluralism
  Legal, 217, 231–32
  Moral and religious, 18, 20–21, 26, 28, 29, 30–31, 51, 52, 58–59, 60, 67–68, 73–74, 76–77, 88, 89, 130–31, 140, 197, 198, 199, 218, 219–20, 221–22, 224, 225, 227, 228–29
  Political, 8–9, 10–11, 12, 13–14, 15–19, 20, 22–23, 26–28, 31, 40n.6, 57–58, 59–60, 67–69, 74–77, 88, 130–32, 133, 142, 170, 190, 222, 233, 235

240 INDEX

Property, 23–24, 40, 41, 47–48, 59, 84, 103–4, 105, 141–42, 149, 168, 188, 204, 232

Public Freedoms in the Islamic State (1993), 5, 9–10, 12, 19, 175, 181, 190, 217

Public interest, 48, 84, 86–87, 89–90, 124, 138, 141–42, 184, 225

Public opinion, 1–2, 19–20, 67, 125–26, 180, 183, 184, 186, 190, 198, 206, 215, 225, 235

Qaradawi, Yusuf al-, 73n.16, 83, 103–4, 106, 116–17, 118, 208–9

Qutb, Sayyid, 18, 40, 91–99, 103, 114–15, 149, 155–57, 160–61, 165, 166, 173

Rawls, John, 26, 27, 29, 30–31, 220, 230

Reform, religious and political, 15–16, 22–23, 38–39, 46–47, 49, 57–58, 80–81, 92, 98–99, 132–33, 165, 173, 174, 179–80, 193, 194, 195, 234

Religious scholars, 11, 12–13, 35, 40, 41, 44, 50–51, 55, 87–88, 92, 115, 118, 122–23, 124–25, 126, 127, 138, 142–43, 151–52, 154, 155, 172, 194, 197, 206–7, 208, 221, 229

Republic of Virtue, Islamic democracy as, 13, 15–16

Revolution
Egypt (1952), 95, 156
Egypt (2011), 2–3, 8–9
English, 53
French (1789), 53
Iranian (1979), 96, 166–67, 169
Tunisian Jasmine (2011), 1, 5, 9, 15, 18, 19, 178, 181, 219

Rida, Rashid, 61, 158

Sahifa of Medina (*see* Medina, Sahifa (Constitution) of)

Saied, Kais, 1, 3–4, 5–6, 25

Salafism, 92, 97, 98–99, 153, 154, 155, 167

Sartre, Jean-Paul, 158, 162, 163, 186, 189–90

Schmitt, Carl, 105–6

Secular political parties, 1–2, 18–19, 24–25, 73–74, 75–76, 88, 89, 178

Secularism, 4, 19–21, 46, 52, 54, 78, 97, 100–1, 105–6, 110, 114, 115, 120–22, 126–27, 129, 143–44, 160, 165, 166, 184, 187, 193, 209, 218, 220, 223, 225, 227, 228, 231, 232, 234

Separation of powers, 1–2, 10, 12–13, 14–15, 190–91, 193, 226, 234–35

Scholars of Islam (*See* Religious scholars)

Shari'a, 3–28, 39, 41, 44, 71, 72, 74–75, 83, 84, 86, 103–4, 107, 113, 114–17, 130–31, 138, 139–40, 141–42, 149, 157, 178, 179–80, 194, 196–97, 198, 199, 200, 201, 202–5, 207, 212, 214, 215, 224–25, 229, 231, 232–33, 234

Absence of in 2014 Tunisian constitution, 7–8, 21–22, 23–24, 26–28, 132

Theory of the Objectives (*Maqasid*) of, 39, 40, 41, 83, 105, 115, 138, 142–43

Shatibi, Abu Ishaq, al-, 84–85, 124, 138, 174

Shi'a, 72–73, 126, 161, 167, 172–73, 213, 231

Shura (*see* Consultation)

Siba'i, Mustafa al-, 160, 165

Social relations, in Islamic law (*mu'amalat*), 124, 205, 206

Sovereignty, 9, 22, 109, 183–84, 186, 193, 196, 204, 217

Divine, 10, 11–12, 157, 200, 209, 221

Popular, 7–8, 10, 14, 15–16, 27–28, 29–30, 57–58, 171, 182–83, 184, 197, 203–4, 208, 210, 225, 230

Sudan, 87, 109, 114–15, 137, 168–69

Tha'alibi, Shaykh 'Abd al-'Aziz, 152

Tolerance, 10–11, 52, 57, 61, 63, 67, 103–4, 126, 224

Turabi, Hasan, al-, 168–69, 198

'Ulama' (*See* Religious scholars)

'Umar ibn Al-Khattab, second caliph of Islam, 43–44, 48, 54, 103–4, 119, 172–73

Umma, 19–20, 44, 51, 56, 71–72, 79, 81, 87–88, 89, 98, 101–2, 111, 124–26, 138, 142, 167, 180, 190, 202, 204, 209–10

INDEX   241

Umayyad Dynasty, 72–74
Unity, moral and religious (in the political community), 10, 11–16, 19, 27–28, 51, 60–69, 71–72, 88–89, 207, 218, 220, 225, 227, 230
Universal caliphate (*see* Mankind as God's deputy on earth)
Universal Declaration of Human Rights (1948), 28–29, 41–42, 137, 143–44, 200, 211

Vicegerency of God (*see* Mankind as God's deputy on earth)

Wasat, Wasatiyya, 60, 83, 88, 91n.1, 108, 135

Zakat, 47, 54–55, 78, 103–4, 111–12, 172
Zaytuna, al- (mosque and university), 131, 147, 149, 150–52, 158, 163, 165, 175, 200.